W9-BZB-617

AN ACT OF PIRACY

THE SEIZURE OF THE AMERICAN-FLAG MERCHANT SHIP *MAYAGUEZ* IN 1975

AN ACT OF PIRACY

THE SEIZURE OF THE AMERICAN-FLAG MERCHANT SHIP *MAYAGUEZ* IN 1975

by
Gerald Reminick

THE GLENCANNON PRESS

MARITIME BOOKS

Palo Alto
2009

Published by The Glencannon Press
P.O. Box 341, Palo Alto, CA 94302
Tel. 800-711-8985, Fax. 510-528-3194
www.glencannon.com

First Edition, first printing.

ISBN 978-1-889901-47-3

Library of Congress Cataloging-in-Publication Data

Reminick, Gerald, 1943-
    An act of piracy : the seizure of the American-flag merchant ship
Mayagüez in 1975 / by Gerald Reminick. -- 1st ed.
    p. cm.
    Includes bibliographical references and index.
    ISBN 978-1-889901-47-3 (alk. paper)
1. Mayagüez Incident, 1975. 2. Mayagüez (Ship) I. Title.
    E865.R46 2009
    959.704'3--dc22
                                        2009019752

Publisher's notes:
1. Although the seizure of the *Mayaguez* was technically not piracy because she was taken by a foreign government, rather than individuals, the title was chosen because it succinctly refers to the incident in the broader sense of "piracy" and because President Gerald Ford referred to it in that sense.
2. Every effort is made to obtain and reproduce the best quality photographs. Due to wartime conditions, and the age of the photos available, a number are of lesser quality. They have nevertheless been used.

Dedication

This book is dedicated to the forty-one servicemen who were killed in the recovery of the steamship *Mayaguez* in May 1975. Their names are the last to be inscribed on the Vietnam Wall Memorial in Washington, D.C.

U.S. Air Force
Jimmy P. Black, Bobby G. Collums, Gerald A. Coyle, Thomas D. Dwyer, Bob W. Ford, Gerald W. Fritz, Laurence E. Froehlich, Jackie D. Glenn, Darrell L. Hamlin, Gregory L. Hankamer, David A. Higgs, Faleagafulu Ilaoa, James G. Kays, Michael D. Lane, Dennis W. London, Robert P. Mathias, Edgar C. Moran II, William R. McKelvey, George E. McMullen, Tommy R. Nealis, Paul J. Raber, Robert W. Ross, Elwood E. Rumbaugh, Richard Van de Geer, Robert P. Weldon.

U.S. Marine Corps
Daniel A. Benedett, Lynn Blessing, Antonio Ramos Sandovall, Gregory S. Copenhaver, Kelt R. Turner, Gary L. Hall, Joseph N. Hargrove, James J. Jacques, Ashton N. Loney, Danny G. Marshall, James R. Maxwell, Richard W. Rivenburgh, Walter Boyd, Andres Garcia.

U.S. Navy
Bernard Gause Jr., Ronald J. Manning.

By the same author:

ACKNOWLEDGEMENTS

There are many people who helped me in writing this book. A very special thank you to my colleague and editor, Professor Joyce Gabriele who has assisted me in all my writings. Thanks also to Professor Kevin Peterman and maritime historian William Hultgren for their assistance with photographs.

The Public Relations Director of the American Merchant Marine Veterans Organization, Gloria Flora Nicholich, was an inspiration. She was also responsible for introducing me to Raymond Iacobacci, captain of the USNS *Greenville Victory*, whose input was vital to the story.

Special thank-you's go out to the veterans of the Koh Tang Beach Club; Dan Hoffman, Fred Morris, Larry Barnett, Tom Noble, Al Bailey and Jim Davis for their interviews and photographs; for the following crew members of the USNS *Greenville Victory*, Karl Lonsdale and Herminio Rivera and Stephen Zarley of the SS *Mayaguez* and James Miller, son of Capt. Miller.

I'm grateful to Dan and Toni Horodysky for their invaluable *American Merchant Marine at War* website. And once again, my editor, Bill Harris, has dedicated his patience and skill in bringing this book to fruition. I appreciate the academic support given me by the Libraries of Suffolk County Community College and the Gerald R. Ford Library.

Of course, none of this would be possible without the emotional support of my wife, Gail.

The friendship and support of Jean Dierkes-Carlisle, daughter of Charles Fitzgerald, the 1st Asst. Engineer killed aboard the

SS *Stephen Hopkins* on September 27, 1942 has become invaluable.

I am truly thankful to all of them for their support and encouragement.

CONTENTS

FORWARD

On May 12, 1975, the U.S.-flag merchant ship, *Mayaguez,* owned by Sea-Land Service, Incorporated, steamed through international waters from Hong Kong to Sattahip, Thailand, loaded with containers. The ship was between six and seven miles off the coast of the island of Poulo Wai, sixty miles from the Cambodian mainland. Early in the morning, a gunboat belonging to the Khmer Rouge, the communist government of Cambodia, seized the vessel.

It was the first boarding and capture of a U.S.-flag merchant vessel since the American Revolutionary War.

President Gerald Ford, faced with his first major crisis, referred to it as an "Act of Piracy."

A hastily drawn up plan put together by the president, Secretary of State Henry Kissinger and the National Security Council was implemented, calling for quick recovery of the vessel. It was felt that fast action was necessary so that the United States, whose prestige was already low because of the unpopular Vietnam War, could demonstrate that she was still a power to be reckoned with.

The recovery of the *Mayaguez* was achieved through acts of heroism by the U.S. military and the American Merchant Marine.

XIV AN ACT OF PIRACY

PRELUDE

The years of 1974-75 were filled with worldwide economic and political unrest. Inflation created an upward spiral on the prices of food and fuel. The Arab oil embargo caused severe oil shortages and stiff price increases in gasoline which further heightened fears of inflation. The leading financial nations of the world showed little economic growth. In 1975, the unemployment rate in the U.S. reached 8.5 percent, its highest level since 1941, when it was 9.9 percent.[1]

In a demoralizing time for America, our personnel and troops had been evacuated from Vietnam on April 30, 1975. The United States ended its attempts to prevent the spread of communism in Southeast Asia. The war in Vietnam was viewed as a tragic error on the part America and tainted its role as a world leader. Nevertheless, this area of the world remained a hotbed of political activity. Cambodia fell to communism as its former president, Lon Nol, surrendered his country to the Khmer Rouge.

On the American political front, President Nixon resigned the presidency in 1974 and was pardoned. Several of his appointees, John Erlichman, H.R. Halderman and John N. Mitchell were convicted for their roles in the Watergate conspiracy and sentenced to prison. President Gerald Ford now led a country in desperate need of political and spiritual uplifting. Unrest was demonstrated by the two unsuccessful assassination attempts upon his life in September of that year. And, looming in much of the American subconscious was the humiliation of the USS *Pueblo* Incident six years earlier.*

---

* The USS *Pueblo* was a U.S. Navy vessel on an intelligence mission off the coast of North Korea. On January 23, 1968, she was attacked by North Korean naval vessels and MIG jets. One man was killed and several were wounded. The ship was captured. Eighty-two surviving crew members were captured and held prisoner for eleven months.

In Cambodia, the Khmer Rouge was also involved in a struggle with Vietnam over control of the offshore islands of Poulo Wai, Koh Tang and Ron Sam Lem. Cambodia had expanded the twelve-mile limit off these islands to ninety miles. This gave them control of the shipping lanes which passed through the area and claims to potential oil reserves in the seabed. To enforce their claim, the Khmer Rouge raided and seized a number of ships between May 2 and May 12, 1975.

AN ACT

OF PIRACY

2 AN ACT OF PIRACY

1

CAMBODIA AND THE

KHMER ROUGE

Cambodia was a French protectorate from 1863 until receiving its independence in 1953, along with Laos and Vietnam (It was occupied by the Japanese during World War II). Remaining essentially neutral even into the 1960s, Prince Norodom Sihanouk became the country's ruler and was popular with its citizens.

During his largely peaceful reign Sihanouk presided over a people that were well-treated. Because there was little political unrest in the country, the Khmer Rouge communists had little success. However, Cambodia and Vietnam had a history of disputes concerning their territorial waters. In 1969, Cambodia, in accordance with international law, extended its territorial waters to the recognized twelve-mile limit.

Dr. Raoul Marc Jenner:

> Cambodia became the first country in the Gulf of Thailand to establish territory waters to be five nautical miles in 1957. Prince

3

> Sihanouk also ordered the Cambodian Navy to protect the islands of Poulo Panjang, Poulo Wai and Koh Tang, whose occupation, he wrote, 'are essential to the good development and maritime future of the Port of Kompong-Som.'[1]

Meanwhile, as part of the war in Vietnam, President Nixon ordered the bombing of Communist bases and supply lines used by the North Vietnamese and the Vietcong in 1969. This caused the North Vietnamese to flee and infiltrate the Cambodian villages which were subsequently bombed. Prince Sihanouk disapproved of this action but there was little he could do to reverse it. Instead he began to support the Vietnamese with aid.

There soon developed a civil war in Cambodia between Prince Sihanouk and General Lon Nol. General Nol gained more supporters as they objected to Sihanouk's new attitude toward the North Vietnamese and the willingness of the prince to let them infiltrate the country with little regard to the Cambodians.

In March 1970, while Prince Sihanouk was in France dealing with health issues, his government was overthrown by General Nol. However, Prince Sihanouk established a government in exile. It was during this turbulence that he expressed his support for General Pol Pot who had become the leader of the North Vietnamese Communists.

Later that year, General Nol abolished the Cambodian monarchy established by Prince Sihanouk and the country was renamed the Khmer Republic. The U.S. supported General Nol in his effort to rid the Khmer Republic of the North Vietnamese.

> The United States moved to provide material assistance to the new government's armed forces, which were engaged against both the Khmer Rouge insurgents and NVA/VC [North Vietnamese Army/Viet Cong] forces. In April 1970, U.S. and South Vietnamese forces entered Cambodia in a campaign aimed at destroying NVA/VC base areas. Although a considerable quantity of equipment was seized and destroyed, NVA/VC forces were elusive and moved deeper into Cambodia. NVA/VC units overran many Cambodian Army positions while the Khmer Rouge expanded their small scale attacks on lines of communication.[2]

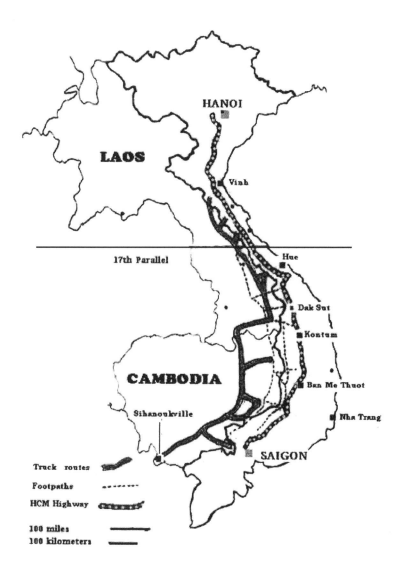

The Ho Chi Minh Trail included footpaths, truck routes and secluded highways that gave the NVA/VC access to South Vietnam. ABC-CLIO.

In all likelihood the "American bombing in Cambodia and the subsequent Cambodian casualties made Lon Nol's government unpopular, and may have caused support for the Khmer Rouge to grow, particularly in the countryside. Support for Sihanouk, in exile in Beijing, was strong in rural areas, and he urged resistance against Lon Nol's regime."[3]

From the very beginning of the new Khmer Republic, the leaders had difficulties. One of the most serious problems was:

> ...transforming a 30,000–man army into a national combat force of more than 200,000 men, and spreading corruption. The insurgency continued to grow, with supplies and military support provided by North Vietnam. But inside Cambodia, Pol Pot and Ieng Sary asserted dominance over the Vietnamese-trained communists, many of whom were purged. At the same time, the Khmer Rouge forces became stronger and more independent of their Vietnamese patrons.[4]

This shift in power was hastened by the act of U.S. Congress cutting aid to Cambodia. Included in the cuts was money to fund the bombing of the Khmer Rouge in 1973. "By 1974, Lon Nol's control was reduced to small enclaves around the cities and main transportation routes. More than 2 million refugees from the war lived in Phnom Penh."[5]

By 1975, the end was imminent for the Khmer Republic.

> On New Year's Day 1975, communist troops launched an offensive that, in 117 days of the hardest fighting of the war, destroyed the Khmer Republic. Simultaneous attacks around the perimeter of Phnom Penh pinned down Republican forces, while other Khmer Rouge units overran fire bases controlling the vital lower Mekong resupply route. A U.S.–funded airlift of ammunition and rice ended when Congress refused additional aid for Cambodia. Phnom Penh surrendered on April 17, 1975 – five days after the U.S. mission evacuated Cambodia.[6]

The Khmer Rouge Communists came to power in 1975. They ruled Cambodia between 1975 and 1979.

> The Khmer Rouge regime is remembered mainly for the deaths of an estimated 1.7 million people, through execution, starvation and forced labor. It was one of the most violent regimes of the 20th century; often compared with the regimes of Adolph Hitler and Joseph Stalin. In terms of the number of people killed as a proportion of the population of the country it ruled and time in power, it was probably the most lethal regime of the 20th century.[7]

After the Khmer Rouge took control of the government a major decision was made to reestablish and extend the territorial waters. The tiny islands of Poulo Wai and Koh Tang were included. The Cambodians had historically included these islands as theirs. The extension of the territorial waters beyond them, however, was new.

There were two underlying reasons for the continued policy and control of these islands. First:

> The administration [Khmer Rouge] … issued a decree in 1972 setting the size of the country's continental shelf and claiming Cambodia's rights over it. The territory covered a third of the waters claimed by Thailand, and three–quarters of the zone claimed by Vietnam. The lure of possible oil and gas contracts in the Gulf [of Thailand] prompted Cambodia and its neighbors to act without consulting each other. Cambodia and Vietnam's claims overlapped by 60,000 square km.[8]

A U.S. Defense Intelligence Appraisal document stated, "It appears that the Khmer Communists (KC) have decided to garrison on the islands before the Vietnamese Communists focus their attention on them. Poulo Wai and Koh Tang Islands are two of the KC garrisoned locations."[9]

The second reason for Cambodian and Vietnam fighting over the islands was that they were strategically located in the middle of major shipping lanes. The basic issue was that Cambodia had extended her twelve-mile territorial rights to ninety miles offshore, including the two islands in question. By claiming these islands and establishing a new territorial boundary, the message from the Khmer Rouge to the Vietnamese was quite clear.

There were important incidents (later confirmed by the GAO [U.S. Government Accounting Office]) that rapidly developed from April 25th to May 12th setting the stage for the *Mayaguez* seizure. On April 25th at a "Special National Congress" held in Cambodia, Sihanouk was declared the Chief of State and Penn Nouth the new Prime Minister. On May 1, a State Department Status Report on Cambodia stated, "At present, to our knowledge, no foreign nation has an Embassy in Phnom Penh. [GAO Note: State Department later said that there may have been People's Republic of China personnel in Phnom Penh at this time but there was no indication that an Embassy had been established.]"[10]

On May 2nd:

> ... a group of Thai fishing boats were seized and later released by Cambodian authorities. On May 4th, a Korean ship was fired upon by a Cambodian patrol boat but it escaped. Korean officials requested U.S. assistance. U.S. officials in Korea discussed the situation on several occasions with State Department officials in Washington by telephone. On May 6th, six vessels fleeing from South Vietnam and a South Vietnam Government craft were seized by Cambodia.[11]

On May 7th, "the new Cambodian regime was focusing attention on which islands they should control because of possible petroleum reserves. Also on that date, a Panamanian ship was seized and released about thirty-five hours later on the authority of the Cambodian hierarchy."[12]

Finally, the GAO later reported that on May 9th, "There was some evidence to suggest the new Cambodian Government was claiming a ninety–mile territorial limit and planned to seize foreign ships violating such limits."[13]

The situation in this part of the world, made volatile by a major war, and fueled by years of disagreements between Cambodia and Vietnam, was disintegrating. The area was ripe for a major political event such as the seizure of another vessel; one unfortunately owned by the United States.

2

S.S. *MAYAGUEZ*

The North Carolina Shipbuilding Company

    … was one of the original nine emergency yards, developed by Newport News Shipbuilding in 1941 with six ways… Its six ways were increased to nine in the second wave of shipbuilding expansion. At its peak, North Carolina Shipbuilding employed 15,000 people and had the best productivity of any of the Liberty shipbuilders. After the war, the yard was held in reserve as a stand-by yard until the 1950s, when it was liquidated.[1]

North Carolina built 243 ships consisting of cargo vessels, military cargo vessels and attack cargo vessels. The first ship, *Zebulon Vance* was launched 6 December 1941 and the final ship, *Santa Isabel* was delivered in October 1946.[2]

She began as hull No. 114 for the North Carolina Shipbuilding Company of Wilmington, North Carolina in January of 1944. Construction on the vessel that would later be named *Mayaguez* was completed after three months and on April 24, 1944 she was christened *White Falcon* by the War Shipping Administration (WSA). She was one of sixty-four (C2–S–AJ1) cargo vessels measuring 8,335 gross tons commissioned by the Maritime Commission. Her length was 459' 2" with a beam of 63 feet. The ship was powered by turbine engines generating 6,000 horsepower. Her top speed was 15.5 knots.

The *White Falcon* was used in the North Atlantic convoys for the remainder of World War II under the house flag of American Export Lines. After the war, in 1947, Grace Line purchased her and she was renamed *Santa Eliana*. For the next twelve years she was used to transport machinery and other equipment to Venezuela and return with bananas and cork.

In 1959 the *Santa Eliana* began the first of two notable periods in her life. She, along with the *Santa Leonor*, was sent to the Maryland Shipbuilding and Drydock Company's Baltimore yard where the process of converting them to container ships began. The rebuilding of the *Santa Eliana* was described thus:

> The main structural alterations included the addition of a 45 ft. long mid-section, extending the beam by 11 ft. with blisters and sponsons, the division of the hull into cellular holds capable of carrying, within each cell, from two to five containers. Three gantry cranes were installed (two forward and one aft) traveling on tracks and equipped with automatic and manual systems for loading and discharging. Among other items of new equipment were special hatch covers and a new high-level bridge above the old one to permit unobstructed vision over the cranes. In their new guise the vessels had a length of 504 ft. 6 in. (o.a.) and a breadth of 74 ft.. Capacity was 476 containers, of which 382 were stored below and 94 carried on deck. The sponsons were equipped to carry petroleum.[3]

The cost of the renovations was $10,500,000.

Containerization would revolutionize the entire shipping industry, affecting not only ships but docks, ports and workers. Containers as long as forty feet could be directly loaded onto ships and off-loaded onto railroad cars or trucks. The cost-savings in eliminating the numerous traditional handling charges

A new mid-section is lined up on the Santa Eliana *prior to being welded to the old engine room and superstructure to create a new "Seatainer" vessel.* Grace Line, Inc.

were tremendous and eagerly anticipated. The savings on pilferage alone, now that the containers were sealed, was a tremendous asset.

On January 12, 1960 the *Santa Eliana* entered New York harbor to great fanfare. Excitement was high concerning her new role. For the first two weeks her mission was one of education. Grace Line offered "sales seminars aboard the vessel. Company

The Santa Eliana *as she appeared on January 12, 1960.* Grace Line, Inc.

officials said they expected that most of the ship's 4,500 dead-weight tons capacity would be in use when the ship sails January 29 on her initial voyage ..."[4]

The cost-savings began in earnest after the two week educational period. On January 29, 1960, the *Santa Eliana* shifted to Port Newark, N.J., and began loading her cargo. The huge gantry cranes aboard swung 176 steel and aluminum containers into the ship's hold while trailer rigs were relieved of their eighteen-ton containers. It was said that this new method of cargo handling, "reduced to thirty-one hours the time it takes to discharge and load a full cargo. This means that 476 containers can be unloaded and the same number loaded in substantially less time than conventional methods would require."[5]

According to Grace Line, containerization meant that a trucker or railroad car could pick up a loaded sealed container from anywhere and then ship it to Port Newark where it would be picked off the truck rig or railroad car by the gantry crane and loaded onto the ship. The process was reversed when the ship reached its destination port.

The *Santa Eliana*'s captain, Ronald Mackenzie, explained in a news conference that, "the container service virtually eliminated pilferage en route. The containers are made of aluminum and steel. The top of the container and a side door are secured with special bolts sealed at the point of origin. They are unsealed on arrival by special representatives of the consignees."[6]

On January 29th, in an historic voyage, *Santa Eliana* departed on her 4,500 mile round trip to three Venezuelan ports;

La Guaira, Puerto Cabello and Maracaibo. She was the first U.S.-flagged container ship. Her cargo consisted of chemicals, clothing, machinery, powdered milk, and radios. However, upon arrival at La Guaira on February 2nd, the Venezuelan dock workers refused to unload the ship because of the new loading equipment. They felt the ship represented a threat to their jobs. A boycott resulted and by February 20 was in its 18th day. Grace Line revealed that the boycott was costing them $2,500 a day.

On the following day an agreement was reached so the *Santa Eliana* could be unloaded.

> A spokesman for the Grace Line said that an agreement had been worked out with terms satisfactory to the workers and that a commission would be established to work out a permanent solution to the mechanization problem. The terms for releasing the *Santa Eliana* were not known here, but the Grace Line were said to have accepted them with the proviso that they would not establish a precedent for future ships.[7]

On February 22nd the terms were released; Venezuelan longshoremen would unload the cargo and, in return, Grace Line would no longer send containerized ships to Venezuela.

The Santa Leonor *later became the* Ponce *for Sea-Land, Inc. Here she is shown in the English Channel in 1967.* Skyfotos.

The *Santa Eliana* and the other Grace Line containership, *Santa Leonor*, spent the next six months tied up in Baltimore awaiting their fate. The idle time at $2,500 a day was now running $75,000 per month. This total didn't include the $4 million investment cost to convert the freighters to container ships or the $3 million invested in buying the containers.[8]

The return on investment to date had been zero, although *Santa Eliana* was entitled to a U.S. government subsidy because she made a single voyage to Venezuela. Even after the six month period, Grace Line did not ask the U.S. government to intervene. The company didn't want an international dispute on their hands. One-and-a-half years later in February 1962, the two ships were still tied up at the Baltimore harbor.

In 1963 Grace Line launched a new 14,000 gross ton ship named *Santa Magdalena* — a combination cargo-passenger ship. She became the largest ship to sail from the U.S. to South

The Santa Magdalena *arriving in New York City for the first time on February 8, 1963.* Flying Camera.

America's West coast. The president of Grace Line, W.J. Mc-Neil, was also confident at this time that a settlement between the Venezuelan government, who controlled the Venezuelan dock workers, and U.S. State Department was imminent.

Grace Line eventually sold *Santa Eliana* and *Santa Leonor* to Sea-Land Service of Menlo Park, New Jersey. The ships were immediately sent to Pascagoula, Mississippi for additional conversion. The container cells on board were enlarged to accommodate the new 35 ft. containers.

The *Santa Eliana* was re-christened with the name *Sea* in 1964. Her sister ship became the *Land*. The *Sea* was put to work between the Gulf states and Puerto Rico. While on this run in 1965, the *Sea* was re-named *Mayaguez,* after a major port on Puerto Rico's west coast.

In 1965, the *Mayaguez* departed from New Orleans for Oakland, and eventually the Far East, to carry cargo and support the U.S. forces in Vietnam. It was while operating in the China Sea during the Vietnam War that *Mayaguez* finally showed her ability. The large gantry cranes were an asset in the deep water ports, enabling the ship to move 274 containers quickly ashore. Her route during this era was to shuttle from Hong Kong to Saigon to Sattahip to Singapore.

On April 21, the *Mayaguez* loaded in the port of Saigon. Her cargo consisted of 274 containers: "(107 routine commer-

The Mayaguez *ex-*Sea *ex-*Santa Eliana *ex-*White Falcon *alongside in New Orleans.* William F. Hultgren collection.

cial cargo, 77 military cargo, and 90 empty; the 77 containers of military cargo consisted of 2 mail, 26 of machine parts, supplies, and replacement equipment, three of subsistence supplies, 8 of commissary supplies, and 38 of post exchange items.)"[9]

3

MAY 12, 1975

GULF OF THAILAND

The *Mayaquez* was steaming approximately sixty miles off the Cambodian coast in a heavily traveled sea lane. According to the manifests, her cargo consisted of food, chemicals, clothing, mail and consumer products. The ship's course took her six to seven miles off the island of Poulo Wai, now occupied by a Khmer Rouge garrison. The Khmer Rouge had recently started enforcing the international twelve-mile sea territorial limit measured from its offshore islands. During the preceding two weeks several incidents occurred in which the Khmer Rouge demonstrated its increasing aggressiveness.

- May 2 — a group of Thai fishing boats were seized and later released by the Cambodian authorities.
- May 4 — a Korean ship was fired upon by a Cambodian patrol boat but escaped. Korean officials requested U.S. assistance. U.S. officials in Korea discussed the situation several times on the phone with Washington.

- May 6 — six vessels fleeing from South Vietnam and a South Vietnamese government craft were seized by Cambodia.
- May 7 — a Panamanian ship was seized and released about thirty-five hours later on the authority of the Cambodian government.
- May 9 — there was some evidence to suggest the new Cambodian government was claiming a ninety-mile territorial limit and planned to seize foreign ships violating such limits.[1]

Nonetheless, there was little concern expressed by the American military command and no warnings were issued concerning the area.

Sixty-two-year-old Charles T. Miller had taken command of the *Mayaguez* in January.

Capt. Charles T. Miller

Capt. Miller was born in 1912. He and his sister were raised in a foster home. After a brief career as a horse jockey he decided to go to sea. According to Miller, he "sailed on forty ships over the next forty years." During those years Capt. Miller worked his way up through the hawse pipe. He "began his slow rise from ordinary seaman to ship's captain learning the ropes mostly on the treacherous South China Sea, working on a succession of cargo vessels, troop carriers and passenger liners."[2]

In the spring of 1953 Capt. Miller took part in the humanitarian effort to help Pakistan. There had been a catastrophic drought in that country causing a famine. After a request by its president, Mohammad Ali, President Eisenhower asked Congress to authorize the shipment of one million tons of wheat to Pakistan. The SS *Anchorage Victory* was chosen to be the first American ship to deliver the wheat. Capt. Miller was master of that ship.

On June 26th 1953, the *Anchorage Victory* left Baltimore with a cargo of 9,860 tons of wheat. Upon arrival in Karachi Harbor, observers saw painted on the side of the ship hands clasping and the statement, "Wheat for Pakistan from the United States of America."

The Anchorage Victory *arrives in Karachi "dressed" with flags from bow to stern.* James Miller.

Speaking in an interview, "Capt. Miller expressed his conviction that he was speaking for the entire crew saying, 'We're proud to bring the stuff over here.'"

Between 1958 and 1966 Miller ran a small shipping company — which owned one vessel transporting Moslem pilgrims from Indonesia to Mecca — but went broke when he tried to finance a "World Trade" ship to carry manufacturers' exhibits around the globe.[3]

Capt. Miller supervises the stevedores unloading wheat from his ship in Pakistan. James Miller.

Stephen Zarley was twenty-eight-years-old and worked in the Engine Department as a wiper:

> Upon our arrival in Hong Kong we were told that we would be making another trip to Sattahip. We took on apples, clothing and general goods for the PX. We set sail on the evening of May 10.
>
> [On May 12] I arose at my regular time of 0630 and went into the chow hall for coffee. There was only one thing planned for us other than the usual cleanup. The chief engineer, Cliff Harrington, asked us to wash down the turbines and the main condenser.

Capt. Miller:

> At 1418 in the afternoon of the 12th, the third mate on watch, Mr. Coombs, called me and told me to get up on the bridge, he saw a gunboat approaching us carrying a red flag.
>
> I arrived on the bridge, and a few seconds later, a burst of machine-gun fire was shot over the bow. They were about a quarter of a mile away from us.
>
> The ship was not fast enough, I could not outrun them, so the only thing I could do was proceed and see if they would fire another burst at me.
>
> The second burst, they put a rocket — they all had shoulder-held rocket guns — over the forecastle head of the ship. I decided it would be best to stop, let them investigate and see what I was carrying, and find out why they wanted me to stop or why they fired shots over the ship. I didn't intend to have any of the crew injured by the next rocket fire or mortars.
>
> I stopped and was boarded by several armed insurgents (seven carrying AK-47's) of the Khmer Rouge army. They immediately came to the bridge, put a gun on me and the gunboat left the side of the ship.

Stephen Zarley:

> It was after two o'clock, and my partner Tyrone Matthews and I were in the lower engine room when I heard the telegraph bell. The telegraph was located next to the throttles, on the next deck going up, facing the turbines and boilers. I wondered what the bell was for since we were sailing in the open sea. The only reason to maneuver was that there must be a problem with the fishing boats which travel in groups and often cross the bow of a larger ship.

Ten minutes later I went up to get a drink of water. On the blackboard was written "X 1420?" The "X" is the symbol for stop engines and 1420 is the time, 2:20 in the afternoon. I was puzzled over the question mark so I asked the first engineer, Vern Greenlin, what was happening.

The first had taken his maneuvering post at the throttles and was speaking with Americo Faria (12-4 Oiler.) He told me that Faria had been topside doing his rounds when he saw two gunboats coming towards the ship and they had fired. The first was a joker and I didn't believe him. I told him to tell me the real reason the ship had stopped. He didn't know what was going on; all he knew was what Faria had said. The bridge hadn't phoned so the first asked me to go topside and find out what was happening and then come back and report.

I went to the chow hall and it seemed like the entire crew was there. Everyone was talking at once and from the looks on their faces and the sound of their voices I knew something serious was happening. It was the chief steward (Andy Anderson) who finally spoke to me. He confirmed what Faria had told the first. He added that our attackers were Cambodian and about fifteen of them were on the bridge.

I left Andy and went to report to the first. The first, Faria, Minichiello (12-4 Third Engineer) and Carlos Guerrero (12-4 FWT) huddled around me as I repeated Andy's words. I had forgotten Tyrone in the lower engine room so I rushed down to tell him.

All of us then, stood around asking each other the unanswerable questions like; What do they want with us? Will they let us go? Are they pirates?

A while later, the chief [engineer] came down the ladder and asked what all the fuss was about. He had been working in the diesel generator room and hadn't heard about the boarding. Again I told the story. The chief took his favorite seat in front of the turbines and the same questions were asked again. At three o'clock, Tyrone and I went up for coffee.

The crew were all gathered together in the chow hall and all wondering what was going to happen next. The *Pueblo* Incident of 1968 was brought up. The thought of a sharing the same fate as they was most discouraging. Eleven months as prisoners and one dead. Torture, disease, hunger, confessions. Our future seemed bleak, indeed. We also remembered that no military action was taken during the seizure of the *Pueblo*. Our most pressing question was if sparks (Radio Operator Wilbert Boch) had gotten off a message.

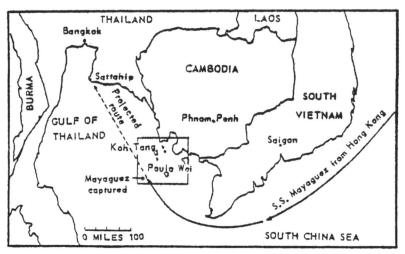

Route of the Mayaguez *from Hong Kong to Sattahip showing where she was captured off Cambodia.* Author's collection.

Capt. Miller:

The gunboat proceeded to the island of Poulo Wai. That is an island that has been in dispute for the last ten years that I know of [as to] whether it was owned by Cambodia or South Vietnam.

There were no people on the boarding party that spoke any English; all they could speak was Cambodian. By sign language they pointed to the gunboat, which indicated they wanted me to follow it, which I did.

We have two speeds, or three speeds on the ship; we have maneuvering speed, which is 20 rpm's on slow, 40 rpm's on half and 60 rpm's on full. That is for maneuvering in and around close quarters. When we are out to sea we run around 75 or 76 rpm's, which gives us around a speed of 14 or 15 knots; it depends on the currents of the area.

When they indicated that they wanted me to follow the gunboat into the island of Poulo Wai, I put her on half speed, which gave me 40 rpm's, a delaying action, because we had already gotten an SOS off on the radio; the radio operator ["Sparks"] contacted two vessels — one a Philippine ship and one a Danish ship — and they were told to notify the American authorities we were being seized by a Cambodian gunboat.

I proceeded following the gunboat; it outran me a little bit but we kept them in sight so we could know where we were going.

Stephen Zarley:

I got my first look at our captors at 3:30 PM. A small, young, dark-complexioned man came into the chow hall. He was completely dressed in black with a scarf wrapped around his neck. He carried an M-16 automatic rifle and wore a cartridge belt across his chest. He motioned with his hand for us to leave the chow hall and go out onto the starboard side deck. We did!

When I got on deck the ship was underway. We were going dead slow and circling a small island, heading towards a group of others. The islands were not too high and have a full, rich tropical growth set behind sandy beaches. There were no gunboats in sight. I saw about six armed Cambodians on deck. One who was guarding the door we had just come through, one near the forward crane, one guarding the ladder leading to the bridge, and a couple on the main deck below us. After a while, the ship stopped and two gunboats came towards us from one of the islands. When the gunboats came alongside, a few of the deck crew lent a hand. It was obvious that the Cambodians knew nothing of seamanship. Jungle boys, Khmer Rouge. (At some point during the rest of the day they identified themselves as Khmer Rouge.)

The boats looked like they just came from the factory. Grey in color and with large white numerals painted on the bow. They each had twin 50-caliber machine guns mounted in a turret above the wheelhouse. On the stern was a larger gun; more like a cannon used for shore bombardment. The boats were equipped with radar and radio. One boat was flying a solid red flag while the other flew the Vietcong flag. The twin 50s pointed at our deck until twenty-five or thirty of their men came aboard.

The Khmer Rouge are a ragged looking bunch. No uniforms or shoes. Most wore sandals but some were barefoot. The hats were all different, some wearing hard shell campaign hats, others had Aussie-style green campaign hats, others had black berets, and some were hatless. All of them had scarves wrapped around their necks. (Later, they would steal blue towels from the linen locker and use those for scarves.) What the Khmers lacked in clothing they made up for in arms. Their weapons consisted of the American M16, the Russian AK-47, Chinese grenades and M79 grenade launchers. There was one gun that I didn't recognize which had a muzzle with a very wide diameter. The men with the M16s and AK-47s had plenty of spare cartridge clips strung around their waists.

Capt. Miller:

The radio operator came up on the bridge at that time; the armed insurgents put a gun on him; they didn't want him to talk to me but he had already gotten the SOS to the two ships.

The insurgents didn't want me to talk to anybody in the crew. The radio operator stood over in one corner and advised me he had gotten the SOS off to the two ships — the Philippine ship and the Danish vessel. I don't know the names; he didn't get them himself.

So I asked the radio operator to go down and get a Mayday out on our single sideband. The Mayday was put out and the tug *Bianca* answered back and we asked the captain to notify the authorities. He was a Philippine tug, and the owner was the Luzon Stevedore Co., in Manila.

The radio operator heard the conversation between the tug and his office that the authorities in Manila had already received word, which, I imagine, was Subic Bay, the military authorities there. So this made me feel a lot better, that our military had been notified that the ship had been seized.

(At 1418 local time the Delta Exploration Company in Jakarta, Indonesia, received a Mayday call from the ship: "Have been fired upon and boarded by Cambodian armed forces at 9 degrees 48 minutes north/102 degrees 53 minutes east. Ship was being [taken] to unknown Cambodian port.")

We proceeded then and went in on the mainland side of Poulo Wai Island into a little cove there. They wanted me to go about a half mile off the beach.

I was steaming in a northwest direction coming up here and was six and-a-half miles off Poulo Wai. There are two islands in the group ... I imagine this is the position that the military authority received when we sent the SOS.

I then followed the gunboat in and around the island into the mainland side. They wanted me to anchor about a quarter mile off the beach but I refused because I knew the SOS had been received by American authorities and our air base in Thailand was only around 280 miles away, U-Tapao Air Base. I figured if there was any rescue people to come to save us they would come out of U-Tapao and I didn't want to get in too close to the land to receive fire from the shore if a rescue party came. They would only have to fight several Khmer Rouge insurgents aboard the ship at the time.

Stephen Zarley:

The ship moved again and we were told that we were going to go to the mainland. Once in a while I could hear the captain speak. I couldn't understand what was being said, but from his actions it was plain that he didn't want to move the ship again. He was stalling. He was trying to tell the Khmers that it was getting dark, he was afraid that the ship would go aground since he was unfamiliar with the area and our radar was out. Sparks had gotten a message out and the captain was holding off in hope that the military would arrive. We were only 100 miles from a U.S. airbase. We moved again but only a short distance and anchored off a group of three islands. We stayed the night there.

The Khmers let us have pretty much the run of the ship but they were everywhere. Earlier we had given them oranges and cigarettes in hope that if they thought we were a friendly lot they might treat us well.

During the evening, I could see firing from one of the islands. Tracers were being used and I could hear gun reports. (Later, I learned that the Khmers had fired on a Japanese and a Scandinavian ship. Neither one was hit.) I went to bed at ten-thirty. Some guys couldn't sleep but I felt the Khmers didn't want to kill us. Not yet, anyway, or else they would have done so before. If they were going to kill us, better that I was asleep.[4]

Capt. Miller:

We laid there overnight, and the following day they wanted me to go in by Baie de Ream. I refused to go in to Baie de Ream because I only had a small-scale chart; I had no large-scale chart of the area and you don't know where the reefs are and how much water is in there. I refused to take the ship in.

They had me heave up the anchor at 6 o'clock in the morning. (I believe the time was) and he wanted me to go in this direction. I told them no because there were no soundings on the chart; I would go in behind Kas Tang Island.

So the gunboat led us in and took us into a little bay there.

The only conversation that I could have was with the Khmer Rouge navy ensign that was on the ship, around thirty-two years old; he knew all about the chart. When I told him there was not enough water, he pointed on my sounding figures, the 18, 19, 20, and he asked me if they were fathoms or meters.

Well, meters is a lot less water than fathoms, so I lied to him and told him they were meters, I couldn't go in, the ship was drawing too much water.

They wanted me to go into a beach here about a quarter of a mile, a little cove off Kas Tang Island. There is a lot confusion here. "Koh" means "island," and "kas" means "island." On the chart it says "Kas Tang"; we call it "Koh Tang."…

I refused and anchored off Koh Tang Island in 15 fathoms of water with five-and-a-half shots of chain on the anchor*. The reason I did that, I still wanted to stay away from land in case a rescue party came so we wouldn't receive the gunfire from the island. We could see they were well fortified. They agreed to let me anchor about a mile off the beach there.

It was around 4 o'clock in the afternoon when the first American aircraft came over the ship. It was a big four-engine Orion recon ship. That came from Subic Bay. He flew over the ship, I would say 500 or 600 feet above the ship, right over the smokestack, and he received fire from the insurgents that were onboard.

Here in the night, anchored off Poulo Wai, they put on more armed insurgents. We had around forty armed insurgents [on board] when we shifted to Koh Tang Island. They were up on the forecastle head and had been patrolling the hotel section of the ship where I and the crew had our quarters.

I anchored off there and the recon plane flew over, as I said, practically over the smokestack of the ship. He made another pass and flew around 70 feet above the forecastle head, and the name of the ship is on both sides of the bow in about eighteen-inch letters. He definitely identified the vessel as being the *Mayaquez*.[5]

---

* A shot of chain is equal to 15 fathoms or 90 feet.

4

MILITARY

RECONNAISSANCE

In Jakarta, Indonesia, John Neal of the Delta Exploration Company received the message on May 12 at 1418. During the next hour, he listened for additional communication from the ship but to no avail. Finally, he contacted the U.S. Embassy in Jakarta. An hour-and-a-half after the message was received, the "U.S. Defense Attaché Office in Singapore, informed Commander of the Seventh Fleet that local shipping agency had received Mayday relayed by a tugboat; 'Being boarded by Cambodian army and commandeered at position 9 degrees 48 minutes north/102 degrees 23 minutes east.' Vessel identified itself as an American flag ship..."[1]

At 1545 the U.S. Defense Attaché's Office in Singapore contacted Command of the Seventh Fleet that a local shipping agency had received a Mayday from an American flag ship. CINCPAC [Commander IN Chief, PACific] Honolulu received the message and forwarded it to Washington.

Between 1554 and 1755 the U.S Embassy in Jakarta sent a series of six messages concerning the seizure to the National Security Agency, the White House, the Central Intelligence Agency, the National Military Command Center and other concerned commands. The six messages concerned the following conditions aboard the vessel:

1. Vessel is under own power slowly following one gunboat to Kompong Som.
2. No casualties were evident.
3. Crew doesn't feel to be in immediate danger.
4. Troops on board do not speak any English.
5. Crew standing by for instructions.[2]

As a result, Washington began to react:

> At 0512 (Eastern Daylight Time)* on May 12th, the Defense Department's National Military Command Center received notification of the seizure and discussed the report with Pacific Command in Hawaii at 0534. Almost two hours later, at 0730, the Center directed the Pacific Command to launch a reconnaissance aircraft from U-Tapao, Thailand, to obtain a photographic, visual, or radar fix on the ship and its armed escort. It was not until 0957 (night time in Cambodia), however, that the first reconnaissance plane, a P-3 at U-Tapao, was launched.

Congressional hearings later questioned the timing of the Command Center's response:

> The question arises as to why almost five hours elapsed before this elementary action was undertaken.
> Although the *Mayaguez* was only moved a short distance from the point of seizure during this five hours, the delay in launching aircraft could have considerably increased the potential search area for reconnaissance and the vessel could have been moved to the Cambodian mainland.
> Defense has stated that, as soon as the report of the seizure was received, the requirement to locate the vessel was immediately

---

* There is an eleven hour difference between Cambodia and Washington.

recognized and the process started. The Thailand-based P-3 was not kept on alert, so it had to be readied, the crew briefed, the mission planned, and all other pre take-off activities completed. Given the situation, Defense said that the aircraft was launched in remarkable time. (A P-3 aircraft in the Philippines was on ready alert but the flying time to the vicinity of the seizure was about four hours. The flying time from U-Tapao was only forty minutes).

According to Defense, the P-3 was the proper craft to be assigned to this mission because of its unique capabilities. The P-3 is a large, propeller-driven aircraft specially equipped for long-range surveillance. Jet fighters were initially considered for reconnaissance but were rejected due to their lack of staying power and the fact that their use might have been interpreted as a military signal. Unlike the P-3, however, jet aircraft were on the alert in Thailand and could have been quickly launched. Other aircraft in Thailand were also available for, and suited to, such a reconnaissance mission. For example, the AC-130, which provided coverage after the *Mayaguez* was located, is specifically equipped to operate at night.

Although other aircraft in Thailand probably could have been launched sooner, the local U.S. command had no operational authority to launch aircraft for reconnaissance purposes closer than twelve miles to Cambodian territory. [Security deletion] Approval for the launch of reconnaissance aircraft into Cambodian airspace originated in the Office of the Secretary of Defense.

Defense acknowledged the need to improve the process of initiating reconnaissance but did not identify any specific steps being implemented.

It did emphasize that because of the sensitive political situation in Southeast Asia action in that part of the world was initiated with extreme caution.[3]

Meanwhile, the Deputy Director for Operations of the National Military Commend Center requested CINCPAC to launch the Orion P-3 Recon planes from the U-Tapao air base in Thailand. Other conditions of surveillance were also reviewed at this time:

1. That CINCPAC provide continuous P-3 surveillance over the Gulf of Siam north of 8 degrees north and east of 101 degrees east, no closer than twelve nautical miles to the Cambodian mainland, islands excluded.

2. That CINCPAC provide photo coverage of Phnom Penh, Sihanoukville, and the island of Poulo Wai at first satisfactory light, regardless of cover...

From this guidance, CINCPAC further instructed CINCPACFLT [Commander IN Chief PACific FLeeT] to report sightings of Cambodian naval units as well as the captured *Mayaguez*, and obtain photos of Cambodian naval units as feasible. This mission was, in turn, passed to the Commander, Philippine Air Patrol Group (CTG 72.3), who had P-3 aircraft located at his primary base of operations, Cubi Point, Republic of the Philippines, and at his logistic base and refueling stop, U-Tapao Royal Thai Naval Air Station, Thailand. At 0166Z hours, 13 May a P-3 aircraft reported positive identification of the *Mayaguez* at 9 degrees 56' N, 102 degrees 58' E.[4]

There was some confusion over the film processing mechanics and "exploitation procedures for photo reconnaissance." The Joint Chiefs of Staff (JCS) hadn't issued complete instructions concerning the processing, duplication and dissemination of photo reconnaissance. "... but after a telephone exchange between CINCPAC J2 and the Defense Intelligence Agency (DIA), the DIA provided instructions to CINCPAC, SAC [Strategic Air Command], and the SAC Reconnaissance Center, with information copies to Air Force headquarters."[5] However, instructions were not passed on to the P-3 Recon planes as directed by the JCS.

This omission was apparently resolved (possibly through operational channels) because approximately three hours after the DIA message, CINCPAC J2 directed COMUSSAG, CINCPACAF, and CINCPACFLT to follow the DIA instructions for processing and distributing .... CINCPAC also directed CINCPACFLT to forward unprocessed P-3 mission imagery to the 432nd Reconnaissance Technical Squadron (RTS) at Udorn for initial processing and rapid readout. The 432nd RTS was to prepare the Initial Photo Interpretation Report (IPIR) and dispatch it to specified addressees as 'Special USN P-3 coverage.' A duplicate positive was to be sent to the Fleet Air Intelligence Service Center (FAISC) Pacific, and the original negative to Fleet Intelligence Center Pacific in Hawaii.

Because the Navy P-3 unit at U-Tapao, Thailand had not been an addressee on the CINCPAC message, COMUSSAG retransmitted the message to the U-Tapao-based P-3 unit, but apparently too late. A little more than six hours after the dispatch of the CINCPAC message, COMUSSAG was informed that the first P-3 film had been sent to FAISC Pacific at Cubi Point, Philippines, for processing.

Subsequent imagery was handled as instructed, however, and, when the operation to recover the *Mayaguez* and her crew was authorized, CINCPAC provided film handling instructions for Fleet tactical aerial photo reconnaissance operations.[6]

CINCPAC instructions to COMUSSAG eventually included providing the following recon photos as the seizure and rescue plans unfolded:

- Photo coverage of Phnom Penh, Sihanoukville, Hon Panjang Island (09 degrees 18' N., 103 degrees 28' E.), and the island groups in the vicinity of 09 degrees 58' N., 102 degrees 53' E. (Poulo Wai).
- Flights over Phnom Penh and Sihanoukville to be restricted to a minimum altitude of 6,000 feet, while flights over the islands were restricted to a minimum of 4,500 feet.
- The Essential Elements of Information (EEI) to include merchant ships, naval craft and paratroop landing/drop zones.
- After the *Mayaguez* was located and under observation, CINCPAC requested initial imagery of Koh Tang Island and daily coverage until after the execution of contemplated recovery operations.
- Flights in the vicinity of Koh Tang Island were restricted to a minimum altitude of 6,500 feet. The EEI now included:

Pier Facilities.
Gun emplacements.
Fortifications.
Small boat locations.
Troop concentrations.
Evidence of ship/shore personnel movement to/
from *Mayaguez.*
One-time readout of building locations and
helicopter landing areas.[7]

The end result was that the vital information was eventually forthcoming but the amount of time it took to gather it was, indeed, questionable. Testimony given said that the "First U.S. aircraft arrived on the scene at about 10:30 AM (2130 in Cambodia). It identified a ship of the same class but could not positively identify the *Mayaguez.* At 9:16 PM (1016 in Cambodia) the third U.S. reconnaissance aircraft on the scene positively identified the *Mayaguez.* It was "dead" in the water at Poulo Wai Island, sixty miles from the Cambodian mainland and only several miles from where it was boarded. From this time forward, the *Mayaguez* was under continuous aerial surveillance.[8]

SS Mayaguez *is dead in the water with two Khmer Rouge gunboats alongside.*
U.S. Air Force.

5

MAY 12, 1975

WASHINGTON, D.C.

During his regular morning intelligence report, President Ford was advised by Deputy Asst. for National Security Affairs, Lt. Gen. Brent Scowcroft at 0740 that the American ship *Mayaguez* was fired upon, boarded and seized. Information was limited so soon after the seizure and Scowcroft could only outline the situation in the area, explain that the Mayday message had been received and define the type of ship and the physical location of the seizure.

President Ford called for a National Security Council (NSC) meeting at noon.

Prior to the meeting the following activities were authorized:

- 0810– 0832. Pacific Command requested authority to use flares/search lights for illumination for photo coverage. The National Military Command Center (NMCC) OK's

USS Harold E. Holt *(FF-1074) was a Knox class frigate named after the Australian Prime Minister Harold Holt. She was built by Todd Pacific Shipyards in San Pedro, California, and launched in 1969. She was one of the first ships sent to rescue the* Mayaguez *crew. U.S. Navy.*

request. Restricted aircraft ordered outside of Cambodian twelve-mile territorial limit and at the orders of Ford, "Get aircraft airborne."

- 0937. CINCPACFLT – Hawaii orders nearest surface ships to area.
- 0957. P-3 Reconnaissance aircraft launched.
- 1005. Pacific Command notified NMCC that P-3 aircraft en route from Cubi Point, Philippines.
- 1019. The destroyer USS *Holt* and supply ship USS *Vega* get underway for the area.[1]

The National Security Council meeting began at 1205, Monday, May 12. The Principals attending were President Ford, Vice President Nelson Rockefeller, Secretary of State Henry Kissinger, Secretary of Defense James Schlesinger, Acting Chief, Joint Chiefs of Staff General David C. Jones and Director of Central Intelligence William Colby. Other attendees included Deputy Secretary of State Robert Ingersoll, Deputy Secretary of Defense William Clements, Assistant to the President Donald Rumsfeld, Deputy Assistant for National Security Affairs Lt. Gen. Brent Scowcroft, and Senior NSC Staff Officer for East Asia Richard Smyser. The meeting lasted forty-five minutes and was held in the White House Cabinet Room.

USS Vega (AF-59) was also sent to aid in the Mayaguez *rescue. She was built in 1954 by the Ingalls Shipbuilding Corp. and launched in 1955.*

President Ford began by requesting an update from CIA Director William Colby. Colby described what was known concerning the seizure, the geographical area, the territorial dispute involving oil rights and the erratic activity involving the Khmer Rouge communists.

President Ford: "What are our options?"

James Schlesinger:

> We can have a passive stance or we can be active. We could do such things as seizing Cambodian assets. We can assemble forces. We could seize a small island as a hostage. We might also consider a blockade. All these options would have to be scrutinized by Congress because, while you have inherent rights to protect American citizens, you would soon run into the CRA [Continuing Resolution Authority].
>
> We do not have such affirmation on the actual situation. Such information as we have indicates that the main purpose of the Cambodian forces in occupying the islands may have been to keep them from their brethren in South Vietnam. It could be a bureaucratic misjudgment or a by-product of an action against South Vietnam.
>
> The Cambodians have already seized three ships: a Panamanian, a Philippine and now an American. They did release the first two ships. We do not know, in handling this sort of thing, how good their communications is.

Discussion then shifted to the proximity of the *Maya-guez* to the islands when she was seized.

William Colby: [She was] "About seven to eight miles."

Donald Rumsfeld: "Isn't this piracy?"

James Schlesinger: "Yes."

Henry Kissinger:

> As I see it, Mr. President, we have two problems: The first problem is how to get the ship back. The second problem is how the U.S. appears at this time. Actions that we would take to deal with one of these problems may not help to deal with the other. For example, I think that if they can get us into a negotiation, even if we get the ship back, it is not to our advantage. I think we should make a strong statement and give a note to the Cambodians, via the Chinese, so that we can get some credit if the boat is released. I also suggest some show of force. What do we have in the neighborhood of the incident?

James Schlesinger: "We have the *Coral Sea*, which is now on its way to Australia for ceremonies."

President Ford: How long would it take to get there?

James Schlesinger: About two to three days.

President Ford: "Do we have anything at Subic?"

General David C. Jones: "We have the *Hancock*, and other vessels, but it would take about a day and a half at least to get them down there."

Henry Kissinger: "We may not be able to accomplish much by seizing their assets, since they are already blocked. Perhaps we can seize a Cambodian ship on the high seas. But I think that what we need for the next forty-eight hours is a strong statement, a strong note and a show of force."

Discussion followed concerning turning the *Coral Sea* around and the use of aircraft. It was stated that aircraft would be over the island, "to see what kind of forces there are."

Henry Kissinger, "Can we find out where Cambodian ships are around the world?"

Adm. James L. Holloway III, Chairman, Joint Chiefs of Staff: "I'm not sure there are any, nor merchant ships of any kind."

William Colby: "They have some coastal stuff, some small vessels and the like. But that is it."

William Clements: "We should not forget that there is a real chance that this is an in-house spat. In that area there have been two discovery wells, drilled by Shell and Mobil. One made a significant discovery. We are talking about 600-700 million barrels … I think that this is what this fuss is all about."

President Ford: "That is interesting, but it does not solve our problem. I think we should have a strong public statement and a strong note. We should also issue orders to get the carrier turned around."

Henry Kissinger: "I think we should brief that this is an outrage. Even if they quarrel with each other, they cannot use us."

President Ford: "We should get the demand and our objection to what has happened out to the press before they get the story from elsewhere."

Robert Ingersoll: "They may want to hold the ship as a hostage to our equipment."

James Schlesinger: "That was our first thought, before we looked into it further."

The discussion then turned to the feasibility of using mines from USS *Coral Sea* and whether she carried any.

James Schlesinger: "We can get the mines in within twenty-four hours."

There was then some discussion of using the USS *Hancock*. At this point General David C. Jones suggested, "we get our contingency plans together as soon as possible and start assembling a task force to go in that direction. We also have other means. We have B-52s that could do it."

James Schlesinger: "The mines are at Subic; the B-52s are in Thailand."

President Ford: "I think we should turn the *Coral Sea* around. We should get everything organized in Subic Bay. We should make a strong statement before the news hits from other sources. We should also get a full photo run of the island and of the harbor where the ship is."

Vice President Rockefeller:

> I think this will be seen as a test case. I think it will be judged in South Korea. I remember the *Pueblo* case. I think we need something strong soon. Getting out a message and getting people ready will not do it. I think a violent response is in order. The world should know that we will act and that we will act quickly. We should have an immediate response in terms of action. I do not know if we have many targets that we can strike, but we should certainly consider this. If they get any hostages, this can go on forever.

James Schlesinger: "They have thirty-nine."
Donald Rumsfeld: "Americans?"
James Schlesinger: "We think so."
Vice President Rockefeller: "Now you can take action before you begin to get protests. I believe the authorities there only understand force. There is an old Chinese saying about a dagger hitting steel and withdrawing when it hits steel, and that is the impression that we should convey."
President Ford: "I think that is what we will do. We will turn around the *Coral Sea*. We will get the mining ready. We will take action."
Henry Kissinger: "If it is not released by Wednesday, we will mine."
Vice President Rockefeller: "Public opinion will be against it in order to save lives. Is there anything we can do now?"
James Schlesinger: "We could sink the Cambodian Navy."
William Clements: "We could hit the patrol ship."
Vice President Rockefeller: "Or we could seize the island."
Henry Kissinger: "I agree with the vice president that we should show a strong position. We should also know what we are doing so that it does not look as though we want to pop

somebody. We could mine their harbors. This will not get the ship. Or we could take the ship, or we could scuttle it."

James Schlesinger: "They will have the ship already. It is like the *Pueblo*. Once it got to Wonson it was hard to bring it back."

Henry Kissinger: "In Korea, some things might be possible, but with this new group it is very uncertain what will happen."

President Ford: "How soon could we take the island?"

Gen. David C. Jones: "We have helicopters in Thailand and we could do it fairly quickly."

Henry Kissinger: "We cannot do it from Thailand."

James Schlesinger: "You know that the reconnaissance missions are being flown from Thailand."

Henry Kissinger: "That we can get away with, but I do not believe we can run military operations from there."

Vice President Rockefeller: "What if we had a series of escalating actions? Some we would take now, the others later. We have to show that we will not tolerate this kind of thing. It is a pattern. If we do not respond violently, we will get nibbled to death. We can announce these things to make clear what we are doing."

James Schlesinger: "The trouble with an announcement of future steps is on the Hill. Anything that we announce, Congress will need to be briefed."

President Ford then questioned the timeliness of the communications regarding the ship's seizure. One of the major issues concerning the seizure was the lack of communication resulting in subsequent command problems, and, as it also developed, the lack of importance attached to a U.S. merchant ship.

President Ford: "We have now looked at the options. We will issue a statement and we will send a message. We will turn around the *Coral Sea*. We will get a task force assembled at Subic and maybe get it underway. Perhaps we will scramble a force to take the island. I'd like to get something straight now.

Brent told me at 7:45 that the ship had been seized, but there should be a quicker way to let us know this."

Gen. Brent Scowcroft: "I agree. That is when I heard of it."

Donald Rumsfeld: "I also."

Henry Kissinger: "I was not told until my regular staff meeting this morning, and then it was mentioned as an aside."

James Schlesinger: "This is a bureaucratic issue. The NMCC did not become alarmed because it was not a U.S. Navy vessel."

President Ford: "This would be alright in ordinary times but not now."

William Colby: "I will get a wrap-up of the sequence of notification."

Donald Rumsfeld: "Can we notify merchant ships of the danger?"

General David C. Jones: "We will see."

Donald Rumsfeld: "I do not see the advantage of announcing the warning. We could make a case on either side. To the extent we want to be forceful, we do not need to make it public."

Vice President Rockefeller: "I do not think turning the carriers around is action. Congress will get into the act. The doves will start talking. But, unless the Cambodians are hurt, this pattern will not be broken."

Henry Kissinger: "The main purpose of using a statement is that we have no choice. We have to have a reaction. But the statement should be very strong. It should demand the immediate release of the ship, and it should say that the failure to do so could have serious consequences."

President Ford: "It should point out that this is a clear act of piracy."

Henry Kissinger:

> Then we should get our military actions lined up. My expectation is that we should do it on a large scale. We should not look as though we want to pop somebody, but we should give the impression that we are not to be trifled with. If we say that it should be released, then we can state that the release is in response to our statement. I would relate what we do to the ship, rather than to seize an island.

William Colby: "We may wish to point out that they released the other ships. This gives them a way out."

Donald Rumsfeld: "They can figure out their own way out."

President Ford: "But, if you take strong action, let us say nothing first. I would like to get the DOD (Dept. of Defense) options by this afternoon."

James Schlesinger: "The action should put them under pressure. If we mine the harbor, they will simply sit. We have got to do something that embarrasses them."

Donald Rumsfeld: "That is why I think we should look at the options."

Discussion followed concerning the various options. President Ford requested to have options that day. Deputy Defense Secretary Clements reminded the council of the oil situation.

Henry Kissinger: "I see a lot of advantages in taking the island rather than in mining the port. Let us find out what is on the island, how big a battle it would be, and other relevant factors."

Defense Secretary Schlesinger advised the group of a reconnaissance report which was due that evening and he felt, "it would not take a large force," concerning a potential attack of the island. Then he asked President Ford, regarding his authority and relationship with Congress."

President Ford: "There are two problems: First, the provisions of summer, 1973. Second, the war powers. Regarding the military options, I would like to know how they would be hamstrung and what we want to do. I assure you that, irrespective of the Congress, we will move."

Henry Kissinger continued: "There are three things we need to know: First, what force is required to take the island? Second, what force is required to take Kompong Som, and to take the ship and the people? On the whole, I would prefer this. Third, what it would take to mine the harbor?

1973 WAR POWERS RESOLUTION
The 1973 War Powers Resolution provided for the sharing of responsibility between the President and Congress concerning the involvement of the U.S. in wars or hostilities with other countries. It was passed on November 7, 1973:

SEC. 2. (a) It is the purpose of this joint resolution to fulfill the intent of the framers of the Constitution of the United States and insure that the collective judgment of both the Congress and the President will apply to the introduction of United States Armed Forces into hostilities, or into situations where imminent involvement in hostilities is clearly indicated by the circumstances, and to the continued use of such forces in hostilities or in such situations.

(b) Under article I, section 8, of the Constitution, it is specifically provided that the Congress shall have the power to make all laws necessary and proper for carrying into execution, not only its own powers but also all other powers vested by the Constitution in the Government of the United States, or in any department or officer thereof.

(c) The constitutional powers of the President as Commander-in-Chief to introduce United States Armed Forces into hostilities, or into situations where imminent involvement in hostilities is clearly indicated by the circumstances, are exercised only pursuant to

(1) a declaration of war,

(2) specific statutory authorization, or

(3) a national emergency created by attack upon the United States, its territories or possessions, or its armed forces.

Consultation

SEC. 3. The President in every possible instance shall consult with Congress before introducing United States Armed Forces into hostilities or into situations where imminent involvement in hostilities is clearly indicated by the circumstances, and after every such introduction shall consult regularly with the Congress until United States Armed Forces are no longer engaged in hostilities or have been removed from such situations.

Reporting

SEC. 4. (a) In the absence of a declaration of war, in any case in which United States Armed Forces are introduced —

(1) into hostilities or into situations where immi nent involvement in hostilities is clearly indicated by the circumstances:

(2) into the territory, airspace or waters of a foreign nation, while equipped for combat, except for deployments which relate solely to supply, replacement, repair, or training of such forces; or

(3) in numbers which substantially enlarge United States Armed Forces equipped for combat already located in a foreign nation; the president shall submit within 48 hours to the Speaker of the House of Representatives and to the President pro tempore of the Senate a report, in writing, setting forth—

(A) the circumstances necessitating the introduction of United States Armed Forces;

(B) the constitutional and legislative authority under which such introduction took place; and

(C) the estimated scope and duration of the hostilities or involvement.

(b) The President shall provide such other information as the Congress may request in the fulfillment of its constitutional responsibilities with respect to committing the Nation to war and to the use of United States Armed Forces abroad

(c) Whenever United States Armed Forces are introduced into hostilities or into any situation described in subsection (a) of this section, the President shall, so long as such armed forces continue to be engaged in such hostilities or situation, report to the Congress periodically on the status of such hostilities or situation as well as on the scope and duration of such hostilities or situation, but in no event shall he report to the Congress less often than once every six months....

Vice President Rockefeller: "Does it make sense to do this if the boat is in it?"

James Schlesinger: "You can perhaps accomplish the same thing by quarantine as by mining."

Henry Kissinger: "I doubt it. We learned in North Vietnam that mines work better. With a quarantine, you have to have a confrontation and a crisis regarding every ship."

James Schlesinger: "We would have to be tough in such confrontations."

Vice President Rockefeller: "I agree with Rumsfeld. Why should we warn them? There must be planes we can use out of Thailand."

Henry Kissinger: "If we bomb out of Thailand, we would be out of there within a month."

With the meeting drawing to a close, President Ford asked for a review of the situation, current options and how they were going present the seizure to the Congress and to the American public.

President Ford: "Let us review it again. Within an hour or so, there will be a public statement. Let us make an announcement ahead of time, and a tough one so that we get the initiative. Let us not tell Congress that we will do anything militarily since we have not decided. I think that is important to make a strong statement publicly before the news gets out otherwise."

Henry Kissinger: "We will be pressed this afternoon."

Donald Rumsfeld: "How about a statement that gives the facts, states that this is an act of piracy, and says that we expect the release. We will not say that we demand the release, because that will activate the Congress. I think you get the same thing without speaking of a demand. Moreover, to demand seems weaker."

James Schlesinger: "It is not weak to say that we demand the release."

Henry Kissinger: "I would demand."

Donald Rumsfeld: "Perhaps not publicly, but privately."

Henry Kissinger: "If Congress takes us on, I think we have a good case."

President Ford: "With the military appropriations bill coming up, they would not want to give a picture of running out."

Henry Kissinger: "Then we should keep quiet. Let them explain about the three ships."

Vice-President Rockefeller: "How long does it take to get the carriers there?"

James Schlesinger: "About one-and-a-half days."

Henry Kissinger: "I would overfly with reconnaissance."

President Ford: "It should be visible."

Henry Kissinger: "That we can get away with, but not bombing."

Vice-President Rockefeller: "Aren't those bases being closed anyway?"

Henry Kissinger: "Not necessarily."

President Ford: "Alright. Let us get a message to the Chinese government as soon as possible."

Vice-President Rockefeller: "Could we not ask Thai permission to use the bases?"

Henry Kissinger: "No."

James Schlesinger: "Only reconnaissance is possible, but if we ask, they will refuse everything."

Henry Kissinger: "Lee Kuan Yew has asked us to stay in Thailand as long as possible to give him time to work on getting the defenses of Malaysia ready. Bombing from Thailand will get us out quickly."

President Ford: "How far away is Subic?"

Henry Kissinger: "To bomb, even from Clark, we would be in trouble. This is a symptom of Vietnam. We can bomb from Guam with B-52s or from the carriers. But we should know what we're doing. I am more in favor of seizing something, be it the island, the ship, or Kompong Som."

President Ford: "This has been a useful discussion. Thank you. I will look forward to seeing the options."[2]

The National Security Council meeting ended at 1350. Shortly afterward the White House issued its first press release on the seizure:

> We have been informed that a Cambodian naval vessel has seized an American merchant ship on the high seas and forced it to the port Kompong Som. The President has met with the National Security Council. He considers this seizure an act of piracy. He has instructed the State Department to demand the immediate release of the ship. Failure to do so would have the most serious consequences.

Later that afternoon:

- At 1412 — The aircraft carrier USS *Coral Sea* and escorts were ordered to the vicinity of Kompong Som at best speed. Included was an Amphibious Ready Group/ Marine assault unit of four vessels; USS *Okinawa*, USS *Duluth*, USS *Barbour County* and USS *Mt. Vernon*.
- At 1544
  — Orders were issued by the Joint Chiefs of Staff to: Provide continuous P-3 surveillance of the seizure area. Conduct two flights of photo reconnaissance of Phnom Penh, Kompong Som port and Poulo Wai at first satisfactory light. There was also to be high altitude coverage of Poulo Wai.
  — CINCPAC subsequently ordered aircraft reconnaissance photo priority to identifying merchant ships, naval craft, and paratroop landing zones.
- At 1630 — A representative of the Liaison Office of the People's Republic of China was summoned to the Office of the Deputy Secretary of State and given a message for the Cambodian representatives in Peking demanding the ship's release. However, the PRC representative refused to accept the message.
- At 1722 — CINCPAC Fleet orders MK 52 mines to be prepared for use in certain areas.

These mines weigh 1,000 lbs., have a charge of 625 lbs., and sit on the sea bottom. They are activated by a ship's signature on the surface, or by a submarine's signal. The aircraft aboard the Coral Sea *were each capable of carrying four of these mines. U.S. Navy.*

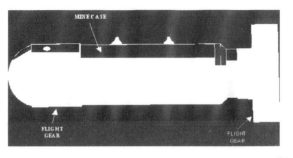

- 1800 — The Voice of America, broadcast to Cambodia, carried the story of the seizure. (*Ironically, it was this broadcast by Voice of America that brought the news of the seizure to the Khmer Rouge leaders. In September 1975 Democratic Kampuchea Foreign Minister Ieng Sary said that, "American technology brings the news faster than our armed forces."*[3]

- 1824 - The second destroyer, USS *Henry B. Wilson* gets underway to the seizure area. Her estimated time of arrival is 8 PM on May 14.[4]

USS Henry B. Wilson *(DDG-7) was named for Admiral Henry Braid Wilson, and built by Defoe Shipbuilding Company in Bay City, Michigan. She was launched in April 1959 and served as plane guard for carriers on Yankee Station in the Tonkin Gulf.* U.S. Navy.

Other actions which came from the first NSC meeting were "that jet aircraft were ordered to make low passes over and to fire near, but not at, small craft in the area, and authorization by the President to use riot control agents in the effort to recover the ship."

Up to this point there had yet to be any positive identification of the *Mayaguez*. Then, the Patrol Squadron skipper, Navy Cdr. J.A. Messegee reported:

> Our first two aircraft arrived on station after dark and discovered several vessels, large and small, within sixty miles of Poulo Wai Island. Systematically each contact was illuminated by parachute flares and examined visually. We assumed the *Mayaquez* would be under way toward the Cambodian port of Kompong Som. Two ships in the area met the *Mayaquez'* general description but several others were similar. The most likely candidate was located seven miles off Poulo Wai. She was fully lighted and apparently dead in the water (DIW), but we weren't able to positively identify her.
>
> As the first two aircraft continued to discover numerous vessels and report their descriptions, courses, and speeds, it became apparent that we would have to obtain positive identifying data – i.e., read the name off the ship. Therefore we directed our third aircraft, which was en route to the area, to make one pass at 300 feet altitude and 1,000 yards offset from the large vessel DIW off Poulo Wai. It was imperative to obtain visual confirmation of the ship's name.

The Lockheed P-3 Orion is a maritime patrol aircraft used by numerous navies and air forces around the world, primarily for maritime patrol, reconnaissance, anti-surface warfare and anti-submarine warfare. U.S. Navy.

Shortly after sunrise on the 13th of May, a VP-17 P-3 made one high-speed pass down the port side of the 500-foot containership laying-to off Poulo Wai. Numerous photos were obtained of the ship and two gunboats tied up alongside. The P-3 crew read the name *Mayaguez* both on the stern and bow of the container-laden merchant vessel. While executing the close-in pass, the P-3 crew observed small arms fire from the *Mayaguez* and AA fire from the twin guns on the gunboats. At the same time a crew member, located near the tail of the aircraft, reported to the pilot that he heard a bullet hit in his area. Consequently, the pilot retired a few miles from the area and inspected his aircraft for low-speed controllability and visually checked it for damage. The plane had been hit by a single .50-caliber projectile which caused superficial damage to the vertical stabilizer. The pilot decided it was not significant and elected to remain on station for his scheduled surveillance period.[5]

Later in the evening at 2143 on May 12 the *Mayaguez* was seen slowly leaving her position at Poulo Wai. The U.S Seventh Fleet directed the Marine Amphibious Ready Group Alpha to be ready to move. The P-3s were directed to locate and track all Cambodian navy units. Finally, at 2137, the *Mayaguez* was reported to be heading north.[6]

6

Morning, May 13, 1975

Gulf of Thailand

When the reconnaissance plane flew over, Capt. Miller was certain his ship had been identified because of the eighteen-inch *Mayaguez* letters on the bow. Capt. Miller:

> We laid there; this was on the morning of the 13th … All this time they wouldn't let me off the bridge: they kept a gun on me so I wouldn't roam around the ship. If I went down to talk to any member of the crew, they sent an armed insurgent with me, armed with a rifle, an AK-47. They had shoulder guns, launchers and American field-pack radios so that they could communicate from the ship to installations ashore in Koh Tang or Kompong Som.[1]

Stephen Zarley:

> At 8:00, the ship was to proceed to the mainland, but for some reason, there was a delay. Our captors were still aboard and several gunboats were alongside. A small fishing vessel was on the port side

midships which had brought food from the island. The boat was perhaps 25 feet long and 7 feet wide. The wheelhouse was set aft with little space between it and the gunwales. There was no radio or compass that I could see. There were no hatches on deck and fish nets were stacked on the bow. The boat was run on diesel and there were two empty fuel drums lying on their side against the front of the wheelhouse. Our pilot ladder was over the side to provide access to and from the ship.

I went down to the engine room at 8:00 as usual, but the first just told me to stand by. Since the shift had been delayed, the two of us sat in the machine shop and swapped lies. The chief came below and asked me to change the oil in the No. 2 generator. I went to do the job and it was at this time the ship got underway. After I finished the oil change, I went topside to have a look around. The *Mayaguez* was now anchored off another island (Koh Tang). This island was higher than most of the others and had a high tower set on top of its highest point. There was a lot of coming and going by gunboats between the island and the ship. For what purpose, I didn't know. I was wondering why we're anchored here instead of proceeding into port as planned. I was glad, however, that the ship was still out in the open where she could easily be sighted.

After lunch, Angel Rios (Baker) brought out the leftover food to give to the Khmers. He was very nervous. He was over-polite to the Khmers and he was wearing his Rosary that he had put on soon after our seizure. The Khmers were reluctant to eat our Western food, but ate up our apples, oranges and bananas.

With lunch break over, I again went down to the engine room to clean up from yesterday. I heard a concussion so I hurried topside to investigate. I didn't see anything, but was told that a jet had passed over and dropped a bomb off our bow. We had been found! I was also told that a recon plane had passed over earlier. What would the Khmers do now, I wondered? They had been very calm which we believe was in our favor, but how would they react to the bomb. I felt that the Khmers might be surprised, but since they still had us, the ship should be free from actual attack. I didn't know the mind of these jungle people. Wait and see was all any of us could do.[2]

Capt. Miller:

Around 2 o'clock in the afternoon this Navy ensign pointed to the Island and he pointed to my second officer, Jerry Maregard, and he pointed to me, he went like this, that we were going to be taken as prisoners ashore to Koh Tang Island.

At the time, I figured pointing at two of us instead of the third mate, who was on the bridge with me at the time — he didn't bother him — I figured they were going to take the second officer and I aboard for interrogation where somebody could speak English to us.

Instead, around 3 o'clock in the afternoon they took me down in my room, made me open up my lockers. When I opened the safe lockers, they saw the two safes and they made me open the two safes. My clothes locker was locked.

(At 1545 an A-7 aircraft fired in the water near Mayaguez *to signal the ship not to get underway)*

Capt. Miller:

They took me out of my room and down to the main deck. As I stepped out of my room — our doors on the *Mayaguez* — they have two little buttons on the side of the door you can push to release the lock and another to lock it — when I grabbed hold of the door, I pushed a button to lock it, so my office, the sitting room and my bedroom were locked and nobody could get in, and I closed the door.

They took me down to the main deck. They had fishing boats — one on the port side and one on the starboard side. They took me down to the starboard side, which was a Thai fishing boat with five Thai fishermen on board. They were seized because they had been fishing in Cambodian waters. I later found out they had been held for five months .

When I got on the fishing boat, I saw there were my second mate and three or four unlicensed crew members. I asked the second mate what was going on, because I was under guard and had not talked to anybody since I left the bridge. He says: "They are removing all of the crew."[3]

Meanwhile, overhead:

- From 1640 to 1700 – F-111 aircraft reported smaller vessels tied up to *Mayaguez* and a ladder over the side of the ship.

- At 1717 JCS directed CINCPAC to maintain constant surveillance of *Mayaguez*, prevent its movement into port on the Cambodian mainland. Authority was also given to fire in vicinity of, but not at, the small boats to prevent movement and proceed within the twelve-mile territorial limit.
- At 1718 on scene aircraft reported two small vessels which had been tied to *Mayaguez* moving toward the island. One vessel flying a red flag appeared to have Caucasian personnel on board while the other was carrying a lot of people.[4]

Capt. Miller:

So I just sat there. They put fifty percent of the crew in the Thai boat, they put fifty percent of the crew in the Cambodian fishing boat that was on the port side, and we headed — when they got all the crew off and the plant secured, they had us head for the island of Koh Tang into a little cove.

There they anchored the boats around seventy-five yards off the beach, a nice sandy beach there. It looked like there were 20mm cannon ashore. That is the biggest gun I saw on the island.

They didn't take us ashore at any time on Koh Tang, but the two fishing boats went in with the crew, and a recon plane was flying overhead all the time.[5]

It was at 1733 when the reconnaissance plane reported personnel being disembarked on Koh Tang Island, along with ground fire during low flying visual reconnaissance. However, the planes weren't being hit. Approximately forty-five minutes later, reconnaissance reported that small boats were off-loading personnel onto Koh Tang Island that they were moving into the interior, but it couldn't be determined how many men were moving.

At 1931 the U.S. Charge d'Affairs in Bangkok reported back to the Secretary of State that the U.S. should "play this by the rules," otherwise the U.S. would lose the cooperation of the Thais.[6]

Stephen Zarley:

After work, I put on a clean pair of Levi's and my work boots. I usually wear shorts and a thong, but I heard from someone that the Khmers were going to take some of the crew to the island for protection against the jets. I wanted to be fully dressed just in case.

The ongoing watch were ordering their supper of prime rib, baked potatoes, greens and ice cream, when two Khmers came into the pantry and motioned for us to get up from the tables. It was 1645. I went straight to my room and told Tyrone that we were going on a little boat ride. I grabbed three packs of cigarettes and went back to the chow hall. The men in the chow hall were still standing around not wanting to leave the ship. One of the Khmers pointed his weapon at me so I moved.

Outside was the same fishing boat that had been there in the morning. The Khmer Rouge pointed again and I climbed down the pilot ladder and sat down on the deck with my back against the two fuel drums. More of the crew followed. The rest of the crew were boarding another fishing boat on the starboard side. There were nineteen of us in this boat. The chief and Juan Sanchez (second engineer) were the only two officers among us. Suddenly there was a burst of gunfire from inside the ship. "Christ, what was that?" I asked.

"They killed somebody," someone else said.

I was getting nervous now. I was thinking that someone had refused to go and was shot. I suggested that we count heads once all of us were together again.

The Khmers kept counting us. They would leave and then come back and count again. We got the impression that they weren't happy with the count. There were forty in the crew and I remembered that someone had told the Khmers yesterday, that there were forty-two of us. Evidently, our captors neglected to check the crew list. There would be questions about those two non-existent men later.

The fishing boat got underway and went around the bow of the ship and headed toward the island. The other boat with the remaining crew followed. Four gunboats were escorting us. In a matter of minutes, two jets flew over my boat. My reaction was to hit the deck and get as low as possible. The other guys did the same and with such a movement, we almost tipped out boat over. The jets kept coming; flying very low, but not firing. I looked at the face of the Khmer firing over my head and he met my eyes. I looked away quickly, not liking what I saw in that face.

As we neared the island, the jets flew over it and were met by ground fire. I was becoming concerned that one of the jets might get hit since there were flying so low. If one of them were hit, would other jets come back and attack? There were six jets now flying in pairs. One would come in low while his partner stayed above him. The firing from the island and our boats continued even after we arrived at the island. As the daylight got dimmer, the jets flew higher and then left just before dark.[7]

7

MORNING, MAY 13, 1975

WASHINGTON, D.C.

At 1022 the National Security Council had their second meeting. Secretary of State Henry Kissinger did not attend as he was in Kansas City. C.I.A. Director William Colby brought the Council up to date: "…U.S. reconnaissance flights observed the crew being transferred from the ship via a tugboat and then being led off toward the interior of the island."

However, in answer to whether they were sure it was the crew, James Schlesinger said, "No."

William Colby:

> Although the men could be moved to the mainland at any time, the Khmer Communists may intend to keep them on the island until some final decisions are made regarding the crew and the vessel. So far, the Khmer Communist government has not made a public statement regarding the *Mayaguez*, and Prince Sihanouk today in Peking denied any knowledge of the incident.

Discussion then moved to any Khmer retaliation possible through the use of Kompong Som harbor. At one time it was a busy port of entry, but U.S. aircraft had been delivering to Phnom Penh bypassing the port.

Vice President Nelson Rockefeller: "Several years ago it was the principal port of entry and supply for the Vietcong. It was built originally in order to give them (Cambodians) independence of the Mekong River which was patrolled by the Vietnamese."

President Ford: "One reason why Sihanouk was asked to leave in 1970 was that he turned his face away from the movement of supplies into the port."

Vice President Rockefeller then brought up the subject of misinformation:

> There is one thing that was a big mistake yesterday. You got the information that the American ship was already in the harbor in Kompong Som. This denied you one option, which would have been to try to prevent the ship from being taken into the harbor. But you were told that the ship was already in the port.

James Schlesinger: "I did not say that it was already in the port. I said it might be."

Vice President Rockefeller: "I do not want to argue, but you said that it was known that when you left your department it was one hour away from the port and by the time you arrived here, it would already be in the port."

President Ford:

> I do think we have to be certain of our facts. Overnight, Brent gave me a series of different reports that we were getting about the ship's location and about what was happening. We have to be more factual or at least more precise in pointing out our degree of knowledge. What do we now know? How certain are we of the facts with which we are dealing?

William Colby: "We think that the ship is off the island as I pointed out. We understand that the people have been off-loaded. We have seen it."

Gen. David. Jones:

I talked to the commander in Thailand who was in contact with a reconnaissance aircraft. Through this commander, I have the following report from the aircraft. He said that the ship had one anchor up, and one down. Our experts tell us that it is very improbable that the Cambodians can run this ship, so that if there is any indication that the ship is moving, it must be the Americans who are running it.

Donald Rumsfeld: "How do we know these things? How do we know that it was the *Mayaguez* that your reconnaissance aircraft saw?"

Gen. David C. Jones:

It is a positive identification. As I said, the anchors are up and down. Some boats have come alongside. Through fighter runs, we kept them off. Some, however, did get to the boat. We saw some people getting off and going to the island. Then we saw them on the island. They had their heads between their legs. They appeared to be Caucasians.

President Ford: "Was all this in daylight?"

Gen. David C. Jones:

This was just before it grew dark over there. This is a sort of thing we use with our gun ships and we can get a lot of information from it. The instructions we have to our commanders are not to let the ship go to port. They are to take any action not to include sinking. We should know when it moves, when it raises an anchor, and when it raises the boiler. We can, if necessary, disable the ship. We can hit it abeam, just off the stern. We will not hit people that way. We can do that with pretty high confidence that we can stop the ship from sailing under its own power. Of course, if it is not sailing under its own power, we would make the tug boat the target.

President Ford: "If they try to move the ship, we must take steps to stop it, without sinking it."

Gen. David C. Jones: "This movement would be noticed and reported by the 7th Air Force Support Group within minutes, barring any inclement weather which would have some effect on our coverage."

President Ford: "And you have people on the ball in the Pentagon?"

Gen. David Jones: "Quite a few."

President Ford: "How do you get the information to Brent and then to me?"

Brent Scowcroft: "Last night, there were long time lags before we got the information, and there was a lot of confusion about its accuracy."

President Ford: "I am very concerned about the delay in reports. We must have the information immediately. There must be the quickest possible communication to me.

"We must get the information to the NSC and to me. Jim, will you now please give us your report on the other options."

James Schlesinger:

> We have reviewed the options. The option to take Kompong Som requires many troops. There are about 1700 K.C.s [Khmer Communists] in the area. So our first objective today is to keep the ship out. If we want to take the ship, there are two options: one, we can use the Marines and the choppers that are at U-Tapao. We can take off tomorrow, or, we can wait until the USS *Holt* arrives, which should be around eight P.M. tomorrow night, or about twelve hours later.

The president then questioned whether the *Holt* would have enough fuel after being at flank speed for thirty-six hours.

James Schlesinger:

> It will not be in that condition. In any case the carrier will arrive the following morning and it will be able to refuel. The Navy people are trained in boarding. It might be preferable to wait for the *Holt* because it will be manned and able to do it. We will then have the dominant force in the area. But, of course, this may give the Cambodians time to change the situation or try to prepare themselves. Therefore, it may be better to go by first light tomorrow.

Discussion continued on using the *Holt* for taking back the *Mayaguez*.

James Schlesinger preferred taking the *Mayaguez* quickly and thought instructions should go out, "to use gunfire to keep personnel away from the anchor chain on deck."

Vice President Rockefeller: "What if they are Americans?"

James Schlesinger: "I do not think they have Americans on board except for people to man the boiler. I think they have the other Americans on the island. Our force to take the island is now in Okinawa. In twelve hours, we can have the Marines there."

President Ford: "Twelve hours from now?"

James Schlesinger: "Twelve hours from your order. We already have 125 Marines at U-Tapao."

President Ford: "They would be intended to take the ship. How about the Marines from Subic Bay? How soon can we get them there?"

Gen. David Jones: "They are coming from Okinawa. They could go by 1844 or 1900 or the second light tonight. One day later, we could have the Marines at U-Tapao. We could use large choppers."

President Ford: "They could be used on the island."

Gen. David Jones: "This would be about 1,000. We do not know what is on the island."

James Schlesinger:

> We asked a Cambodian defector and he told us there were about sixty troops on the island. For the island operation, I think it is preferable to use the *Coral Sea*. It gives us dominance over the area. Also, we have its forces and helicopters. The danger for the Americans on the island is that we do not know what the Cambodians would do. I think there is less danger if we have the dominant force. We will have Cambodians on the choppers who will be able to say that we can take the island unless they give us the Americans or the foreigners. This message would be bull-horned from the choppers at a time when we are ready to act.

Brent Scowcroft: "This means that the force of 1,000 Americans from U-Tapao would be for operation to take the island, not the ship.

James Schlesinger: "Right."

William Colby: "We should realize that the Cambodians are tough fellows. We know that they took a Vietnamese ship and killed seven people without thinking anymore about it."

James Schlesinger: "When cornered, they could execute the Americans."

Robe T. Hartmann: "Do we know why they took off the Americans?"

Gen. David Jones: "… whether or not they actually did and why they might have done it."

Discussion followed concerning the lack of information concerning how many Khmer Rouge gunboats were in the area.

Gen. David C. Jones said, "We hope to have better intelligence as soon as the infrared photographs are developed in Thailand."

Scowcroft stated that nothing was new on the diplomatic end.

Vice President Rockefeller:

> I do not think the freighter is the issue. The issue is how we respond. Many are watching us, in Korea and elsewhere. The big question is whether or not we look silly. I think we need to respond quickly. The longer we wait, the more time they have to get ready. Why not sink their boats until they move? Once they have got hostages, they can twist our tails for months to come, and if you go ashore, we may lose more Marines trying to land than the Americans were on the boat originally. Why not just sink their ships until they respond?

James Schlesinger:

> We have several objectives: first, to stop the boat from being taken into port. Second, to get our people back. Third, to attack

and sink the Cambodian Navy, later, after we have our ship and our people out, in order to maximize the punishment.

We do not know their motive. If we sink their vessels, it might precipitate sinking of the freighter and jeopardize getting the Americans out. It seems to me that there is the sequence of priorities. Starting that way, their reaction would be prudent.

Vice President Rockefeller:

> I do not think the Communists respond this way. I remember the story by Mao Tse Tung about sticking a blade in until you hit steel and then you pull out your sword. If you do not meet steel, you go in further. I think you should do everything you can as soon as possible. Later, you can destroy the port as retaliation.

James Schlesinger: "I would prefer for us to first get the ship, and then to proceed against the island."

President Ford: "Brent, what are your views?"

Brent Scowcroft:

> I see two operations. The first is against the ship. The second is against the island. The urgency of the island operation is to stop the Americans from going to the mainland. On the ship, it is to stop it from going to Kompong Som. The optimum situation with the ship is to get the *Holt* between that ship and Kompong Som. We cannot do that until tomorrow.

Discussion continued on the necessity of destroying the Khmer boats with our gunships so that the *Mayaguez* crew would not be taken ashore that evening in the dark.

Vice President Rockefeller: "The longer we take, the worse it gets. If the Communists do not think that you will react strong and fast, they will keep on doing this. We must do it as the Israelis do; we need to respond fast."

Lt. Gen. Brent Scowcroft: "We must recognize that we have a problem with regard to Thailand."

President Ford: "Are we running our reconnaissance and our freighters from Thailand?"

Lt. Gen. Brent Scowcroft: "So far it has been OK. But if we use force, we may be in jeopardy."

James Schlesinger: "There is the possibility of the opposite reaction. If they see us acting, they may change their attitude. Publicly, they may protest, but privately, they may agree. They have done this before."

Vice President Rockefeller: "I agree with that."

Gen. David C. Jones: "Earlier, we had no forces to operate to free the ship. As we discussed yesterday, we had to get our assets into place. We have them."

President Ford: "Let me review the sequence: first, that we use the aircraft to stop any boats leaving the island. You do not sink them, necessarily, but can you take some preventive action?"

Gen. David C. Jones: "Probably."

> … We also have searchlights and flares. We will want to see if there are any Americans on board. We will need to decide whether to fire across the bow or to sink it. We would have some time. They are slow boats. That is one point. We could, with some confidence, interdict the island."

President Ford: "Second, I think you should stop all boats coming to the island. Third, I think we should be prepared to land on the ship tomorrow morning."

Gen. David Jones:

> This is not an easy operation. On a container ship, we can only land our helicopters one at a time. There is not much space. The containers are aluminum. They would not be strong enough to support the helicopters, so we would have to rope people down. They would come down three at a time and they would have to drop twenty feet to the deck. Of course, we would have helicopters alongside to keep heads down as we land. Still, it would be very tricky.

President Ford: "But we could have gunships as well. Fourth, to have the Marines from U-Tapao, 1,000 strong, go to the island. How soon could they get there?"

Gen. David C. Jones: "They can launch within ten hours after I leave here. They could launch at the second light."

Donald Rumsfeld: "The President wanted it tonight."

Gen. David Jones: "Right."

For the remainder of the meeting, it was clear that the various principals had questions concerning the time differences between Washington and Cambodia, and the time frame therein for planned sequences to unfold.

Donald Rumsfeld: "Let's put all this on paper, with the exact times, so that we know what we're talking about."

President Ford: "The landing on the ship can take place tonight. What about the island?"

Gen. David C. Jones: "It could be twenty-four hours later."

Donald Rumsfeld: "I suggest we stick to one set of times."

President Ford: "When does the destroyer get there?"

James Schlesinger: "Eight o'clock."

President Ford: "Dusk, tomorrow night, their time?"

James Schlesinger: "Yes."

President Ford: "Same time as the Marines?"

James Schlesinger: "No."

Lt. Gen. Brent Scowcroft: "Let's use one time for all this."

James Schlesinger: "At seven P.M. tonight, Washington time, we can have some Marines ready. At eight A.M. tomorrow, Washington time, the *Holt* will be in position. Somewhere between that time, the additional Marines will be in U-Tapao."

Donald Rumsfeld: "This is a different set of times from what we were given earlier."

Lt. Gen. Brent Scowcroft: "Right."

President Ford: "I have to go meet some Congressional people. Can somebody please put all this down so that we have it in writing?"

(Schlesinger showed the schedule to the President.)

President Ford makes a point during a National Security Council Meeting concerning the Mayaguez. Courtesy Gerald R. Ford Library.

President Ford: "The *Coral Sea* gets in at eight. What about the *Holt?*"

Gen. David C. Jones: "We are trying to speed it up."

President Ford: "I think the first two steps can be done. Let us take them. I would like to have the next steps written in sequence as to when they can take place."

Vice President Rockefeller: "I think we have some questions about operating on land against the Cambodians."

John Marsh: "Also, there is a war powers requirement."

President Ford: "First, I want to know the times. There should be a logical sequence so that we can have a chance to decide. Let us do it one and two and three, etc."

Lt. Gen. Brent Scowcroft: "I have reservations about landing on the ship."

Gen. David C. Jones: "So do I."

James Schlesinger: "Landing on the ship is to send them a signal. If we start to hit the boats, they know we are up to something. They could kill the Americans, but I doubt it. We have that element of surprise."

President Ford: "But they can take the people out."

Vice-President Rockefeller: "I agree."

President Ford: "Let's get the facts on the times lined up."

Vice President Rockefeller: "We do not want a land war in Cambodia."

The meeting ended at 1117.[1]

By the end of the second National Security Council meeting, the *Mayaguez* had been moved and was seen dead-in-the-water (DIW) approximately one mile off Koh Tang Island. Visual recon had reported "lots of people" were leaving *Mayaguez* and were moving toward Koh Tang on a small vessel. A further report indicated that a small vessel was seen moving toward Koh Tang flying a red flag and with possible Caucasians aboard.[2]

At 1110 a representative of the U.S. liaison in Peking had delivered a message to the Cambodian Embassy warning them of the attitude of the American government regarding the seizure of the *Mayaguez*. A similar message was delivered to the Foreign Ministry of the People's Republic of China. Twenty minutes later a warning was sent by the Defense Mapping Agency Hydrographic Center to all mariners at sea to avoid the area in which the *Mayaguez* had been captured.[3]

At 1800 the Thai response to the situation was released to the press:

> It is recalled that on May 13, B.E. 2518 [*sic*] the prime minister in his capacity as acting minister of foreign affairs had informed the charge d'affaires of the American Embassy that Thailand does not wish to become involved in the dispute between the United States and Cambodia over the seizure of the vessel *Mayaguez*, and that Thailand will not permit its territory to be used in connection with any action which might be taken by the United States against Cambodia.

In the same message it was stated that:

> On May 14, the Thai Government learned that the United States Government has sent some elements of its Marine forces into Thailand as part of its reaction against Cambodia.
>
> The Thai Government considers that this action by the United States Government is not consistent with the goodwill existing between Thailand and the United States, and unless these forces which have entered against the wishes of the Thai government are withdrawn immediately, the good relations and cooperation existing

between Thailand and the United States would be exposed to serious and damaging consequences.[4]

Earlier a memorandum had been sent to President Ford:

THE SECRETARY OF DEFENSE
WASHINGTON, D.C. 20301

MEMORANDUM FOR THE PRESIDENT

Subject: Seizure of U.S. Merchant Ship MAYAGUEZ

Early on the morning of 12 May (Washington Time), the U.S. merchant ship MAYAGUEZ was seized in the Gulf of Thailand in international waters by a Cambodian boarding party. The MAYAGUEZ has a U.S. crew, and her cargo consists of general commercial cargo destined for Singapore and military exchange store and other general supplies for Sattahip, Thailand. The ship is a container carrier owned by Sea Land Corporation, and was en route Hong Kong to Sattahip. Although initially uncon-firmed reports had the ship headed for the port of Kompong Som, P-3 reconnaissance at 122116 EDT revealed the MAYAGUEZ was dead-in-the-water in-company with two Cambodian gunboats near Poulo Wai Island. The ship then started to move towards port; however, more recent reports confirmed that the ship appeared to be dead-in-the-water 25 miles off Kompong Som in the vicinity of Kas Tang Island.

In order to provide a capability for U.S. military response to counter this belligerent act, certain actions have been taken to increase the readiness of selected combatant units. Aerial reconnaissance has been underway since the incident and now that positive identification of the MAYAGUEZ has been made continuous fighter surveillance will be maintained. CORAL SEA and its accompanying escorts have been ordered to proceed to the area and their arrival time is estimated

In summary, the following diplomatic and military events had taken place:

1. One recon plane had been slightly damaged.
2. There had been no response to the letters given to the Cambodian Embassy in Peking or the Foreign Ministry of the People's Republic of China.
3. Cambodian authorities learned of the capture and crew being taken to Koh Tang Island.
4. The Thai Prime Minister said the U.S. would not be allowed to use its bases to retaliate against Cambodia. However, the U.S. Charge d'Affaires said the U.S. would inform the Thai government of any Thai-based actions involving the U.S planes already present in the country.
5. The U.S. Secretary of State was informed by the Charge d'Affaires that the U.S. should "play by the rules, otherwise it stands to lose a great deal in terms of Thai cooperation."[5]

Actions being developed were:

Designated LPH-3 (Landing Platform, Helicoptor) USS Okinawa *was routed to the scene.* U.S. Navy.

The Navy version of the CH-53 was nicknamed the Sea Stallion. The Air Force Version was the Jolly Green Giant. Shown are a flight of Sea Stallions taking off from an LPH. U.S. Navy.

1. The second aircraft carrier (USS *Okinawa*) was ordered underway from the Philippines with the Amphibious Ready Group/Marine assault unit aboard.
2. CINCPAC was ordered by the Joint Chiefs of Staff to isolate Koh Tang Island by intercepting any incoming or outgoing vessels but not to destroy any except upon approval.
3. JCS also ordered the following movement: all available helicopters in Thailand, 125 US Air Force Security police from Nakhon Phanom Air Base in Thailand, two Marine platoons from the Philippines, and a Maine battalion from Okinawa to U-tapao, Thailand Air Base.
4. One Cambodian gunboat had been sunk.[6]

There were a total of sixteen CH-53C helicopters involved in the airlift. One of the helicopters fell out of formation and crashed killing all twenty-three occupants aboard. The dead included eighteen US Air Force Security personnel, four crew members and a linguist.

> To this day, the cause of the crash has not been established with certainty. According to some sources, the crash was due to a technical malfunction. One source claims that one of the main rotor blades separated from the rotor head, while others claim that the crash was due to enemy action. The whole truth about the crash may never be known. The crash caused a major rift between the Marines and the USAF Security Police. According to an article in the *Bangkok Post*, published a few days after the rescue attempt, the "Disagreements between Marines and Air Force security forces became heated almost to the point of violence." The remaining Security Police wanted to be the ones rescuing the crew of the SS *Mayaguez* taking a bloody revenge on the Khmer Rouge. The remaining CH-53s continued to U-Tapao, from where the various elements of the rescue operation were being coordinated.[7]

8

EVENING, MAY 13, 1975

GULF OF THAILAND

C apt. Miller:

From the day the recon plane flew over the ship, we were always under surveillance by a military recon plane, the big four-engine line ship. They saw the two fishing boats go into Koh Tang. They didn't know what happened; they didn't know whether we were taken ashore. Actually we didn't go ashore. We stayed on the fishing boats all night.

Around 7 o'clock, just around dusk, two more gunboats that seized me, *P-128* and *P-133*, came up alongside and one tied up on the one side of the fishing boats; the other tied up on the other side of the fishing boats. The young Cambodian came aboard on the fishing boats and started talking to us in French. Nobody in my crew could talk French or understand with the exception of one man by the name of the Patrano. He lives in Mobile. He talked a little Cajun French and, between their conversations, we understood that this young quartermaster of this *P-128* that seized us wanted to know what was in all the quarters that were locked on the ship.

I told him they were just living quarters. I told him to tell the young man they were just living quarters on the ship for myself and the crew.

He wanted to know if we had electronic surveillance gear in the rooms that were locked. I told Patrano to inform the young man that I would go aboard the ship and open all the doors for him with my master key if he wanted.

He took us out on a gunboat. I requested the chief engineer to go with me. He was my right arm during all this time. So we started out to go back to the *Mayaguez* — the chief engineer and I. We got up alongside the ship. The young quartermaster — he went up the pilot ladder first and then the chief engineer and I followed by two armed insurgents that were going to guard us around the ship. They still had the other armed insurgents on the forecastle head, on the bridge wings and on the fantail.

We got up on the main deck and two of our jets, the first two jets I had seen since our seizure, flew one on the starboard side, one on the port side from bow to stern and let off illumination bombs. They spaced them, four illumination bombs on each side of the ship. When they blew up and illuminated the ship, it was just like daylight. They were taking pictures to see what was happening to the ship. The young quartermaster insurgent was definitely afraid of it, so he didn't even bother to go into the rooms. He ordered us off the boat right away and we went back down on the gunboat and proceeded back to Koh Tang Island. Later I found out when we got back on the vessel that they kicked in all the doors to find out what was in them.

We laid there overnight.[1]

Stephen Zarley:

I felt better when we arrived at Koh Tang. The noise from the low flying jets and rapid firing by the Khmer Rouge had shaken me up during the trip from the ship. The trip only took about twenty minutes, but at the time it seemed much longer. I felt helpless and wanted to hide. I didn't know what my fate would be, but for some reason, the island meant safety.

My boat was the first to arrive and the second one with the remainder of the crew came alongside. We anchored about thirty yards off shore, unable to get closer because of the shallow water and coral bottom. There was a lot of talk among our captors. I got the impression that they were trying to decide what to do with us. To leave us in the fishing boats or to take us ashore. We stayed in the boats. The crew aboard the second fishing boat were made to transfer to mine. We were really cramped now. We counted heads remembering the shooting back on the ship. All were present and unhurt. To this day I don't know what caused that shooting.

I couldn't make out much of what was on the island. I did see some huts set back in the trees and smoke rising. A mongrel dog scampered across the narrow beach. Some of the Khmers had gone to the island and returned with food. They sat in the other fishing boat and ate. The meat they had had been chopped up in our wheelhouse and I thought it was prime rib. They ate in shifts so there was always someone in the gun turrets. From time to time they would fire at the recon plane circling high above us that had replaced the jets.

When nightfall came, one of the gunboats went back to the *Mayaguez*. It seemed like hours until it returned and water had been brought for us. The water was passed around and we made sure everyone got a good share. This was the first sign of true comradeship between us. From then on, this feeling grew; we were all in the same boat!

The captain was called to a man who wore only a pistol. The captain was asked to go back to the ship so the ship could be searched. Many of the rooms were locked, so all the keys were turned over to the captain. The captain agreed and took the chief engineer with him. Before he left, he said, "Don't worry fellows, we'll be back. I'll bring some oranges."

Off they went and we lost them in the darkness. The recon plane was still circling. We could see the lights forming a colored triangle in the sky; white, green and red. The gunboats and shore batteries would open fire and the lights would go out. The guns would cease and again fire when the triangle would form again. This procedure continued throughout the entire night. It was like a game the pilot was playing with the Khmers, egging them to fire and try to hit him.

As we watched the show above us, the sky lit up with a brilliant white flash. The jets had returned over the ship and dropped flares. My thoughts were of the captain and chief. What would happen to them now? I was also very interested in the jets maneuver. I had not seen or heard the jets in hours and the ship and gunboats were blacked out. How was it known that there was renewed activity aboard the ship? My only conclusion was that the recon plane had seen the gunboat depart (white water breaking from the bow) and had called in the jets to investigate. Beautifully done, I thought. The jets dropped flares once more then left. The *Mayaguez* was again covered by darkness.

Awhile later, the gunboat with the captain and chief aboard returned. The commander told us to put out our cigarettes, but we continued to smoke. We did however cover the butts with our palms to hide the glow. What difference did it make if the planes could see us? The pilots knew exactly where we were and proved that they could hit their target, even in the dark.

The captain stepped into my boat and sat down next to me on the gunwale. He told everyone that the search didn't get started and that the boat commander had told him on the way back that we would be returning to the ship at four o'clock in the morning. The Cambodians were afraid of the jets and wanted the captain to radio our military and call off the planes. They seemed shook up over the flares so the captain told them not to be concerned. The planes only dropped flares for taking pictures. No bombs would be dropped as long as the crew was unhurt. The commander still insisted that the planes be called off first thing after returning to the ship. The captain agreed.

The captain and I had a smoke together and he told me that when he contacted Sattahip, he was going to tell the military to give him twenty-four hours to get the ship out himself and if we weren't out by then, to come on and get us out. I kept this to myself since he hadn't said anything to the rest of the crew about his plan.

Besides the shooting gallery above us, the rest of the night passed peaceably. Even with our cramped conditions, some of the crew had no trouble sleeping. I couldn't. I found it very hard to sleep in a sitting position and when I tried to lie down, the bosun's (James Mullis) feet were in my face. Earl Gilbert (4-8 AB [Able-Bodied seaman]), Bill "Mac" MacDonald (4-8 AB), Bob Zimmermen (8-12 FWT [Fireman WaterTender]) and I stayed up pointing out the star constellations and watching the fireworks.[2]

That evening these events also took place:

1. The Joint Chiefs of Staff directed CINCPAC to prevent the *Mayaguez* from sailing toward the mainland, to use whatever control agents/or gun fire necessary to disable the ship with the minimum risk of lives and *not* to sink the ship.
2. USS *Holt* was directed to be prepared to disable and move the *Mayaguez* upon arrival.[3]

9

EVENING, MAY 13, 1975

WASHINGTON, D.C.

T he third National Security Council meeting began at 2240 and ended just after midnight at 0025 Wednesday May 14, 1975. It opened with President Ford asking Lt. Gen. Brent Scowcroft for an update on the situation.

Lt. Gen. Brent Scowcroft:

> With regard to the boat that I told you about, we do not have much time. Our aircraft has used riot control agents twice. That has delayed the boat but has not stopped it. It is now about six miles from Kompong Som, according to the pilot. The pilot is not at all sure that he can disable the boat without sinking it.

Discussion followed concerning the three boats: the first reaching the island, the second being sunk and that just mentioned. The pilot was uncertain as to whether the riot control agents would work or whether there were Caucasians on board this boat. The Council discussed how difficult it was to identify the men by eye and color because of the evening darkness. There was concern that if they did reach the island there might be problems.

Henry Kissinger: "They will hold them for bargaining."

James Schlesinger: "I would think that avoiding bargaining chips is less of an objection than not being in a position where the Cambodians can say that the F-4s killed our own men."

President Ford: "What do we do? Should we let them go into port?"

James Schlesinger: "Let's continue to try and stop them with riot control agents. We understand there are eight to nine men on board who seem to be Americans. There are others below who may be Americans. The pilot thinks there may be more Americans."

President Ford: "What do you recommend?"

James Schlesinger: "I recommend we sink the speedboats. I do not think we should sink the boat but should rather continue to use the riot control agents."

Brent Scowcroft: "The pilot is reluctant to attack if he is under instructions not to sink the boat."

James Schlesinger: "That is true. He originally thought that he would disable the boat without sinking it. Then he became reluctant."

President Ford: "What you think?"

Henry Kissinger:

I've just come back into this problem, having been out of town all day. My instinct would have been as follows: we have two problems: First, the problem of the crew and the ship and of how we win their release. Second, our general posture which goes beyond the crew and the ship. But that sort of thing comes later.

In the immediate situation, I think I agree with Jim. We will take a beating if we kill the Americans. At the same time, we must understand that we cannot negotiate for them once they are on the mainland. If you are willing to take that position, then I think we can let them go. We should not let them become bargaining chips.

Lt. Gen. Brent Scowcroft: "We have already done it on one."

President Ford expressed his concern and anger that the order to stop all boats did not go out from the first Security Council meeting until 3:30.

President Ford: "I gave the order at the meeting to stop all boats. I cannot understand what happened on that order, because I heard that order did not go out until 3:30."

James Schlesinger: "It went out by telephone within half an hour after you gave it."

Gen. David C. Jones: "We talked to Burns, the commander out there, immediately. The confirming order went out later. But our communications are so good that we can get all the information back here immediately to Washington in order to make the decisions from here."

President Ford:

> Was the order given, and at what time, not to permit any boats to leave the island or come into it? I was told it was not given until 3:30. That is inexcusable … Let's find out what happened. It's inexcusable to have such a delay.
>
> Now let us talk about the problem of the moment. It is a different situation, and I reluctantly agree with Jim and Henry.

James Schlesinger: "I think we should destroy the boats that still remain on the island."

President Ford: "That is your recommendation. What do you think, Henry?"

Henry Kissinger:

> I'm afraid that if we do a few little steps every few hours, we are in trouble. I think we should go ahead with the island, Kompong Som, and the ship all at once. I think people should have the impression that we are potentially trigger-happy. I think that once we have our destroyer on station, that is ideal.

James Schlesinger: "I agree. It will go in at noon."

Henry Kissinger: "In the meantime, I think we should sink the boats that are at the island."

Donald Rumsfeld: "I thought the *Holt* would get in at eight A.M."

James Schlesinger: "We understand it is doing twenty-one knots, not twenty-five."

Lt. Gen. Brent Scowcroft: "I've got to get the word out. What should I tell them?"

President Ford: "Tell them to sink the boats near the island. On the other boat, use riot control agents or other methods, but do not attack it."

John Marsh: "Supposing the boats near the island have Americans on it. Should we send some order to use only riot control agents there?"

Henry Kissinger: "I think the pilot should sink them. He should destroy the boats and not send situation reports."

President Ford: "On one boat, there's a possibility of Caucasians. On the others, we can't be sure."

Gen. David C. Jones: "Suppose we say in our order that we should hit all the boats in the cove, not just two."

Henry Kissinger: "We don't need to decide on the cove right now. We have some time."

President Ford then wanted to know how many hours away the *Holt* was and Henry Kissinger answered fourteen hours.

Gen. David C. Jones:

> I have tried to put all this in a chart, indicating when the key actions would take place. The *Holt*, we expect, will arrive at 12:30 Washington time tomorrow. The *Coral Sea* and *Hancock* will arrive later. We are not sure of the latter's arrival time because it is having trouble with one propeller shaft. The Marines are all airborne. They are on the way to U-Tapao. That is the 1,000 marines. The 150, with their helicopters, are already there and on alert. The 1,000 Marines will arrive around 0300 tomorrow morning. That is a time for the first one. After that the others arrive every few hours.

USS Hancock *(CVA-19)off San Diego in the early 1970s.* U.S. Navy.

President Ford: "Then the *Holt* arrives 11:30 Eastern Daylight time tomorrow. That is 2330 Cambodia time. And the *Coral Sea* about twenty-eight hours from now."

Gen. David C. Jones: "It is making twenty-five knots. The plots are pretty good. It is moving towards the spot."

President Ford: "That is not flank speed."

Gen. David C. Jones: "That is the best time that they can do."

President Ford: "Flank speed is thirty-three knots."

Gen. David C. Jones: "The Navy says that this is the best time that they can make."

Donald Rumsfeld: "The information this afternoon was that the *Hancock* would arrive on Friday."

Gen. David C. Jones: "This is very tenuous. They are working on one of the shafts."

James Schlesinger: "We are in serious trouble on the mechanical side. One shaft is out on the *Hancock*. The *Okinawa* has a boiler out. It is making only ten knots. There has been a series of mishaps."

President Ford: "What can be done before daylight ends over there today?"

James Schlesinger:

> We have eleven choppers at U-Tapao. We can run operations against the vessel. In addition, we can land on the island with

120 marines. We can support that with force from Okinawa. All together, we would have 270 Marines. In all probability, we could take the island. The Marines estimate that there might be about 100 Cambodians on the island. We would prefer to land with 1,000.

President Ford: "If you do not do it during the daylight, you have a delay. How long would it be?"
James Schlesinger:

> Twenty-four hours. We do not have the *Holt* there yet. The *Holt* will arrive at noon tomorrow our time. If it is to do anything, I would prefer to wait until the first light on the 15th. Until the *Coral Sea* arrives, all we can use are the helicopters at U-Tapao.

Henry Kissinger: "How would the Marines get down?"
Gen. David C. Jones: "On ladders."
James Schlesinger: "The helicopters would hover."
Henry Kissinger: "But if there were 100 troops on the island, why do we not attack it?"

The Council now began to focus on safety and daylight factors involving the attack on the island and the location of enemy ships and American ships. Considerable discussion developed concerning what to attack, the timing and the potential repercussions.

President Ford: "In this daylight cycle, you could put 120 on the ships, and 270 on the island?"
Gen. David C. Jones:

> The total lift is 270. Our plan was to seize the ship with 120, and then use the Marines from Okinawa to try to go on the island. It is hazardous to go onto the island with this first group because you do not have the time to recycle. We would have to let them remain there overnight, against a force that we do not know.

Henry Kissinger: "Does the *Coral Sea* have helicopters?"
Gen. David C. Jones: "No. It has only two or so that it uses itself. But we could take the Marines on to the *Coral Sea*, and thus get them close to the island."

Henry Kissinger: "I understand we only have eleven choppers."

William Colby: "Couldn't the 270 protect themselves against a force on the island?"

Gen. David Jones: "We have nothing to confirm the exact force on the island."

Henry Kissinger:

> I do not see what we gain by going in with that force tonight. If you sink the boats in the area, and all who approach, it does not matter if we have anybody else on the island. At that point, nothing will be moving.
>
> My instinct would be to wait for the *Holt* and the *Coral Sea*. You can then work with the Marines from the *Coral Sea*. Nothing can happen in the meantime. Then I would assemble a force and really move vigorously.

President Ford: "In other words, the time you gain in this cycle is not worth the gamble."

Henry Kissinger: "Later you can do more. It might work with the 270. But it is a risk. It should be decisive and it should look powerful."

Gen. David C. Jones: "But it cannot be in twenty-four hours, only in forty-eight. Once you start cycling, it takes time."

James Schlesinger: "I think that Henry is thinking of going tomorrow night."

Donald Rumsfeld: "But you have only a few hours left of daylight."

Gen. David C. Jones: "That would not be enough."

James Schlesinger: "We need the morning of the 16th for a coordinated assault."

Henry Kissinger: "We are talking about forty-eight hours."

President Ford: "In other words, you are talking about Thursday night our time."

Gen. David C. Jones: "On Wednesday night, the *Coral Sea* will help a little with its fighters. But not with Marines. Maybe the *Hancock* will do it."

Henry Kissinger: "You also have the *Holt*."

Gen. David C. Jones: "With the *Coral Sea*, and you have other vessels as well. You will have a total of five ships. You would have a good force, but is very late at night to begin to cycle the Marines."

William Colby: "Our estimate was that there were 2,000 in Kompong Som. There's not a large force on the island."

President Ford: "Do you think we can figure with 100?"

William Colby: "Yes. The KC (Khmer Communists) have just arrived in power. They have probably not had time to man the island more fully."

William Clements: "In the time frame that you are talking about, there will not be an island worth taking. All the Americans will be gone."

President Ford: "Not if we knock out the boats. Unless of course they leave at night."

William Clements: "Right. I think they will get out. The *Holt* will protect the ship. But that is not what matters. I doubt that there will be anything on the island."

Donald Rumsfeld: "Can we not use flares for this?"

Gen. David C. Jones: "The main thing we use at night is infra- red. We can read it at night. The P-3s also have searchlights and flares."

Donald Rumsfeld: "The P-3s should be good at keeping the boat under control."

Gen. David C. Jones: "Yes, unless the weather is bad."

William Clements: "The small boats can get through. You cannot get control."

William Colby: "The KC may say something soon."

President Ford: "It seems that at a minimum we should wait for the next daylight cycle, with the *Holt* getting there."

Henry Kissinger: "The *Holt* will be there then."

President Ford: "Right. Is it the unanimous view that we should withhold action until after the *Coral Sea* has a full day there?"

James Schlesinger: "I think you should wait."

William Colby: "This is not my business. I do not think you should go tonight. But I worry about what might happen later.

If they get locked in, if they take reprisals, it would be very difficult for us."

William Clements: "I like to take a middle position. Once the *Holt* gets there, we will have some control. We can do a great deal."

William Colby: "I think that with the Marines, you have to go soon."

Henry Kissinger: "I'm very leery about that operation using ladders."

James Schlesinger:

> If there's token resistance on the island, the Marines can handle it. If there is more, they can try to lock in and get more Marines to land the next day, with the *Holt* for additional support. It is a close call. There are other pressures of time. It is also possible that the Cambodians will decide to execute our men.

William Colby: "Once we take that ship, the clock is ticking."

William Clements: "The *Holt* can get them, by speaking to them with loudspeakers. It can let them know our position."

Henry Kissinger:

> But that is not the issue. We should not look as though people can localize an issue. We have to use the opportunity to prove that others will be worse off if they tackle us, and not that they can return to the status quo. It is not just enough to get the ship's release. Using one aircraft carrier, one destroyer, and 1,000 Marines to get the ship out is not much. I think we should seize the island, seize the ship, and hit the mainland. I am thinking not of Cambodia, but of Korea and of the Soviet Union and of others. It will not help you with the Congress if they get the wrong impression of the way we will act under such circumstances.
>
> As for the 270 Marines, it had several components. There is an advantage in speed. The problem is if anything goes wrong, as often does, I think against 100 KC you would lose more Americans because you do not have overwhelming power. I am assuming we will not negotiate. We must have an unconditional release. On balance, I would like to get a more reliable force.

William Clements: "If you want the ship and the Americans, why not let the *Holt* do it? Let the *Holt* broadcast that if the Americans are not released, all hell will break loose."

Henry Kissinger: "What would hell mean in a case like that?"

President Ford: "Let's do an add-on to Colby's suggestion. The *Holt* is there. You land 270 marines. You bomb the airport at Sihanoukville."

William Colby: "My schedule is to land the Marines today."

James Schlesinger: "Until the *Coral Sea* gets there, we have only the aircraft from Thailand. The inhibitions on the use of the aircraft from Thailand are greater."

President Ford: "No, you have the B-52s on Guam. They can be used."

William Colby: "If you knock out every boat, you have effectiveness."

Henry Kissinger: "That is still localizing it. We will not get that many chances. As Jim says, it would exacerbate the Thai problem."

President Ford: "If we order the Marines to go from U-Tapao, we could get 270 in there."

Gen. David C. Jones:

> That was before we lost two helicopters on SAR. I would urge against doing this in daylight. The Marines would just be landing at U-Tapao. The helicopter pilots would be tired. Nobody would be mated up yet. It would be a difficult operation to be launching at that time, especially since we could not follow up the same day.

Henry Kissinger:

> If you were to give the orders now, Mr. President, there would still be some hours of delay before the messages were received and before the preparations were made. By then we would really only have three more hours of daylight left in order to conduct the operation.

President Ford: "So we rule out any action on this daylight cycle. Then, on the next day, the *Holt* gets there. We then have some more options. The *Coral Sea*, however, doesn't get there until the next cycle."

Henry Kissinger: "If you wait twenty-four more hours, you have the *Holt* and you also have the fact that you can use 270 Marines."

Gen. David C. Jones: "And, in fact, you have 250 more that you can put in. You also have the *Coral Sea*."

Henry Kissinger: "I am not sure that I would let the *Holt* go up against the vessel. It may be best to keep the *Holt* where can it blockade the island. Then we can seize the island."

James Schlesinger: "I agree with Henry Kissinger. But we have to keep in mind that there are forces on the island. That gives them time to prepare. It also gives them time to scuttle the ship."

Henry Kissinger: "But they can still scuttle the ship, even with the *Holt* alongside. If we could seize the ship quickly, I would agree. I did not know that the *Holt* could board."

President Ford: "Unless sailors are different now, they are not good boarders."

James Schlesinger: "Could any Marines do it?"

Gen. David Jones: "We could get the Marines on the ship, but then we could not use them for other things. The suggestion is to go with the first light on the 15th, to get the *Holt* and hold the island."

Henry Kissinger: "My suggestion is to seize the island. We cannot do anything tonight. By tomorrow morning, we can put the Marines on the *Holt*. They can operate. I would go for the island at daybreak of the 15th."

James Schlesinger: "The problem with that is the *Coral Sea* will not be there. If you want an overwhelming force on the island, you should wait until the 16th."

Henry Kissinger: "The ideal time for what I have in mind is the 16th. That would not just include the island but Kompong Som, the airport and boats."

President Ford: "If you wait until the 16th, you have maximum capability. But the people in U-Tapao should be prepared to operate as soon as the *Holt* gets there, at 11:30 tomorrow night. The Marines should be alerted."

Henry Kissinger: "The *Holt* gets there at noon tomorrow. So we can go from first light. We could seize the island and the ship. That, however, would not give us the *Coral Sea* for such operations as we would wish to run against Kompong Som."

James Schlesinger: "You can get 250 Marines in helicopters."

William Colby: "That would mean 500 in two cycles."

President Ford:

> The operational orders should be set up so that the *Holt* and the Marines can go. We do not know what will happen in twenty-four hours. They have options also. We can make a decision tomorrow if they want to. But we should have orders ready to go so that they can move within twenty-four hours. That would be for the *Holt*, the Marines, and the B-52s.

Donald Rumsfeld: "When would it start, then?"
Henry Kissinger:

> At 2200 hours tomorrow. I think that when we move, we should hit the mainland as well as the island. We should hit targets at Kompong Som and the airfield and say that we are doing it to suppress any supporting action against our operations to regain the ship and seize the island. If the B-52s can do it, I would like to do it tomorrow night. Forty-eight hours are better militarily. But so much can happen, domestically and internationally. We have to be ready to take the island and the ship and to hit Kompong Som.

President Ford: "I think we should be ready to go in twenty-four hours. We may, however, want to wait."

James Schlesinger:

> We will be prepared to go on the morning of the 15th. We will see if we can get the Marines on the *Holt*. At first light, we will have

A Boeing B-52 on a bombing run. U.S. Air Force.

plans to go to the island. Simultaneously, we will go for the ship. We will have the B-52s at Guam ready to go for Kompong Som. But I think there are political advantages to using the aircraft from the *Coral Sea*. You will have more problems on the hill with B-52s from Guam.

President Ford: "Why?"

James Schlesinger: "The B-52s are a red flag on the hill. Moreover, they bomb a very large box and they are not so accurate. They might generate a lot of casualties outside the exact areas that we would want to hit."

President Ford: "Let's see what the chiefs say is better, the aircraft from a carrier or the B-52s. It should be their judgment."

Henry Kissinger: "But the *Coral Sea* would delay us twenty-four hours."

Donald Rumsfeld: "But do we have to wait for the *Coral Sea* actually to arrive?"

Lt. Gen. Brent Scowcroft: "No. Their planes can operate at considerable distance."

President Ford: "On the 15th, we can use the B-52s from Guam. On the 16th, we also have the aircraft from the *Coral Sea*."

Gen. David C. Jones: "Except, if you use the *Coral Sea*, it limits some assets. Everybody is now on alert. We can do it when you say. We are ready to go."

Donald Rumsfeld: "Is it not possible that the *Coral Sea* aircraft could strike Cambodia even when the *Coral Sea* is still hours away?"

James Schlesinger: "I'm not sure it would be close enough. Let me check."

Donald Rumsfeld: "The *Coral Sea* could be there near that time."

James Schlesinger: "Let me check."

President Ford: "You may have an operational problem. If you have to turn the carrier into the wind in order to dispatch and recover aircraft, you may lose time."

James Schlesinger: "Yes, but if you go for the 15th, you do not need its presence so soon if you can use the aircraft from a distance."

Henry Kissinger: "What do we have on the *Coral Sea*?"

An F-4J Phantom II landing aboard the aircraft carrier USS Saratoga *(CV-60) underway off the coast of Florida in 1980.* U.S. Navy.

A-7E Corsair II aircraft on the flight deck of the aircraft carrier USS Independence *(CV-62) in December 1983.* U.S. Navy.

Gen. David C. Jones: "We have fighter aircraft, including F-4s and A-7s."

Henry Kissinger: "Would they be more accurate than the B-52s?"

Gen. David C. Jones: "Not necessarily. It depends on the type of target."

Philip Buchen, Counsel to the president: "I see two problems: The first is Cooper-Church Amendment. The second is international law."

President Ford: "On international law, I do not think we have a problem. They have clearly violated it."

Philip Buchen: "We had the right of self-defense, but only self-defense. The Cooper-Church Amendment says no actions in Indochina."

Henry Kissinger: "I think you can legitimately say that our aircraft are suppressing hostile action against our operation."

President Ford: "We cannot be that concerned in this instance."

John Marsh: "This afternoon, we had the NSC prepare a paper saying what we would do. It showed that you would use force in general terms. The reaction from the people we talked to was very favorable."

THE COOPER-CHURCH AMENDMENT

The original Cooper-Church Amendment was first brought to bear in 1970 as Congress tried to prevent President Nixon from deploying more troops in the Vietnam War. It was the first time such an amendment was used to restrict an American President. The amendment sought the following:

1. To stop funding of U.S. troops and advisors in Cambodia and Laos after June 30, 1970.
2. To stop the air operations in Cambodian air space and the support of Cambodian forces without Congressional approval.
3. To stop the support for South Vietnamese forces outside Vietnam.

The bill passed on January 5, 1971. By this time U.S. forces were out of Cambodia, however, U.S. operations continued over Cambodia.

The complete shut down of U.S. forces in Southeast Asia finally came on June 19, 1973 via the Case-Church Amendment. This amendment prohibited any U.S. military involvement in Southeast Asia without Congressional approval.

William Clements: "I hate to have us lose sight of our objectives in this case. Those objectives are to get the Americans and the ship. If we want to punish people, that's another thing. I think that dropping a lot of bombs on the mainland will not help us with the release of the Americans."

President Ford: "I think we have to assume that the Americans were taken from the island and that some were killed. This is tragic, but I think we have to assume that it happened. Does anybody disagree?

(*General expressions of agreement*)

Vice President Rockefeller: "At a briefing yesterday, Congressman Zablocki, one of the proponents of the War Powers Act, said that he would tell the press that the U.S. could bomb the hell out of them."

James Schlesinger: "We are not inhibited by the War Powers Act, only by Cooper-Church."

William Colby: "We think there are about three T-28s at Kompong Som airfield. They could use them. So there is a potential threat of Kompong Som against our forces."

President Ford: "Can we verify this?"

William Colby: "This is from a photograph taken on the 12th."

Donald Rumsfeld: "How are those aircraft equipped?"

William Colby: "With bombs and guns."

Henry Kissinger:

> I think the worst stance is to follow Phil's concern. If we only respond at the same place at which we were challenged, nobody can lose by challenging us. They can only win. This means, I think, that we have to do more. The Koreans and others would like to look us over and to see how we react. Under certain circumstances, in fact, some domestic cost is to our advantage in demonstrating the seriousness with which we view this kind of challenge.

President Ford: "Phil and I have argued for years."

Philip Buchen: "I have to state the problems that we face."

President Ford: "In this daylight cycle, unless something unusual comes up, we will try to prevent boats going to and from the island."

Henry Kissinger: "The latest intelligence shows that there are several small patrol boats near the island in the cove. I think we should sink them."

President Ford: "I agree."

James Schlesinger: "There are four boats."

President Ford: "I think we should sink any boats that can be used to try to move the Americans."

Donald Rumsfeld: "But not the ones that carry Americans."

James Schlesinger: "I disagree with Henry in one case. The legal situation in Indochina is unique. We should emphasize that. The restraints of our actions are different from the restraints anywhere else."

Henry Kissinger: "I would hit, and then deal with the legal implications."

President Ford:

> Bill (Colby) should verify that the T-28s are there. At the second daylight cycle, we are prepared to do more. The *Holt* will be there and the Marines will be ready to go on it and to be put on the island, with the B-52s and perhaps the aircraft from the *Coral Sea* prepared to strike Kompong Som. But, unless there is some unusual development, the actual action will take place twenty-four hours later.

James Schlesinger: "On the 16th."

Henry Kissinger: "You can decide it then."

President Ford: "The preferable time is twenty-four hours later."

Henry Kissinger:

> That is when the best forces will be available. But that has to be weighed against other considerations for the extra twenty-four hours that you lose. I remember 1969, when the EC-121 was shot down off Korea. We assembled forces like crazy. But in the end, did not do anything. Maybe we shouldn't have. We will never know.

William Colby: "There was one other justifiable target in Kompong Som area. The old Cambodian government had twenty-five patrol boats in the Ream Naval Base."

(The President, Henry Kissinger, and James Schlesinger almost simultaneously remark along the lines that might be a worthwhile target.)

James Schlesinger: "But this sort of thing would require the gunships out of Thailand."

Henry Kissinger: "I think we should do something that will impress the Koreans and the Chinese. I saw Teng Hsiao-Ping's comments in Paris."

President Ford: "Are there an airfield and a naval base there in Kompong Som?"

William Colby: "Yes."

President Ford: "Why not hit both of them? There would be as many objections to hitting one as two of them."

James Schlesinger: "The question is whether you use the B-52s or the carrier aircraft. The B-52s may represent the best image for what Henry is trying to accomplish. But, for Congress and others, other aircraft would be better."

President Ford: "Bill has to verify what there is at the Airport."

James Schlesinger: "We'll put some T-28s on the base."

President Ford: "Tomorrow we will still have the options as to what we should do."

Gen. David C. Jones: "On Guam, if we are to do anything, we have to start pretty soon. But there are lots of press there."

Donald Rumsfeld: "You would be launching at about four P.M. tomorrow."

Henry Kissinger: "How long does it take to load?"

Gen. David C. Jones: "There are many planes to load and to get ready."

Henry Kissinger: "Is the first thing tomorrow still time enough?"

Gen. David C. Jones: "I'm not sure."

President Ford: "Are there any others in the Far East?"

Gen. David C. Jones: "Only at U-Tapao."

President Ford: "We do not want that."

Donald Rumsfeld: "It should not take long to calculate the answer on the question of using the *Coral Sea*."

Vice President Rockefeller: "Everybody wants to know when you are moving. In New York, where I just was, people expect you to be doing things. So any steps you take in preparation will be understood."

President Ford: "How many B-52s would you use?"

Gen. David C. Jones: "Perhaps six or nine."

President Ford: "Let's say nine. How many do you have on Guam?"

Gen. David C. Jones: "I am not sure. About twenty or more."

President Ford: "Every time I have looked at a B-52 base, they are always doing something. It would not be that unusual. I think you should load them, and get them ready."

Gen. David C. Jones: "There are about fifty reporters on Guam right now, because of the refugees."

Henry Kissinger: "Can you tell the commander to shut up?"

James Schlesinger: "It will get out, no matter how hard you try."

Vice President Rockefeller: "Perhaps it would be good to have it get out. I don't think we should cavil."

President Ford: "Let's have them get ready to carry out the mission if we decide to do it."

Robert T. Hartmann:

> I am not an expert on military affairs. I'm just an old retired captain in the Reserve. I have been listening in terms of what the American public wants. I think the American public wants to know what you're going to do. This crisis, like the Cuban Missile Crisis, is the first real test of your leadership. What you decide is not as important as what the public perceives. Nothing, so far as I know, has gone out to the public so far, except that we are taking steps. It may be that we should let the public know something of the steps that you are taking. The public will judge you in accordance with what you do. We should not just think of what is the right thing to do, but of what the public perceives.

Henry Kissinger: "I would say nothing until afterwards. That will speak for itself. Then you can explain what you have been doing. If you say something now, everybody will be kibitzing."

President Ford: "But the press should know of the NSC meeting."

Robert T. Hartmann: "I think we should consider what the people think we are doing."

Donald Rumsfeld: "The delay worries me."

Robert T. Hartmann: "Yes."

Henry Kissinger: "If we are going to do an integrated attack, I think we have to go in twenty-two hours. We should not wait for a later cycle. I cannot judge if there will be a problem in taking the island. We are saying that it will be one annihilating blow. I cannot judge if 270 Marines can do it."

Donald Rumsfeld: "There would be 500."

Henry Kissinger: "But there will be 270 for four hours. They will have the *Holt* support. Perhaps they will also have some support from the *Coral Sea.*"

President Ford: "Do we have Marines on the *Coral Sea*?"

Gen. David C. Jones: "I'm not sure."

Henry Kissinger: "If the *Coral Sea* can launch against Kompong Som, it can launch against the island. We have to be sure that the landing has a chance of success."

Gen. David C. Jones: "The probability that the Americans are gone causes the problem. I think we have a high probability."

Henry Kissinger: "Then my instinct is with Rummy. We should go tomorrow night or earlier."

President Ford: "Everything will be ready. But, if you do it in the next cycle, you have the problem of Thailand."

Henry Kissinger:

> The ideal time would be Thursday night. But I am worried that in the next forty-eight hours some diplomatic pressure will occur, or something else. So we have to weigh the optimum military time against the optimum political time. For foreign policy and domestic reasons, tomorrow is better.

President Ford: "The Thai will be upset."

Henry Kissinger: "That is correct, but they will also be reassured."

Donald Rumsfeld: "Can we be sure there is anybody on the island? We might just take a walk."

Henry Kissinger: "If the Americans are on the mainland, then we have to rethink."

Donald Rumsfeld: "If we look at this tonight, we will know tomorrow."

President Ford: "If Jones goes back to the Pentagon tonight with the orders to prepare, we will have details tomorrow."

Gen. David C. Jones: "Everything is now moving, except the B-52s."

Robert Ingersoll: "What is the flying time of the B-52s?"

Henry Kissinger: "About six hours."

Gen. David C. Jones: "Maybe longer."

James Schlesinger: "Can we tanker them out of Guam?"

Gen. David Jones: "Yes."

Henry Kissinger: "What will we say about the boats that have been sunk?"

Buchen: "We have to make a report to the Hill."

James Schlesinger: "It may not get out that quickly."

President Ford: "My answer would be, that we have ordered that no enemy boats should leave the island or go out to it, but that if they did, they would be sunk."

Henry Kissinger: "I think a low-key press statement can be issued, saying what has happened. We should tell the truth. We should say it in a very matter-of-fact way, at a DOD briefing."

James Schlesinger: "It will not stay low-key."

President Ford: "The order was issued that no boats should leave."

Henry Kissinger:

> We should say nothing about the riot control agents. We should say that there were Americans possibly being moved, and that lives were at stake. Some Americans are still on the island. In pursuit of these objectives, the following boats were sunk. One other reason is that it is not inconceivable that the Khmers will cave, and they should come in response to something that we had done.

James Schlesinger: "Should we say that they were sunk from aircraft from Thailand? That is your problem."

Henry Kissinger:

I am worried about it getting out of hand. We will look sneaky and furtive about something we should be proud of. But the Thai thing does give me trouble. I think the Thai military will love it. But the Thai government will say that it does not like it. The Liberals on the hill will put forward a recommendation to withdraw our forces from Thailand. They will match this with some requests from the Thai government.

Donald Rumsfeld: "I think that is a good issue."

Hartmann: "Bob Byrd, whom I regard as a good antenna of sentiment, says that we should act."

Marsh: "Case says we should go in."

Vice President Rockefeller: "In our statement, should we not call them launches?"

James Schlesinger: "The boats are of different sizes."

Henry Kissinger:

I would urge that the spokesman make a short announcement at noon tomorrow. He should explain why we are doing it. He should say that it was ordered by you, executed by the National Security Council, and then answer no other questions. This would be noon. By eight o'clock, we will have decided the other. That will add to your strength.

(General concurrence, meeting adjourned.)[1]

By the end of this meeting the whereabouts and condition of the *Mayaguez* and crew were as follows:

1. U.S. jets were unsuccessful in stopping the Cambodian fishing boat with the American prisoners aboard. Shots had been fired across the bow and riot control agents were dropped on the boat. Both failed.

2. A pilot reported that a fishing boat had docked at 11:15 P.M. in the port of Kompong Som with between thirty to forty possible Caucasians aboard. A Pacific Command intelligence report said eight to nine possible crew members were aboard.[2]

Meanwhile:
1. The message to Cambodia via the People's Republic of China had been returned.
2. An official from Communist China in France said that China wouldn't intervene if the U.S. attacked Cambodia.
3. The U.S. tried to rescue ten Cambodians from the sunken gunboat but were unsuccessful.
4. A helicopter transporting eighteen U.S. Air Force Security personnel from North Thailand to U-Tapao Air base crashed in Thailand killing twenty-three Americans aboard.[3]

In summary, the following plans and statements were made:
1. Finalization of Marine assault plan to land on Koh Tang Island Thursday morning.
2. Boarding the *Mayaguez.*
3. Bombing the Kompong Som mainland area.
4. Using fourteen Marine helicopters to transport 400 Marines from the USS *Hancock* to arrive 6 A.M. Friday morning on Koh Tang Island.
5. Delivery of letter to the U.N. Secretary General requesting assistance in releasing *Mayaguez* and crew.
6. The U.S. sunk one more Cambodian gunboat and two smaller vessels.[4]

Meanwhile, the U.S. Senate Committee on Foreign Relations unanimously approved the following Resolution:

> [The] Committee condemns an act of armed aggression on an unarmed U.S. merchant vessel in the course of innocent passage on an established trade route.
>
> The President has engaged in diplomatic means to secure release and we support that.
>
> Third, we support the President in the exercise of his constitutional powers within the framework of the War Powers Resolution to secure the release of the ship and its men.

We urge the Cambodian Government to release the ship and the men forthwith."[5]

Additional planning and developments involved:

1. Thailand formally requested the removal of U.S. Marines in Thailand.

2. A U.S. Embassy in the Middle East reported to the Secretary of State that a third country official had learned from a senior diplomat that his government was using its influence with Cambodia to seek early release of the *Mayaguez* and the ship was expected to be released soon.

3. U.S. defense press said that there were indications that the Cambodians had tried to move the crew from Koh Tang Island to Kompong Som. One boat was successful.

4. The B-52s based at Guam were 'tasked' to recapture the *Mayaguez.*

5. Using discretion, any vessels in the vicinity of Koh Tang Island were to be sunk.[6]

10

MORNING, MAY 14, 1975

GULF OF THAILAND

The sky above the *Mayaguez* crew became increasingly busy with American military planes. Not knowing the future course of the Khmer Rouge weighed heavily on the captain and his crew.

Capt. Miller:

> We laid here until around four o'clock in the afternoon [May 13] and then proceeded into Kompong Som. They were going to take us into Baie de Ream. They wanted me to take it (*Mayaguez*) into Baie de Ream. I refused so they took us [the crew] into the Baie de Ream. The next morning when we started out they took only one [fishing boat]. Our reconnaissance planes saw two fishing boats and saw only one fishing boat leave the following morning. That is why our military thought half the prisoners were held on Koh Tang Island and the other half had been removed to the mainland to be taken into a military compound either at Baie de Ream or Phnom Penh.
>
> This morning the skies were full of jet aircraft. F-4s, F-111s, and they made passes on the gunboat, the Thai fishing boat we were

on. They didn't fire. I later learned in a conversation that President Ford had issued orders the night before not to let any boats go in Koh Tang, or to the mainland, or any boats from the mainland back to Koh Tang, or any boats to the *Mayaguez*, to blow them out of the water.

The pilot that over flew us — I think he reported there was around nine to twelve bodies laying on the deck and this was relayed from the aircraft to probably the carrier *Coral Sea* which was laying out. We couldn't see the *Coral Sea*; we didn't know the Navy had arrived. But the *Coral Sea* was out there and they launched the aircraft and had aircraft at U-Tapao Air Base.

I found out later from conversations with the President that the pilot informed them there was around nine to twelve bodies on ship, I believe it was, and the President ordered them not to blow the fishing boat out of the water but to try to prevent it from reaching the mainland.

At that time the jets tried to divert the vessel; they started bombing and firing 20mm cannon and machine gun fire ahead of the vessel. They started shooting out ahead the rockets and 20mm cannon. When I saw it wasn't going to work, they came in closer and got to about ten feet off the bow of the ship.

Never doubt that our fly boys don't know how to shoot. They can thread a needle a mile away with their gunfire. If we were bombed once, we were bombed around a hundred times with rockets and 20mm cannon fire.

When we got in close to the mainland of Cambodia out where they didn't want us to land, because we would be lost then, the jets saw that they couldn't turn the ship around, so they gassed us. They came from the bow to stern and dropped tear gas on us figuring if they could gas us enough, maybe we could overcome the ten or fifteen Cambodians aboard the vessel and go back to the *Mayaguez*. It wouldn't have done any good because they still had the armed insurgents on the *Mayaguez*. The only thing, if we tried to overtake the guards there, we had no place to go because there were gunboats around that would capture us again. So I told the crew to lay down, so we wouldn't get hit by shrapnel because when the rockets were dropping in the water around us, there was shrapnel. Three of the men were hit. The engineer was hit in the arm, my third engineer was hit in the leg. Later we found a machinist had a piece of shrapnel in his eye.[1]

Stephen Zarley:

The night had been pleasantly warm, but the grey dawn came in with a chill. I felt tired and my mind was filled with apprehension. I wanted to get back to the *Mayaguez* so bad I could taste it. The captain was waking the crew that were still asleep. It was four o'clock but the Khmers didn't seem concerned. David English (8-12 Third Mate) said something about lies. "We aren't really going back to the ship." I didn't like the way English talked, but maybe he was right. Perhaps the promise last night was only a pacifier.

It was around six o'clock when we all transferred to the second fishing boat. This boat was larger than the one we slept on; especially the wheelhouse. The fishing boat was about forty feet long and eight feet wide. A solid red flag flew from a post atop the wheelhouse. Civilians operated the boat. There was a lot of activity among the Khmers. Our escort was being picked. Eleven came aboard and others manned three of the gunboats. I had seen six (boats) in the area since our seizure. The sun was shining now and the clouds were red from the sun's rays.

We started out of the cove with three gunboats; one in front and one on each side. I looked to see if the recon plane would follow us. It did, circling wide overhead. We were not heading toward the ship, but a right angle to it. We all started muttering about the change in direction. It looked like we were being taken to another island. The convoy turned again and passed the ship far off her port. We all knew then. We were proceeding to the mainland; to the only Cambodian seaport, Kompong Som.

The jets appeared; two, four, then six. The recon plane stopped circling above us and moved off to our port and circled. All eyes were turned to the sky. The Khmer guns began firing furiously. I remember a man asking me what I thought President Ford was doing now. "Probably at Camp David swimming with his dog," I said. How wrong I was. The calm waters around us exploded. Geysers of spray shot into the air near the gunboats. The gunboat peeled away from us zigzagging across the open water firing as they went. Our jets turned from flying ornaments into active instruments of death. Rockets were being placed between the gunboats and us and between them and the mainland. The boat with the commander aboard turned about and sped backwards toward the *Mayaguez*, a jet following and firing. Cannon fire ripped around the other boats and now the recon plane had opened up. One boat was trying to make its way somewhere to our starboard and the third was trying to head in the general direction of the mainland.

After a while we were alone. I got on top of one of the hatches and tried to rest. It was hot and even at this early hour I was beginning to burn. I got back down and sat on the wooden deck. "They got one!" someone said. Sure enough, a cloud of smoke rose from the direction taken by the boat that was heading to the mainland.

Two jets circled around our stern to the starboard side, dropped in altitude and came straight in for our midships. One followed the other a bit higher. "God, they're low," someone said.

"They dropped one," yelled Ed Reyes (crane maintenance man). I ducked and curled up in a ball keeping my head below the hatch cover. I was sure we were going to be blown to bits. Everything seemed to happen at once. I heard the rocket explode and the rapid cannon fire. Our guards, two in the bow, one next to the wheelhouse, one inside and the rest on the stern, were firing their small arms. Spray and shrapnel flew about the boat. The jets screamed above at about twenty feet then swooped sharply skyward. I raised my head to see if anyone had been killed. Al Rappenecker (8-12 third engineer) was lying prone on the hatch cover were I had been earlier. Blood oozed from the right knee of his white coveralls.

"He's hit," yelled the chief.

Rappenecker said that he was all right, but I could see that he was in pain. His wound was washed and bandaged with a handkerchief. Rappenecker was sixty-four and had a heart condition.

The guards were wide-eyed. They just couldn't believe that our planes would attack us. They also were alone. Their commander was gone and, probably for the first time in battle, they were caught out in the open and had nowhere to run. This wasn't the jungle warfare they knew so well.

"Here they come again," shouted Mac.

The attack plane came like the first. The air became heavy with the smell of sulfate and the deck was strewn with shrapnel. I even picked pieces out of my hair. Mac became our best lookout. He called out the jet's positions like the hours on a clock and knew just when an attack was coming. The attack started about 100 feet away from us, but as time wore on they came closer and closer and increased in number.

We were trying to convince the civilian helmsman to turn about. The jets will stop attacking if we head toward the sea. All they want is to keep us from going to the mainland. All attacks can come on our starboard side and the sea lay to our port. It was quite evident that the pilots knew who we were and were not trying to hit the boat. They could have sunk us at will. The chief finally got the helmsman to turn around and we cheered. However, a Khmer Rouge put a gun to the man's head and we continued on our original course. The jets did not attack during that maneuver, but came in fast once we went back on course.

The Khmers had stopped their firing now and protected themselves as the rockets and cannon fire came even closer than before; coming to within ten feet of the hull. How those pilots could fire the rockets so close and not blow our boat up was incredible. The whole crew was amazed at their accuracy.

Some of the crew members wanted to act to overpower our guards. Third mate English was the most outspoken. He felt that he should take command saying that he was an ex-marine officer. I was against the move. We could have taken out the two guards on the bow without much problem, but there was no way we could have gotten to the guards on the stern. One Khmer had an armed M-79 grenade launcher; the kind that burns on impact then explodes. I was imagining what would happen if that thing went off in such close quarters.

For all that was happening; there was some levity. I don't remember what was said now, but everyone contributed. The humor kept our spirits up. Jokes were even made of the attacks. We were happy that the military was making such an effort to free us and I know I felt better knowing that my country was concerned.

I had developed a slight headache. The smell of the gunpowder, the heat and tension finally got to me. It passed and my mind drifted to my family. I prayed. My wife and I have had so little time together because of my seagoing career. What would happen to her and my only daughter should I die? I prayed to God to help them. I thought of my parents and sisters. How were they going to take this? They must know by now about the piracy. I was also mad. Here I was stuck in the middle of a small war and I had nothing with which to protect myself. Hell!

As we neared the sea buoy, the planes pulled up and left. The recon plane had been gone since the first attack on our boat. What would happen now? I was thinking that the attacks were finished. Wrong! Two jets appeared and came straight towards the bow. This was new. I ducked as the jets closed in. As the jets roared above, I heard what sounded like hail falling on the deck.

"We're on fire! Fire," I screamed, as I jumped up. My right leg was burning. Smoke was everywhere. I slapped at my leg in an attempt to pound out the fire. My eyes started burning and watering. My face began to burn. Then it hit me. Gas! I choked, gagged and spat. I fought for breath and felt like passing out. I resisted the darkness and my senses returned. I breathed in as shallow as I could and exhaled hard. I spat to keep the obnoxious taste out of my mouth. I kept my hands away from my eyes so not to irritate them further. My tears would wash them. I stayed away from the water container, knowing that if I drank, I would probably vomit. Some of the crew did. I looked over the side. Jump? The smoke started to dissipate and the fishing boat was leaving it behind.

I wasn't sure for what purpose the gas was used. Either the pilots were giving the Khmers more to think about since the other attacks had failed or this was to give us a chance to overpower them. The gas hit forward of the wheelhouse so only the two guards in the bow were gassed. The crew got the full treatment and now we couldn't have overpowered a kitten. The Khmers were determined to deliver their human cargo to the mainland. They still had the prize.

Ed Reyes was upset. He figured that we should have gone over the side. He felt that the gas was to create confusion giving the crew a chance to make a break. My reason for not jumping was that I and anyone else in the water would have been sitting ducks for the Khmers. Our pilots might think that we were being slaughtered and unload their rockets on the boat. Certainly many of the crew would have been killed.

While we were recovering the jets came again. Another direct hit. For some this was worse than the first time. I prepared myself this time. I covered my face with my sweaty T-shirt and breathed slowly. Of course I couldn't completely keep the gas from getting to me. My lungs filled with smoke again and I became very weak. Juan Sanchez (second engineer) had collapsed on the hatch. I comforted him and the chief brought over a wet towel. One man was crying. "Why were they doing this to us?" he sobbed.

I was terribly weak and lost my composure. I and about four others got on the bow and tried to wave the jets off that were coming again. The jets kept coming. "Hell, they are going to do what they have to," I said. I climbed back to my familiar spot. The planes flew over and the plumes of smoke rose off our stern. I guess our pilots felt like we had had enough. They must have understood our waving.

We were close to the buoy now. Would the jets let us proceed into the bay? The captain said, that as a last resort, the pilots might try to blow off the wheelhouse and stern. They were sure good enough to do it. It might not be a bad idea. It was risky, to say the least, but all efforts had failed to get us turned around. A prison camp didn't seem to be a desirable way to spend the rest of our lives. That is, if we were going to be left alive. We all crowded as far forward as possible, leaving a space between us and the wheelhouse. The Khmers stared at us wondering what was going on. Nothing happened. We had reached the buoy and our jets climbed high and away. The attacks on us had lasted more than three hours. As we came to the mouth of the bay, four jets crossed high off our bow and waved their wings. Goodbye and good luck![2]

Capt. Miller:

After the two gassing attacks, the planes went up to 5,000 to 7,000 feet. They were afraid they had SAM missiles in the military boats in the Baie de Ream. But they kept us under surveillance all the time.

We went in — there is a little pier here. It's a lot bigger than it actually shows on the large scale chart. You can put two ships alongside it, two big cargo ships. We went in between the land and the pier... This is the pier they wanted me to go into with the *Mayaguez* to discharge my cargo to see if I had guns, bombs, ammunition. I refused to go in there. I had no charts to go in there so they just decided to leave the ship anchored off Koh Tang Island.

We didn't tie up to the big pier. They had two Red Chinese ships discharging cargo. We were a little too far away from the Red Chinese ships to see what the cargo was, whether it was military or foodstuffs for the Cambodians.

We tied up to a little fishing pier alongside another Cambodian boat. Along the beach there were 500 to 600 people watching us sitting on deck. We laid there for about a half hour to three-quarters of an hour and the gunboat came alongside the fishing boat again and told us we would have to move to another area.

When we left, there were around 2,000 people standing along the shore around the fishing pier. Ninety percent or better were armed — young boys from nine years old right on up to around fifty or sixty years old – they all had either grenade launchers or AK-47s, a Chinese-manufactured gun. They were manufactured off a copy of the Czechoslovakian AK-47, which is a real good rifle.[3]

Stephen Zarley:

Many of the crew were gathered around the water container quenching their thirst and wetting handkerchiefs. For some odd reason I didn't feel thirsty, so I just stood up, stretched and looked around. Jared Myregard (second mate) had been hit in the left elbow by shrapnel and his wound was being bandaged. Rappenecker's knee was also getting some attention. The fishing boat had come through the ordeal pretty well. The only damage were the wheelhouse windows which were shattered.

The entrance to the bay was narrow. A small island was on our port and a long flat sandy beach was on our starboard. On the beach stood a cement block building surrounded by high barbed-wire fencing. The building looked like a barracks. Two small outriggers were also beached there. We were heading towards a small wooden dock where there was a small space with a couple of large wooden craft lashed together. Behind this dock and extending further out into the bay was a cement dock where two Chinese Communist freighters were berthed. The freighters looked new and were perhaps 25,000 DWT. No cargo was being worked, the hatches were closed and the booms secured. I didn't see a soul on the decks. On the wharf was a large warehouse. Some white substance (lime?) was smeared on the concrete.

Standing on the dock was a welcoming committee of about five hundred black-clad, armed Khmers. The guards were cheered when one of the guards ("Mr. Storyteller") spoke to the crowd. From the hand motions, it was plain he was telling the story of the attacks. In a short time the five hundred swelled to over a thousand. I felt like an animal in the zoo. The other guards kept us seated and also kept some of the crowd members from coming into the boat.

Someone said, "We're dead! They'll torture us to death to revenge their dead buddies."

I told the man to be quiet and I said, "They didn't bring us through all that just to kill us now. They want us alive to bargain with."

The first mentioned that he thought they might strip us and march us down the middle of the town to be spat at and stoned like the American flyers during the Korean War.[4]

Capt. Miller:

They moved us down the harbor about a mile-and-a-half and they anchored off the beach about fifty yards. On the beach, there was a military compound in the prison. There was barbed wire all around and the house was built in a square, an open area in the middle. I figured we were going ashore here and be locked up in this military compound or prison camp.

All this time we had around, I would say, sixty or seventy aircraft-jet fighters, up over the area of Kompong Som and the Baie de Ream.

I have an idea that they were afraid to take the crew ashore in Kompong Som because if our military crew knew we were there, they would bomb the military installation, the oil refinery, the military dock, and their commercial dock. They didn't want that to happen. The Thais cooked us dinner, or lunch. They only had a meager supply, after being there for five months. We had some greens that looked like tops of fresh onions. They had the strong taste of garlic and we had boiled rice and onion tops or greens.[5]

Stephen Zarley:

We had been at the dock for a long while when two American jets flew over at about two hundred feet from the opposite end of the bay. It was such a surprise that no one noticed them until they were over the Chinese ships. The crowd watched in silence. A crewman said, "They're not going to let us go. They're watching our movements so they won't lose us on the mainland."

I smiled and Zimmerman (Engineering Dept.) said to me, "Beautiful."

Our only hope was that the jets wouldn't fire or else we would be dead for sure. The jets came again, headed inland, and no bombing or shooting was heard.

A gunboat arrived and came alongside of us. The commander seemed upset and got into an argument with "Mr. Storyteller."

The gunboat left for the small island on our port. After sitting there for awhile we got underway again to leave the bay. We let go of the dock and chugged about one hundred yards toward the entrance and anchored. The barracks was right across from us and we couldn't take our eyes off what we thought was our new home. The two outriggers were launched and started for us, but our guards waved them off.

The two civilians brought plates and pots full of food out on deck and placed them on the hatches. They were smiling and urged us to eat. No one held back. This was our first meal since noon the day before. Not only were we hungry, but we also wanted to eat because we didn't know when our next meal would be. We had boiled white rice, small green stalks of some kind (very good), fish and water. There weren't enough plates and spoons to go around so we shared the plates and ate with our fingers...[6]

Capt. Miller:

Another gunboat, this time P-131, came alongside the Thai boat and talked to the armed insurgents on the Thai boat and they ordered us to heave up the anchor and proceed. They took us from an island called Tulong Som Quign into a little cove in there. There had been a big lumber mill in there; there was a smelter in there and looked like it was for tin or lead.

Then the second military command post of the Kompong Som area was based here. The second military commander of Kompong Som was a gentleman, well built, about five feet, ten inches; he couldn't speak any English but they had a young speaker there.

When we arrived at the dock (the speaker) was standing on the dock and he spoke to me and very fluent in English. He asked who was the speaker of the group. I told him I was the master of the ship, that I would do the talking for anybody in the crew. So he welcomed me into Cambodia and he said, "We will go ashore. We will serve you some tea. And he says later in the afternoon, "We will serve you dinner."

All the houses in the area here were built over the water on stilts, bamboo stilts, and on teakwood piles. The houses were ten or fifteen feet apart. There were around forty or fifty houses built over the water. To get to the shore we had to walk bamboo poles with a little bamboo hand guide to assist us across. It took as about twenty minutes to reach the beach.

He took us in a big house that had several cots in there and they had a table that would seat eight to ten people. He sat at the head of the table, my chief engineer on one side of the table, myself on the other side of the table and the rest of the crew who wasn't out hunting for coconuts to get a drink, or looking for tobacco - we ran out of cigarettes and all were having a nicotine fit about that time.[7]

Stephen Zarley:

The gunboat which had been in the bay earlier came back. Some instructions were given and we weighed anchor and followed the gunboat out of the bay. I wasn't so sure I wanted to go back out into the open. I didn't want to go through another attack. A few of us kept trying to communicate better with the civilians; trying to find out where we were being taken. The guards quieted the civilians.

After about a half hour, we started towards an island (Rong Sam Lem), with a wide beach and a good sized village. As we neared, two jets flew over the village. We bore to port and entered a cove. The cove was sheltered on three sides by high hills. A lighthouse stood high at the cove's entrance on our port. The cove went back quite a way ending at a small bamboo dock. The gunboat we had followed us there along with two others. The Khmers were busy camouflaging the gunboats.

A small, broad-shouldered man was waiting on the dock. He looked to be in his thirties and was dressed in black and wore a red scarf. The most noticeable thing about him was that he was unarmed. "Good afternoon," he spoke in good English. The captain introduced himself and the man reached out his hand. "Welcome to Cambodia," he said.

The captain replied, "You speak English? You're the first guy that we have been able to speak to."

"Do you speak French?" the man asked.

"No."

"Then we will speak English. Please speak slowly. Are these your friends?"

The captain said, "This is my crew."

The man said, "Some of you have been hurt. Did you smell the gas? Planes no good. No good."

We all clamored out of the fishing boat and followed the small man to our new home. It felt good to walk again! We were led through an area with a spacious planked floor covered by a thatched roof. There were no walls. Large uncovered smoke-blackened clay bowls sat side by side on the floor. I didn't see anything to indicate what these bowls were used for. The first felt they were probably used for smelting.

We walked along a shaky bamboo walkway, about three feet wide in most places, built above stagnant water. The whole area was a marsh. The walkway wasn't in good condition and we had to watch where we set our feet so not to fall through.

We came upon an open area. Four small, one-room "cabin-like" structures were standing on stilts in a row on our right. Next to them was a larger structure. This was better built than the other buildings and had a long covered porch. We stepped on solid ground and were led to a big house. At least, it was larger than the cabins but not as large as the building with the porch.

To the right and a little behind this house was a compound that the Khmers kept us from getting too near. By watching the Khmers, we thought that this was their armory.

To the left of the big house was a small bamboo bridge about five feet long. Six more of the one room cabins were standing on the other side. Two scavenging mongrel dogs ran about. A few chickens and a white pig were seen.

The crew spread out to reconnoiter. The captain, a few of the officers and me, followed the small man into the big house. Two mattress-covered army cots were on the left near the doorway. We were led to and sat down to a long wooden table in the back of the room where warm water and white sugar was served. The man spoke, saying, "He had no authority. He was only the interpreter for the second-in-command of the Kompong Som area." We named him the "Speaker." He began to question the captain.[8]

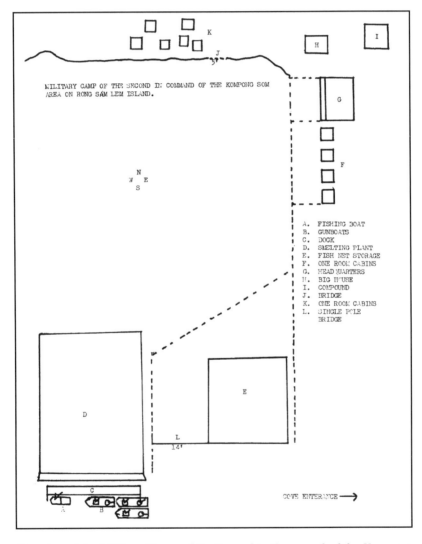

Drawing of the Military Camp of the Second in Command of the Kompong Som area on Rong Sam Lem Island. Stephen Zarley.

11

AFTERNOON, MAY 14, 1975

GULF OF THAILAND

Interrogation began with hot tea being served to the prisoners. Not knowing their fate, their apprehension was high. Would they become prisoners of war? Would they be tortured, killed, or possibly released?

Capt. Miller:

> Then the interrogation started. They served us tea, hot water and cane so we could make a cane tea which they like in that part of the country. Sugar cane tea they call it.
>
> At no time did they accuse me of being in territorial waters. I was six-and-a-half miles off the island of Koh Tang. When I got abeam of it, the ship would be actually five miles off. The territorial waters for any commercial shipping by any country in the world is a three-mile territorial limit. There is no twelve-mile limit, there is no 200-mile limit so long as you use the island for a safe navigation purpose from one port to the next and we don't stop for any commercial operation to make money. The international law says three miles is the limit for anything.

They never disputed that. They never claimed I was in territorial water. The thing they claimed was I was a spy ship, and the big containers I had on the deck, I had 274 containers. Each container is 8 1/2 by 35 feet long, and they are two high on deck and five deep in the container cell. I had eight rows of containers, five in the fore part of the vessel, in the hotel section of the ship, and then the stern. I had three rows of containers aft of the house.

He wanted to know if I had any surveillance equipment. No, I'd told him that we were just civilian merchant seamen out here working for a company, earning a living to support our families back in the United States. I had no ammunition. I had no bombs. I had no guns. As a matter of fact, I don't even have a gun on the ship. The company I work for doesn't permit it. They gave me a mace canister. A little handheld mace gun. If I had any difficulties with the members of the crew, I can knock them out with a shot of mace and secure them.

He asked me how the aircraft found out that I was seized by the Cambodians. I told him that the morning of the 13th I was supposed to arrive in Bangkok. My original port of arrival was Sattahip. I told them I wasn't going to Sattahip. I was going to the commercial port of Bangkok. If they thought I was going to the military port of Sattahip, they would probably have removed us out of the area, figuring we did have arms and military equipment aboard the ship. I told them I was going in to Bangkok. I told the young man I would take him out to the ship and open the vans so he could see. I only had frozen beef, frozen chicken, lettuce, tomatoes, celery, and the commercial cargo was all. PX supplies, aircraft parts, commercial cargo for the city of Bangkok, and all the commercial cargo I had was taken into Singapore.

He asked if there was any CIA on the ship, and the chief engineer and I told him no. He asked if there was any FBI in the crew. I told him no. I told him that we were just a common carrier that supplied the markets from Hong Kong to Bangkok to Singapore and returned to Hong Kong.

"Oh," he says, "you don't go back to United States?"

I said, "No this is just a feeder vessel for the company that makes the trip to Hong Kong-Bangkok-Singapore-Bangkok. We stay out here a year.

The young fellow was very pleasant. Up to this time nobody had abused us at all. If they wanted us to do something, they didn't speak to us, they just shoved the rifle in our back and pointed which direction they wanted you to go.

I finally convinced them — I could see he was deathly afraid of the jets in the air. I finally convinced them that if they would release my crew, put me back aboard the *Mayaguez* and I could fire up the plant again and get enough steam to generate electricity, I would call my company by radiotelephone and request the company to get the military authorities to remove the jet aircraft over the Cambodian soil.

At this point he told me that our aircraft had already blown four of their gunboats up. The gunboats were all American built. They are in the *Janes* manual as swift boats. They are around sixty-five feet long, have two GM [General Motors] engines, twin screw and their top speed is around twenty-eight knots. They were furnished by our government for river patrol for the South Vietnamese and the Lon Nol government of Cambodia. The Lon Nol government of Cambodia collapsed and they seized the gunboats along with it. So we were being escorted by our own American-built ships. They have two .50-caliber antiaircraft machine guns mounted above the bridge, one .50-caliber machine gun mounted on the stern, and above that they have two mortar guns.

We started negotiations, and at six o'clock he had a scheduled negotiation for the first military command post in Kompong Som. I promised them faithfully that if they would put us back on the ship, we would notify the company, and the company would get the military to remove the aircraft out of the Cambodian skies, and there would be no more bombings of their gunboats or their cities or anything.

He got on the phone — in the meantime they fed us. At six o'clock he got on the walkie-talkie. They are very proud of the American equipment they had, these field pack radios. He pointed to it, "American, U.S. We are friends, but you are American boys, we are not going to harm you. At the same time they are out there sharpening knives about that wide, and about that long, and I could see my head rolling off in the sand there.

The crew with me were very good. I had a good crew. They all behaved. One of my fears was that if somebody did get out of line or went berserk from being captured, they would make an example of one of us to show us to stay in line while we were in their captivity.[1]

Stephen Zarley:

The "Speaker" asked why the ship had come into Cambodian waters. The captain explained that his charts didn't show that the Wai islands belong to Cambodia. The reason why he was so close was that our radar was out and he was taking a line of sight off Poulo Wai for an accurate position.

The "Speaker" asked what the ship's cargo was and where was the ship going. The cargo was made up of food, clothing and other dry goods. No munitions were aboard the ship. The ship was heading to Bangkok. (The captain didn't tell the "Speaker" that our actual destination was Sattahip because of the naval base in there.)

The "Speaker" then asked why the captain had called the planes. The captain denied that he did. The planes came looking for the *Mayaguez* because it was overdue in port. The "Speaker" didn't believe this and kept pressing. All during our time in the camp, the captain was singled out by the Khmers as the one responsible for the situation.

The "Speaker" went on and asked about the two missing men. Were they CIA or FBI? The captain said that the entire crew was there and no one in the crew was a government agent. The "Speaker" didn't believe this either and would, from time to time, bring this subject up.

The "Speaker" went back to the planes again. Finally, the captain told them that if the crew were released, the planes would leave. As long as the crew were in Cambodia, the planes would stay.

The "Speaker" stopped his interrogation and walked out and went to the building with the porch. It's interesting to note, that the "Speaker" would always refer to Cambodia as his "Friendly" and his countrymen as his "Friendlies." The ship was always referred to by name, by the "Speaker" and also by the captain. The captain always referred to himself as "Charlie." This is his name; of course, but it did sound strange to hear him say "Charlie" instead of "I."

Most of the crew were lounging on the porch by now. Warm water and sugar were set on a couple of tables for us to drink. Ed climbed a coconut tree and felled some young coconuts. The coconuts were cracked open and the meat distributed to the crew. Nas found a Guava tree and so we had guava to eat along with the coconuts. English was looking at the M16 that the Khmers were showing off. They also showed the field pack radio standing in the corner. The Khmers were proud that some of their weapons were made in the USA. I remember the "Speaker" asking the captain if he could call our planes from the field radio.

The "Speaker" came up to the captain after a while, and introduced another man. He was the Second in Command of the Kompong Som area. I would judge the commander to be in his forties and of slight build. He was also a little taller than most of the Khmers that I had seen so far. He was unarmed and unlike the other men, wore no scarf. The captain was told that we would be going back to Kompong Som and the First in Command would decide what to do with us. The *Mayaguez* still had to be brought into port. The captain asked how long we were to be kept prisoners. He was told perhaps two months but that was up to the First in Command.

Food arrived from the back of the building (we decided that it was the headquarters) and it was spread out on the porch. I ate boiled white rice, fish and eggplant. Also served, but I didn't eat it, were the lower part of chicken legs with claws attached. After the crew had finished eating, the "Speaker" and commander ate.

A little later, mattresses were brought around and laid down for us to sleep on. It was still light, but I guess the Khmers felt we could be watched better if we were asleep. The "Speaker" and commander came up to the captain. He was asked if he and two other men were willing to go back to the ship and radio the military to stop the jets. The rest of the crew would follow once the planes were gone and bring the ship into port. Third Mate English protested but the captain agreed. They wanted to know exactly how the captain would contact the military and they wanted to know if the captain really had the authority to call off the planes. The captain explained that he could, if necessary, talk to the president. However, more than three men would be needed to get up steam to generate electricity to operate the radio. The "Speaker" didn't understand so the captain went through the process of steam generation as simply as he could. I don't think the "Speaker" understood even then, but agreed to let the captain take the men needed.

The men picked to accompany the captain were Sparks (radio operator), the chief, the first, Rappenecker, Myregard, Zimmerman, Suilaimen (8-12 oiler), and myself. Ed Reyes was asked but refused since he didn't want to leave his father, Guillermo (chief cook.) Nas, though not asked, tagged along with no protest from the "Speaker." The "Speaker" told Capt. Miller that is was very important that the planes be stopped from flying over Cambodian territory because three gunboats had been sunk and their crew were left swimming far from shore.

The captain said that he wanted us to go to the ship on the fishing boat, since the jets were destroying the gunboats. He also asked that the guards be instructed not to shoot at the jets when they flew over to look at us. The "Speaker" agreed.

When we left the ship, we felt that we wouldn't be seeing our shipmates for a long time, if ever. We didn't think the jets would allow the ship to be taken to port or that they would leave us as long as any of the crew were still captive. We felt that the Khmers felt this way too. We believed that we were being sent back to the ship, not to radio the military, but as a concession. We walked out, bidding those left behind good luck.

We missed a turn somewhere and came to a building vacant except for fish nets. As we walked through, Rappenecker picked up a long bamboo pole to use as a hoist for a white flag. We then crossed a single poll bamboo bridge about 14 feet long. We did a high wire act and this led us to the smelting plant on the other side. Our fishing boat was there but the gunboats were gone. The Thais were all smiles and offered us ice from the holds. A white T-shirt was attached to Rappenecker's pole and given to me to wave at the jets.

We sat and sat. Sunset was approaching and we were getting edgy at the thought of venturing out in the dark. The gunboat came into the cove and we were asked to take it since it was faster than the fishing boat.

"No!" It was a unanimous. We climbed out of the fishing boat and went back to camp.

The captain explained to the "Speaker" that the day was too late and it would be suicide to go out at night, especially in a gunboat. The "Speaker" agreed and told the captain that at six the next morning, the whole crew could go. The captain questioned him further. Did the "Speaker" mean that the crew was to be released or that we were to bring the ship to port? The "Speaker" only said that the crew would go back to the ship at six. At least the crew would be together for whatever happened. I told the captain when we were waiting on the fishing boat that I didn't like the idea of the crew being separated. Of course there wasn't anything we could do about it. The "Speaker" also said that four gunboats had been destroyed and one hundred of his friendlies were wounded. Did he mean four more boats had been sunk or the total was now four? There had to be some dead. One of the Khmers came over to Zimmerman and I and said, "Lon Nol, no good. No good. Sihanouk good." Then he said with a wide grin, (I won't forget it), "American finis. American finis." We just walked away.

The crew began to settle down to sleep. Some slept on mattresses outside, while others slept on sheets of white paper found in the cabins. The rest of us slept on bamboo mats spread out on the headquarter's floor. The captain and Frank Pastrano (third cook and father of Willie Pastrano; former light-heavyweight boxing champion) slept together on an army cot at my head. The mosquitoes were pesky at first but I guess I was too tired to let them keep me awake. I woke up once to the sound of voices. The captain had gotten up to take a leak, but the guards outside told him to go back to bed; using their weapons as prodders. It was completely dark in the camp. No lights shone for the jets to see.[2]

As the negotiations began at 1800 Cambodian time on May 14, the following events were unfolding for the U.S. early that morning:

- At 0029 the U.S. sunk three boats and damaged three others. CINCPAC and supporting commanders were briefed on the outcome of the Third National Security Council meeting that had ended two hours earlier. Military plans were put into action to recover the ship and its crew as follows:
- At first light 15 May, U.S. Forces would be prepared to secure Koh Tang Island and simultaneously board the *Mayaguez*. Also planned were strikes against Kompong Som complex using B-52s from Guam and tactical aircraft from the USS *Coral Sea.*
- USS *Hancock*'s estimated arrival at Kompong Som: 0500 on the 16th.
- The helicopter carrier USS *Okinawa*, one of four vessels in a four vessel Amphibious Ready Group-Marine assault

President Ford briefs the leadership on the seizure of the Mayaguez. Courtesy Gerald R. Ford Library.

unit — estimated arrival at Kompong Som at 1000 on the 18th.

- The F-111 aircraft during a 1½ hour observation tour observed two boats together off Kompong Som port area, later separating, one going into Kompong Som port and the other to Koh Rong Som Lem Island — a Cambodian Island a few miles offshore and the movement of patrol boats around Koh Rong Som Lem Island.
- Koh Tang Island was also flown over at 6,000 feet to determine the best landing zones for the Marines. [3]

In addition, the Secretary of State was sent the following report from the U.S. Embassy in the Middle East:

> A third-country learned from a senior diplomat that his government was using its influence with Cambodia to seek early release of the *Mayaguez* and that it was expected to be released soon.[4]

At 5:00 A.M. that morning the Thai Prime Minister "whished" the U.S. Charge d'Affaires an Aide Memoir protesting the landing of marines at U-Tapao despite Thailand's request that Thailand facilities not be involved in U.S. action to recover *Mayaguez* and pointing out that unless such forces were withdrawn immediately, the relations between the United States in Thailand would be exposed to serious and damaging consequences.[5]

Capt. Miller:

> At 6 o'clock he got on the field-pack radio and talked to the military commander in Kompong Som, and he promised me the military commander in Kompong Som would talk to the supreme military commander about our release if I could get the aircraft out of the Cambodian skies.
> Around 7, or 6:45 at night, it was just becoming dusk, I made out a statement of facts because we were off the vessel from the afternoon of the 13th until 12:05 on the 15th, and I didn't keep any log from the time we were seized. They wouldn't let me write any

log. They wouldn't let me use any telephones, and I had to have something for the Coast Guard when we finished our log which was October the 12th. So I made a statement of fact.

Around 7, or 6:45, we got word over the radio that the supreme commander of Phnom Penh said he would permit seven men to go aboard the ship and light the plant off, get enough electricity to use my radiotelephone and talk to my company.

They asked me if I could talk to the aircraft. I have no means of communication with the military aircraft. I could not talk to the military ashore. I have no means of communication to talk with the military ashore. The only ones I communicate with would be the Sea-Land Office in Bangkok.

The understanding was if I could talk on the radio to my company in Bangkok, that I would ask the company to withdraw the military aircraft over the Cambodian soil. My agreement with the young gentleman was that the crew would be returned to the ship, I would get steam up. I would ask my company to get the military to remove the aircraft the day I sailed, not before. I was not going to remove our aircraft while we were still captive by the Cambodian Khmer Rouge.

I asked that we be returned to the vessel, get steam up, I would notify my company and that I would be able to sail from the territorial waters of Cambodia within twenty-four hours. That was the agreement that I stuck to all during the negotiations.

When the aircraft first came over the Cambodian skies, several people asked me what I thought about it, and I told them I thought they were angels from heaven. I still believe it...

We couldn't begin to go back to the ship with only myself, the radio operator, and four men in the engine department to get the plant in operation. I requested more men. The second commander of the military post where we were held agreed that I could take nine, including myself, which was sufficient to get steam up on one boiler and enough electricity to operate that radiotelephone.

They took us out to where the boats were tied, we had to go through these houses built over the water, and it was just beginning to get dusk. They put us on the gunboat again. I told them I didn't want to go in the gunboat, I would rather go out in a fishing boat, because if our aircraft saw another gunboat after he told me they already sunk four of them, then the eight men with me probably would have been killed, including myself.

The chief engineer and I discussed it and decided we wouldn't go out that night on the gunboat, and they didn't have another boat to take us out on. So we returned to the three houses we were confined to.

The young Cambodian who spoke English promised me that Phnom Penh would send word down by six o'clock the following morning to release all crew and take them back to the *Mayaguez*, and we would be permitted to sail out of the Cambodian waters with the aircraft in the sky as long as they didn't do any firing or bombing of the soil. This I promised to do.

In the situation that we were in, I would have promised them the Moon between two slices of bread.

They served us tea, confined us into three houses that were built over the water. Each house had a catwalk or a gangway built in front of it with a big open porch on it, and the house was enclosed. We all slept out in the open porch area. There was a few bamboo mats issued. There was not enough for forty members. There were two or three cots that some of the unlicensed crew slept on, two men to a cot, they were unusually large military cots, about four feet wide, and eight feet long, canvas cots. I slept on the split bamboo deck under the roof porch.

They put armed guards on us so no one could go ashore down the gangplank to the mainland. I didn't get too much sleep. I woke up at 3:00 o'clock in the morning (*May 15th in Cambodia*) and I went out on the catwalk to get a little exercise, and the next thing I had was a gun in my ribs. They told me to get back in. So, I lay down on the deck again and waited until 5:30, and I woke up all the crew at 5:30. It was beginning to get daylight. I woke up the crew to be prepared to go back on the *Mayaguez* on the fishing boat, which they promised me they would have back in the area.

At 6 o'clock they had communications with the military command at Kompong Som, and the word had not been received from Phnom Penh at this time to release us, so after several promises that there were going to take us back to the ship at Koh Tang Island, they bypassed it. The crew was becoming very disgusted with nothing but lies from these people.

They were about ready to mutiny with me. I told them, just behave yourself fellows, the only thing we can do is what they request of us, and wait until Phnom Penh sends word down that we can be released. The crew did. They all gathered around me like we were going to have a meeting. The young English-speaking Cambodian was sitting alongside me by the field-pack radio on a table on the porch. We discussed several points. He wanted me to write four points that he wanted me to put out to the American people or the military of the United States. How the Cambodians felt toward the crew and toward the United States.[6]

12

PLAN OF ATTACK

The fourth meeting of the National Security Council was convened at 3:52 P.M. Wednesday, May 14. As a result of the meeting President Ford issued the orders to commence military operations to recover the *Mayaguez* and her crew. This action would "include air attacks against the military facilities near Kompong Som to prevent reinforcement and support from the mainland for Cambodian forces detaining the ship and its crew."[1]

Subsequently the Joint Chiefs of Staff issued verbal orders to CINCPAC to complete the following:

1. Seize and secure the *Mayaguez*.
2. Conduct a Marine helicopter assault on Koh Tang Island.
3. Destroy all Cambodian craft that intervened in the operation.

4. CINCPAC ordered the USS *Coral Sea* to conduct strikes against targets in the Kompong Som complex with first attack targeted at 2045 to coincide with estimated capture of the M*ayaguez*. The first strike was to be armed reconnaissance with the principle targets aircraft, the military, and watercraft, "avoiding merchant ships in Kompong Som harbor until clearly identified as a Cambodian." Subsequent strikes were to use precision-guided munitions to attack military targets of significance in the Kompong Som complex.[2]

The fourth meeting of the National Security Council was adjourned at 1742.

Twenty-seven minutes prior to adjournment …

the first troop-carrying helicopter lifted off from U-Tapao Airfield, Thailand, where all available USAF helicopters and the Marine ground security force had been pre-positioned. At about the same time, tactical aircraft also began to launch to provide continuous coverage for the operation, and an airborne command post assumed on-scene control. Thirty minutes later the USS *Holt* was in position to receive the Marine boarding team. B-52 aircraft in Guam were placed on one-hour alert.[3]

At 1830 President Ford briefed seventeen Congressional leaders of his plan supported by the National Security Council to recapture the *Mayaguez*.

Approximately three-and-a-half hours prior to the orders given for military assault, the U.S. Ambassador to the U.N., John Scali, delivered a letter to Kurt Waldheim, Secretary General of the U.N., requesting intervention to help release the *Mayaguez* and her crew:

His Excellency Mr. Kurt Waldheim,
Secretary General of the United Nations,
New York.

Dear Mr. Secretary General: The United States Government wishes to draw urgently to your attention the threat to international peace which has been posed by the illegal and unprovoked seizure by Cambodian authorities of the U.S. merchant vessel, *Mayaguez*, in international waters.

This unarmed merchant ship has a crew of about forty American citizens.

As you are no doubt aware, my Government has already initiated certain steps through diplomatic channels, insisting on immediate release of the vessel and crew. We also request you to take any steps within your ability to contribute to this objective.

In the absence of any of a positive response to our appeals through diplomatic channels for early action by the Cambodian authorities, my Government reserves the right to take such measures as may be necessary to protect the lives of American citizens and property, including appropriate measures of self-defense under article 51 of the United Nations Charter.

Accept, Mr. Secretary General, the assurances of my highest consideration.

Sincerely, John Scali[4]

The planning for the assault of Koh Tang Island progressed and by 0300 May 14, the 1,000 man battalion had arrived at U-Tapao. Plans were prepared to capture the *Mayaguez*, seize Koh Tang Island and hold it for forty-eight hours if necessary. Priority one was to locate any crew members on the island. The only pre-assault restriction was that "the island would not be softened up," because this might harm the crew. However, as soon as the Marine's attack began, "jet aircraft suppressive fire would be used in support of the operation."[5]

A significant obstacle, and a crucial piece to the puzzle, was the lack of any maps of Koh Tang Island. The only map on hand was an un-detailed and enlarged photo from April 17. In addition, planes were restricted from flying below 6,000 feet. Consequently:

1. The visual sightings were difficult to analyze because of heavy foliage; hence there were no visual sightings.
2. Only two potential helicopter landings were surmised, without any possible landing zone pre-analysis.

3. Point C on the map on page 162 was determined to be a possible antiaircraft site (which was never destroyed.)
4. Besides the landing zones, the use of eleven helicopters had to be determined. Each helicopter carried twenty-five Marines and the round trip from U-Tapao to Koh Tang Island was four hours.
5. Reinforcements would not arrive until another four hours had passed.
6. Information at U-Tapao indicated that the *Mayaguez* crew was probably not aboard the ship.[6]

The plan of attack was to use three helicopters (sixty personnel) to take the *Mayaguez*. The remaining helicopters with 175 Marines on board would then take the island. Four hours later, ten more helicopters would return with 250 reinforcements, providing a total of 475 Marines on the island. "Bringing only 175 personnel in the first wave was felt to be a reasonable risk, given the Marines understanding of eighteen to twenty Cambodian irregulars on Koh Tang."[7]

There was one major change in the overall plan. It involved the simultaneous landing on the *Mayaguez* and Koh Tang Island. CINCPAC later explained that it wasn't known if there were any Cambodians aboard the *Mayaguez*. If there had been, it would have made it impossible to land the Marines from helicopters because of enemy gunfire.[8]

Several other command decisions were made just prior to the assault. One was the potential use of the largest conventional bomb in the U.S. arsenal; the BLU-82. The BLU-82 was a 15,000 pound bomb delivered by parachute from a C-130 cargo plane. It was designed to clear pads for helicopter landings in the jungle because of the large explosive radius, sound and flash. It was also designed to psychologically intimidate the enemy. Decision to use the bomb was left up to the assault commander. In addition Riot Control Agents would be used on the *Mayaguez*, but not on Koh Tang Island. Another decision provided for the inclusion of Cambodian linguists, a doctor, and an explosive ordinance specialist to the assault force.[9]

Right, the BLU-82/B Daisy Cutter Bomb in the U.S.A.F. Museum. Below, a Daisy Cutter explosion at a test site in Utah. U.S. Air Force.

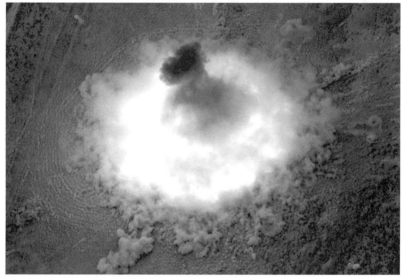

By 12:00 P.M. May 14 the operational plan was set and approved by local command. It was, however, only a verbal plan between the local U.S. command and the Marines at U-Tapao Air Base. In the normal scheme of operations, a written operational plan would have included the

> … expected enemy threat. The local U.S. Command view was that the Marines knew the task, their own capabilities and limitations, had the advantage of first-hand observation of the objective area from an observation aircraft and were the best qualified and proper unit to plan the landing and ground maneuvers they would have to execute. The Marine assault plan was considered 'gutsy.' The local U.S. Command, which had a coordinating role during the incident, incorporated the Marine assault plan into an overall concept plan for

the operation. This plan was received in Washington at 1:30 P.M. on May 14, and approved, as modified by CINCPAC.[10]

On the day of the seizure, the Defense Intelligence Agency supplied the following statistics of what was believed to be the Communist Khmer Rouge strength on Koh Tang Island. "Possibly 150 to 200 Khmer Communists were on the island, armed with 82mm mortars; 75mm recoilless rifles; 30-caliber, 7.62mm, and 12.7mm machine guns; and B40/41 rocket propelled grenade launchers." Also, the defense intelligence agency estimated that:

1. An additional 1,500 to 2,000 Khmer Communists were in the Kompong Som/Ream area.
2. There were twenty-four to twenty-eight Khmer Communist naval craft armed with 3-inch guns, 20/40 mm antiaircraft weapons, and 50-caliber, 7.62mm, and 12.7mm machine guns.
3. An unknown number of 23/37mm AA weapons were at known sites at Ream airfield.
4. There were a small number of T-28, AU-24, AC-47, and helo gunships with unknown operational status and locations.[11]

Late in the afternoon of May 13, Intelligence Pacific in Hawaii issued its estimate of Khmer Communist strength on Koh Tang – a maximum force of 90 to 100, reinforced by a heavy weapons squad of ten to fifteen.[12]

Intelligence Pacific in Hawaii and the Defense Intelligence Agency were supposed to coordinate their estimates. Intelligence Pacific estimates reached the local U.S. command five to six hours before the assault. There was "no evidence of the Defense Intelligence Agency estimate of 150 the 200 ever reaching the local command. Intelligence Pacific estimate was communicated verbally and in written form… The Marine Corps personnel responsible for planning and carrying out the assault stated that the intelligence estimates available to them indicated there were only eighteen to twenty Cambodian irregulars and their families on Koh Tang. From reports of numerous Cambodian patrol craft in the vicinity of Koh Tang and evidence of the antiaircraft sites, Marine assault personnel concluded that the intelligence estimates available to them were probably inaccurate. Therefore for planning purposes they assumed that there were possibly 100 people on Koh Tang, including women and children. On May 17, two days after they were recovered from Koh Tang, officers in charge of the Marine assault force saw accurate pre-assault estimates of Khmer Communist strength for the first time. Assault personnel have estimated that there were actually about 150 Khmer Communists on Koh Tang. We were not able to determine why the pre-assault estimates did not reach Marine assault personnel. (A Marine officer estimated between 400 and 600). We were told by Marine assault personnel that had more accurate information been available; the assault would have been conducted more covertly.[13]

There was a string of events that began which soon led to release of the *Mayaguez* and her crew. From 0600 to 0622, three helicopters carrying forty-eight Marine ground security force combat troops plus the six MSC volunteers were being placed on board then USS *Holt*.

Meanwhile in Phnom Penh, Cambodia at 0607 15 May, a lengthy nineteen-minute press communiqué regarding the *Mayaguez* was read by the Minister of Propaganda, Hu Nim. The communiqué was entitled, *Cambodia Announces Intent to Release* Mayaguez:

> Since we liberated Phnom Penh and the entire country, U.S. imperialism has repeatedly and successfully carried out intelligence and espionage activities to conduct subversive, provocative acts against the newly liberated new Cambodia in an apparent desire not to allow the Cambodian nation and people to live.
> It explains why the RGNUC has detained U.S. imperialist ships off the Cambodian coast, charging that these ships, including the *Mayaguez*, are CIA spy ships. It also charges the U.S. of using airplanes to attack the Cambodian naval vessels and then says: "Our RGNUC will order the *Mayaguez* to withdraw from Cambodian

territorial waters and will warn it against further espionage or provocative activities. This applies to the *Mayaguez* or any other ships, like the ship flying the Panama flag which we released on 9 May 1975."[14]

This broadcast was picked up by the U.S. Foreign Broadcast Information Service. At 2015, Kissinger informed President Ford of a domestic Cambodian broadcast of about one hour earlier.[15]

From 0620 to 0715, the Cambodians holding the *Mayaguez* crew on Koh Rong Som Lem Island received orders from Phnom Penh to release the captives.

President Ford and senior staff members stay late into the night to learn of the recapture of the S.S. Mayaguez *and her crew. Left to right: President Ford, Counsellor Robert T. Hartmann, Counsellor John Marsh, Deputy Assistant for National Security Affairs Brent Skowcroft, Press Secretary Ron Nessen, Chief of Staff Donald H. Rumsfeld, Secretary of State Henry A. Kissinger.* Gerald R. Ford Library.

13

SS *GREENVILLE VICTORY*

As a three-pronged attack to rescue the crew, recover the vessel and retaliate against the Khmer Rouge was developed by the National Security Council and the American military, it was realized that an integral phase would be reboarding the *Mayaguez* by American Marines. It was decided the boarding party should include six volunteer civilians from

The SS Greenville Victory *was one of the faster Victory ships with an 8,500 horsepower engine that drove her at 17-plus knots.* Capt. Ray Iacobacci.

133

the USNS *Greenville Victory*. Their expertise would be needed to activate the engines and get the ship underway.

The USNS (United States Navy Ship) *Greenville Victory*, crewed by civilian mariners had a long, successful history. Her keel was laid March 21, 1944 at the California Shipbuilding Corporation. She was one of 531 Victory Class ships built during World War II. She was also one of 141 faster Victory vessels because she had an 8,500 horsepower engine capable of doing 17 knots, compared to the earlier Liberty ship which could only reach 11 knots.* Victory ships were built for the long distances of the Pacific Ocean in the war against Japan. The *Greenville Victory* was 455 feet long and 62 feet wide. She was launched on May 28, 1944 and named in honor of Greenville, South Carolina. She was turned over to the War Shipping Administration on July 8, 1944.

The *Greenville Victory*'s World War II service was noteworthy as she delivered cargo in both the Atlantic and Pacific theaters. Following the war, she was chartered by the Seas Shipping Company of New York for two years and in the spring of 1948, was transferred to the Army Transportation Service. In March 1950, the *Greenville Victory* was purchased by the U.S. Navy and assigned to the Military Sea Transportation Service (MSTS), designated T-AK-237, and from 1950 to 1953 sailed in the Atlantic and Caribbean. There she transported:

> ... military cargo to French, English, and German ports; Guantanamo Bay; and the Canal Zone. Between 19 February and 9 May she sailed out of New York to the Far East and back, loaded with ammunition for Korea. After completing a run to Europe and back, she again departed New York 9 July for the Far East. She reached Yokohama, Japan, 9 August and during the next 2 months operated in the Western Pacific, carrying ammunition to Formosa and to French forces fighting communist Viet-Minh guerillas in French Indochina. Sailing from Yokohama 4 October via San Francisco, she reached New York 6 November 1953 to resume cargo runs to Europe.[1]

---

*   Most of the other Victory ships had 6,000 horsepower engines and did 15 knots.

During the next eight years, *Greenville Victory* supplied American bases throughout the world. One operation involved her with Task Force 43 during 1955-56. This included setting up "Operation Deep Freeze" in the Antarctic. The U.S. Navy was responsible for supplying the American contingent of an international group to further studies of Antarctica as part of the International Geophysical Year. The *Greenville Victory* made two additional trips in this capacity. The "*Greenville Victory* would travel more than 26,000 miles to and from the Antarctic. She would also travel some 6,000 miles to the Arctic. The ship holds the distinction of being the first MSC [Military Sealift Command] ship to carry cargo to both polar regions."[2]

Another important mission for the *Greenville Victory* was transporting the heavy equipment overseas in 1959 to set up the first U.S. missile battalion:

Moored three miles from Ross Island, HMNZS En-deavor, foreground, and USNS Greenville Victory, *background, brought construction materials to Ant-arctica. Taken in January 1957.* National Science Foundation.

January, 1957, the USNS Greenville Victory *brings supplies to the U.S. Naval Williams Air Operating Facility (now called Mc-Murdo Station).* National Science Foundation.

... known as the 46th artillery group (Redstone) it had its own organic and assigned fire and support units. It was a unique organization, being one of the three such units ever to be activated in the U.S. Army. It was the smallest unit, in strength and structure, to contain members of practically every branch of service. Among the different branches recognizable in the Group's Tables of Organization are Artillery, Engineer, Ordnance, Military Police, Signal, Adjutant General, Quartermaster, Medical Corps and Chaplain core. In effect it is a hard-hitting, self-sufficient task force providing "field artillery atomic missile support for field army."

... By the end of March 1959 all the equipment, and a caretaker party had been loaded aboard three ships and sailed from the port of Beaumont, Texas. The heavy equipment had been moved overland by rail and then loaded aboard the two liberty [sic] ships, USNS *Greenville Victory* and USNS PVT *Towle* while the LOX [Liquid OXygen] plants were placed on board the converted "baby Flattop" USS *Croatan*. The troops left Fort Sill on 1 April 1959 and sailed from Brooklyn aboard the troop transport USNS *General Rose* on 3 April 1959. Troops and equipment rejoined in Bremerhaven, Germany on 18 April 1959. After hasty processing the Group undertook a 500 mile march to its new home station, at Artillery Kaserne, Neckarsulm, which it reached on the afternoon of 24 April 1959.[3]

Additional operations included deploying with the 6th Fleet five times between 1956 and March 1964, transiting the Suez Canal twice, and then in October 1964 participating in a massive transatlantic troop lift exercise ...[4]

The *Greenville Victory* then became a vital cog in the Vietnam War effort, the humane rescue of the Vietnam refugees at the war's end, and the release of the SS *Mayaguez*. During 1974-75:

Greenville Victory's normal operations had taken her to forty-four ports from the Atlantic to the Pacific to deliver material required by the Department of Defense units. She carried ammunition from the U.S. East Coast to South Vietnam, and helped supply the Navy installation in Diego Garcia in the Indian Ocean. The vessel transited the Panama Canal five times during that year. During the evacuation of South Vietnam, she carried one group of 7,000 refugees and another of 3,029.[5]

A key figure behind the success of the *Greenville Victory* was her master, Capt. Raymond Iacobacci. Capt. Iacobacci was born in Brooklyn and came up through the "hawsepipe." When he was a young boy he watched ships dock and unload. The seed was planted and he made up his mind to work his way toward becoming a ship's captain.

Iacobacci began his career in the summers by working for the Sutton Line, Hudson River, NY, side-wheelers on weekend night cruises.

Capt. Ray Iacobacci, taken aboard the Marine Fiddler *(AK-247) on August 28, 1972.* U.S. Army.

His first full time job was on the *Johnson*; a troop and independent coastal carrier running from New York to the Caribbean, and San Juan to Cristobol, Panama. Iacobacci was the 4th officer, coxswain, and senior watch officer.

Capt. Iacobacci then went to work for the Military Sea Transportation Service. He worked for forty-two months on the USNS *General R.E. Callan*, obtained his AB (Able Bodied seaman) papers and passed the exam for a third mate's license, but couldn't get an officer's job so he went back to work as an AB. Ten months later he got a job as the junior third officer on the *Callan*.

Ray Iacobacci climbed the career ladder and eventually became a master. He eventually served in the Military Sealift Command for thirty-eight years and five months. His first ship was the LST *287*. Other ships he commanded were the SS *Marine*

Fiddler (a heavy lift ship), an attack cargo dock ship, a landing ship dock, the USNS *Comet*, the USNS *Robinson Victory*, and then finally transferred to the USNS *Greenville Victory* in 1972.

In 1975, Capt. Iacobacci's ship was in Sunny Point, North Carolina, loading ammunition for Vietnam: The first port was Cam Ranh Bay, then Danang and on to Qui Nhon where half the cargo was discharged. From there, *Greenville Victory* sailed to Sattahip, Thailand, where she discharged the remainder of her ammunition.

The ship was then ordered to Queng Nam to pick up refugees.[6] The following account is from Captain Iacobacci's Refugee Evacuation Report:

> The refugees came in many different small boats. Both accommodation ladders were rigged over the sides and four debarkation ladders. The highline transfer bag was used to hoist small babies and those unable to traverse the gangway. Every member of the crew that could be spared was assisting in loading the refugees and their personal gear. In addition, some crew members were delegated to search troops coming aboard for weapons. At one time, two barges jammed with approximately 4,000 refugees came alongside and were made fast to the port side. Commenced loading same from port side and continued loading other refugees from small boats on the starboard side. It was apparent that most

Barges loaded with Vietnamese refugees approaching the Greenville Victory. Capt. Ray Iacobacci.

of the refugees had come from the Danang area. The crew worked continuously until all the refugees were aboard, many times having to physically carry people and possessions off the ladders. It rained off and on throughout the day but the crew stayed at their tasks and the refugees kept coming. Refugees were loaded until the capacity of the vessel was reached. Any remaining refugee boats were diverted to the SS *American Challenger* who was also anchored in Cam Ranh Bay along with the USNS *Miller* which was tied up to the Delong pier loading refugees. The ship then proceeded out of the harbor to Phu Quoc.

The first night out the passengers were quiet and content. The next morning word was somehow received by the refugees that the ship was not destined for Vung Tau, RVN, as they believed, and the mood of the passengers became restless. Our immediate problem, however was in getting food to the refuges since many of them stated they had not eaten in four to five days. Since we had sufficient food and water on board, it appeared that all would be fed with no problems, but the distribution of the food proved that to be a fallacy. The first servings of food brought out to the refugees caused a mass rush with much pushing and shouting and the men trying to distribute were in danger of physical injury. Requested the aid of several ARVN troops in maintaining order but this proved to no avail. We did however receive the assistance of approximately sixteen Vietnamese Red Cross workers who did their best in serving the refugees. It was impossible however to cook and distribute enough food at one time for all the passengers. They were informed that we would cook and serve food as often as capable and for the refugees to please give everyone a chance of obtaining at least one serving. This proved fruitless as many of the ARVN soldiers would fight to the head of the lines or else stand back and wait for someone going back to their area and then steal their food. The refugees that had brought their own food aboard were allowed to cook on deck by the Master to take some of the load off of the ship's galley force who were working up to twenty hours a day making food for the refugees in addition to maintaining food service for the ship's crew. It helped some.

Many weapons were collected by the crew from the ARVN upon boarding the ship but due to the great influx of refugees from both sides of the ship it became apparent that approximately 200 weapons of various types had slipped by or been concealed. The ship was packed and deck space was a premium. The master, first officer and chief engineer staterooms were opened for use by selected refugees. The ship's hospital was in use twenty-four hours a day by sick and wounded refugees and the troop compartment was also being used as a hospital as previously anticipated. Two ARVN doctors on board treated as many cases as they could handle, both in the hospital and on several occasions circulating through the crowds on deck and in the holds for those unable to make it to the hospital for treatment. It was estimated that we were carrying approximately 7,000 refugees and in all likelihood it was closer to nine or ten thousand. Prior to our arrival at Phu Quoc, radio messages were received indicating that adequate security in addition to food and water would be available for the refugees upon arrival. Upon arrival at Phu Quoc it was immediately evident that the refugees were unhappy over being sent to this remote island. It was stated by some of the English-speaking passengers that Phu Quoc was never considered part of Vietnam by the Vietnamese. Its history is most noted by the South Vietnamese as being a prison camp.[7]

We had a civilian intelligence officer aboard disguised as a refugee who would hang around my first officer, Harriman. They would both report to me about what was going on down below with the refugees. The refugees resented being taken to Phu Quoc. Word got around that they were going to hijack the ship. We got to Phu Quoc, dropped anchor and you could just feel the tension in the air. I pleaded with the administration to send a LCU (Landing Craft Utility) or a LCM (Landing Craft Mechanized) to take some of the refugees off the ship or "it" was going to hit the fan.[8]

We arrived at Phu Quoc in party with the USNS *Miller*, SS *American Challenger* and the SS *Pioneer Commander*. The mood of the passengers aboard this vessel was that of discontent. Security by the South Vietnamese consisted of two small gunboats and one harbor gunboat. At no time did they communicate with the master of this vessel regarding the security measures while at anchorage. One of the patrol craft made a sweep by this ship with a loudspeaker aimed at the refuges informing them that they would stay at Phu Quoc where there was adequate food and water and that after a few days rest, aircraft would be available for transfer to the mainland to any city in South Vietnam. This announcement was met with what appeared to be cheers and catcalls. The mood of the passengers was growing increasingly hostile and after two hours of sitting at anchorage none of the landing craft promised for the transfer of refugees had come alongside to start the discharge operation. One passenger said that he did not "believe his government anymore. They had promised a safe refuge in Cam Ranh Bay and had not received it — they promised food and water at Cam Ranh and had not receive it — now they are sending us off the mainland and we do not ever believe they will let us go back." One of the ARVN officers made a statement to one of the crew members that if they did not start offloading *now* that there would be trouble.

A call was made to the SS *Pioneer Commander* by the USNS *Miller* stating that the situation aboard his vessel was serious and would he please notify the RVN Navy Officer in charge of the offloading who was aboard his vessel to please get one of the LCM's over to his vessel to start offloading which may perhaps quiet his passengers down. This same plea was repeated by this vessel. The offloading was being done by LCMs which could only handle approximately 250 to 300 personnel and was only going to the SS *Pioneer Commander* and the SS *American Challenger*. The total number of refugees aboard the vessels in the harbor at that time was estimated at 30,000. At approximately 1200 hours two hand lettered signs were raised by the refuges aboard this vessel reading "Phu Quoc No Vung Tau." This sign was greeted by cheers and applause by the passengers. At approximately 1215 hours local time a delegation of refuges made up of Catholic Lay Brothers, ARVN officers and village elders forced their attention upon the master of the USNS *Greenville Victory* and threatened his life and the destruction of the vessel if it was not immediately put underway to Vung Tau. Considering the safety of the crew and passengers, and the welfare of the vessel, the possibility of this act giving similar ideas to refugees aboard the other vessel, the only course of action was to capitulate to their demands. Upon announcement to the passengers that the vessel would be going to Vung Tau, all open hostilities and threats ceased and reserved atmosphere came over the crowd as they settled down for the journey to Vung Tau.[9]

As Capt. Iacobacci explained to the author:

If we didn't consent to take them where they wanted to go, they were going to lob a grenade down into the number three hatch! My main concern was that nobody got hurt. I didn't want to have to start writing letters to answer why a son or husband got killed. It just wasn't worth it.

I had never read or received any instruction on what to do with hijackers. All I knew was that if planes were hijacked that's where you went, where they wanted you to go. That's what I based my decision on. Instead of resisting I would take them where they wanted to go. No one got hurt, and no one died.

So we started to head south and I told the crew that the ship had been hijacked. Meantime, I notified my commanding officer MSC Far East of our course, speed and position. As we were going south around Cambodia, the next morning a destroyer was coming over the horizon from the southwest at full speed toward us. The tension aboard the vessel went right down. I was so happy and later that day a helicopter came down to investigate us on the starboard side of the bridge and looked in at the standing watch personnel and me. There was an Air Force officer aboard the helicopter and seeing everything was OK, he took off. I dropped the hook and waited for orders.

Meanwhile the *Transcolorado* came in anchored and drifted down to us. They had a load of Marines on board. They could have jumped on board our ship they were so close. We got orders to proceed to the dock. After receiving these orders I got the pilot on the VHF and told the *Colorado* so they halted what they were doing. The refugees were taken off the ship.

We then went down below and the ship was a mess and stunk terribly. We got orders to proceed to Saigon. All the cargo holds were washed down three times with disinfectant. We then loaded more provisions for the refugees and proceeded to Vung Tau where our orders were to rendezvous with other ships.

We then received orders to pick up more refugees so we moved closer and waited near a buoy. You could see all the fishing boats on the horizon loaded with refugees ready to come over as soon as the Communists released them. They wanted to know why I was hanging around the sea buoy. I told them I was six miles from shore and they had rockets on shore because I delivered them. Those rockets had a six-mile range and that's where I was going to stay. Again, I didn't want anybody getting hurt, killed or damage to the ship.

Eventually the Commies released the fishing boats and they drifted down to us as fast as they could. We picked up 6,200 on board and fifty-two Marines were now on board in their own compartment. They searched the refugees for weapons and explosives as they came aboard. All the weapons were put in a pile in the pilot's room one deck below the bridge deck. When we proceeded to leave the area the pilot's room was half-filled with weapons and ammunition. So, I put McGee, a wiper, as guard to make sure no one entered the pilot's room. McGee said to me as I was passing one time, "that if we picked up any more refugees he was going to launch a life raft and become one himself." He was always the comedian!

We proceeded to Subic Bay, Philippines where we anchored and put some barges alongside. The refugees were discharged onto the barges and the *Transcolorado* took them. The *Transcolorado* had larger water reserves than we had. They could accommodate more refugees and make more water. Orders were then to go to Cubi Point. Rumors were flying and orders were to go back to Vietnam and go up and down the coast picking up stragglers.[10]

Capt. Iacobacci's final summary statement regarding the evacuations:

> The operation must be considered a success although marred by several ugly instances of looting and misconduct by ARVN soldiers and commandeering of the vessel from Phu Quoc to Vung Tau. On the plus side of the record my officers and men are to be commended for their outstanding efforts and dedication to service. Due to our rush sailing orders from Thailand, we had to leave five crew members behind in addition to one crew member previously hospitalized and another crew member on light duty. To fill in the gaps, crew members worked fourteen and fifteen hours a day to provide assistance to refugees and complement the deck department in their watch duties. We were also fortunate in having two ARVN doctors on board who worked continuously for four days and deserve a special recognition. We also became enriched by three new U.S. citizens born aboard the ship while in international waters. (*Later a fourth baby would be born on the* ship). The parents were presented official birth verification papers signed by the Master. Awaiting further orders for the night of 5 April 1975.[11]

More rescues were in order. The April 29, 1975 *Greenville Victory* report while loading refugees from Saigon and Vung Tau:

> Loading refugees by cargo booms, ladders and nets. The sight was unbelievable… At least twenty or more in each cargo net with ten to fifteen women with babies in their arms and hanging onto the nets. … at least 100 boats alongside with hundreds of more streaming towards us. …The situation was pitiful, unbelievable and heart rendering. No assistance from other ships …[12]

The magnitude of the refugee situation can be seen in the following May 2, 1975 message to CINCPAC Honolulu requesting rations:

Refugee Logistical Requirements — Minimum ration per day per man. (Est. 5,400 aboard)

1. 1 Noodle instant portion
2. 4 Slices of bread
3. ½ lb. of meat/fish
4. 3 oz. Veg. fresh or canned, canned fruit if possible
5. ½ lb. of rice
6. If rice is instant, remove bread

Daily Consumption:

Paper cups – 8 cases
Paper plates – 10 cases
Plastic spoons – 4 cases
Toilet paper – 8 cases[13]

Vietnamese refugees aboard the Greenville Victory. Capt. Ray Iacobacci.

14

THE

MERCHANT MARINE

VOLUNTEERS

Meanwhile, The Joint Chiefs of Staff ordered MSC Commander Rear Admiral Sam H. Moore to find merchant marine volunteers in Subic Bay that would join the U.S. Marines in retaking the ship. Their mission would be to get the ship underway and sail it to international waters. During the night of May 13, Capt. Iacobacci and his first officer, Clinton Harriman were relaxing at the Subic Bay Officers' Club when Capt. Iacobacci was called to the telephone.

Captain Iacobacci:

At approximately 2200 hours 13 May while in the Officer's Club at Subic Bay, I received a phone call from MSCO, Philippines that six volunteers were needed for a special mission concerning the SS *Mayaguez*. A vehicle was dispatched from the MSC office to pick up the master and first officer Harriman who was in my company and we were brought to the MSC office for a briefing and

145

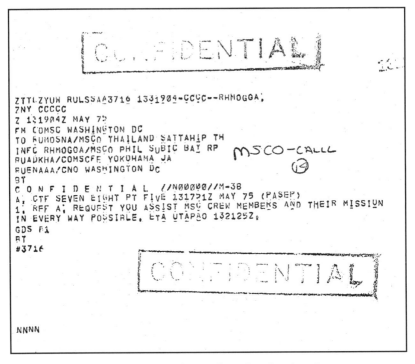

```
                    CONFIDENTIAL

ZTTLZYUW RULSSAA3716 1331904-CCCC--RHMOGOA,
7NY CCCCC
Z 131904Z MAY 75
FM COMSC WASHINGTON DC
TO RUHOSNA/MSCO THAILAND SATTAHIP TH
INFO RHMOGOA/MSCO PHIL SUBIC BAY RP        MSCO-CALL
RUADKHA/COMSCFE YOKOHAMA JA                    (4)
RUENAAA/CNO WASHINGTON DC
BT
C O N F I D E N T I A L  //N00090//M-3B
A, CTF SEVEN EIGHT PT FIVE 131721Z MAY 75 (PASEP)
1, REF A, REQUEST YOU ASSIST MSC CREW MEMBERS AND THEIR MISSION
IN EVERY WAY POSSIBLE, ETA UTAPAO 132125Z,
GDS R1
RT
#3716
                        CONFIDENTIAL


NNNN
```

Confidential Order to Capt. Iacobacci. Capt. Ray Iacobacci.

requirements for the mission. From the office we walked back to the ship and immediately searched for volunteers.[1]

Clinton H. Harriman:

We learned that a message had been received asking for six volunteers to accompany a detachment of U.S. Marines to Cambodian waters to re-take the SS *Mayaguez* and sail her out of their territorial jurisdiction. After this short briefing, the master and myself returned to the ship where we joined Lt. Cdr. Capie, COMSCO, Phil. for further briefing. The dangers involved were brought out and the possible difficulties to be encountered were discussed briefly, but the time was running short and volunteers were needed. The captain was absent at this time, being busily engaged in the rounding up of proper personnel for the task at hand. I left Lt. Cdr. Capie and sought out the captain and asked him if I could go. Thankfully, he accepted my offer to volunteer for this most exhilarating mission. As senior ranking officer present, I was put in charge of the crew and shortly afterward around 2400 we left by car for the U.S. Naval Air station at

Cubi Point. Captain Iacobacci's last words to me before we departed were, "Harry, try not to let anybody get hurt, but get that ship out of Cambodia."[2]

There were two third mates aboard *Greenville Victory.* One, Karl Lonsdale, had recently graduated from SUNY [State University of New York] Maritime College, the oldest Maritime school in the U.S.

Karl Lonsdale:

First Officer Clifford H. Harriman. Sealift Magazine.

When I first heard of the Khmer Rouge taking the *Mayaguez* and its crew, I was on the *Greenville* alongside the dock in the Philippines. We had discharged our cargo of human beings, the shore gangs had cleaned up the ship, and we were awaiting orders.

I thought it was outrageous that the Cambodians had taken one of our ships and its crew and that the U.S.A. should use whatever force it took to get them back. Since the *Greenville* was sitting idle at the dock, I thought perhaps they might send our ship over there to assist in some way.

Not too long afterwards, I was standing watch on the ship when a U. S. Naval officer came aboard to see the watch officer which was me. He said that Admiral so-and-so had sent him. They wanted six volunteers to go on a mission to recapture the *Mayaguez.* A skeleton crew familiar with merchant ships, to sail the ship to a safe port in the event that the regular crew was not recovered. It would be dangerous and there was a possibility of even getting killed. They wanted as volunteers a minimum of a second mate, a couple able seaman, the second engineer and a couple of firemen/oilers. The captain and Harriman were ashore at the Officer's Club and had been contacted and they were on their way back to the ship. In the meantime, I was to go spread the word and knock on doors looking for volunteers.

I wanted to volunteer right away. Here was a chance to help my country and fellow mariners, go on a military adventure and be part

Third Officer Karl P. Lonsdale. Sealift Magazine.

of the headline news. But they wanted a second mate at least and I was only a third. Oh well, the second mate was seventy years old, so I didn't think he'd be going. The captain had to stay with the ship, so I figured Harriman would be going. Well, I went about looking for volunteers on the ship. The response I got was not all that positive as I thought it would be, but I didn't have a wife and kids either.

Next I went to the captain's office where the captain, five volunteers and naval personnel were meeting. They had the engineer volunteers, but they had only Griffin and Harriman for the deck. One more hand was needed, so I said I'd go. They mulled it over and I got accepted. Sometime later we were issued helmets and flak jackets and were flown to Thailand on a military cargo plane.[3]

Second Assistant Engineer Michael A. Saltwick:

At 2230 hours on Tuesday, May 13, Capt. Iacobacci asked me if I would like to volunteer to attempt the rescue of the SS *Mayaguez*. The captain informed me that this request came from the Joint Chiefs of Staff in Washington. I was informed I could pick two men to assist me should I decide to volunteer my services. After thinking the matter over for a few minutes I told Capt. Iacobacci I would go but I would require the assistance of Mr. Epifanio Rodriguez and Mr. Herminio Rivera. Having sailed with these two men I knew their competence was of the highest order and that we would function extremely well as a team.

Shortly after my decision the U.S. Navy had produced Mr. Rodriguez and Mr. Rivera. I took them aside and briefed them as best as I could regarding the job ahead; the possible risks involved and the fact that I considered it vital that the team that went would have to be able to work smoothly under possible extremely trying and unpredictable conditions. A few moments later they informed me they would go if I would. I then took them to the captain and presented them and myself as the engineering team for further briefing.

After the short briefing we were told to pack whatever few work clothes, etc., we might need. The chief engineer, Mr. Yuen Woo, gave me a comprehensive rundown of what I might expect to find aboard a C2 (*Cargo ship*) and the best and quickest way to get the plant on the line. After quickly packing clothes, flashlights, hand lanterns, spare batteries, gloves, etc., we left the ship about 2400 hours and very soon found ourselves on the airstrip at Cubi Point Naval Air Station. When I entered the

Second Assistant Engineer Michael A. Saltwick. Sealift Magazine.

plane at the forward entrance the interior was wall to wall Marines. After finding a comfortable seat on the floor of the aircraft, we were soon airborne and the first leg of the mission was now underway.[4]

Yeoman-Storekeeper Robert A. Griffin:

While in my hotel room on liberty I received a telephone call from the MSC Phil Office requesting I report to the MSC Office at the request of the master. I queried as to the reason but was told that the information could not be divulged over the phone. I immediately thought of trouble at home and rushed back to the base. I arrived at the MSC Office and was informed of the need for volunteers to go to Cambodia and take control of the SS *Mayaguez*.

I informed the MSC officer that I was the Yeoman-Storekeeper aboard the USNS *Greenville Victory* and did not understand what purpose I could serve on this mission, but yes, I would certainly be willing to go. From the MSC office I walked to the ship where I met the master, first officer and Lt. Cdr. Capie, COMSCO Phil. I was shown a message which requested six volunteers to sail the SS *Mayaguez* from Cambodian waters and advised of the dangers I would probably be facing. I told them I still would volunteer and was honored that I was considered for this mission. I was then

Yoeman-Storekeeper Robert A. Griffin.
Sealift Magazine.

informed of the names of the other volunteers and knew that a capable crew was involved.

I was still a little puzzled over why they would need a man in my position and I was informed that I would be a helmsman and also assist in duties on deck. Since I had handled our own vessel before I had no doubts about my capabilities. I also informed them that I had eight years communication service with the U.S. Air force and that I could handle the communications and signal lights if required during the journey. After the briefing I was given a short time to pack and at midnight we departed the USNS *Greenville Victory* for the Naval Station at Cubi Point, Republic of the Philippines.

On arrival at the aircraft we were informed that there was no more space available and that the MSC personnel would have to wait for another aircraft. Lt. Cdr. Capie then stepped in and made space for us on the aircraft. Needless to say I was excited at this opportunity to be a part of this important operation.[5]

Oiler Epifanio Rodriguez:

While in town on authorized liberty, two military policemen knocked on my hotel room door with orders to report to the MSC Office immediately for important orders. I queried them as to the reason for taking me back to the base and they stated it was due to no personal problems at home, but it was important that I report immediately. Upon reporting to the MSC Office I was briefed by Lt. Cdr. Capie, COMSCO Phil on the *Mayaguez* incident and then was asked the whereabouts of Mr. Rivera. I stated that as far as I knew he was still aboard the ship.

Upon arriving back to the ship with Lt. Cdr. Capie I saw Mr. Rivera in the passageway with Mr. Saltwick, second assistant engineer. I then reported to the master and confirmed my attention as a volunteer since I felt it my duty as a United States Merchant

Seaman. Since our ships constantly sail the waters where the *Mayaguez* was captured I felt that the U.S. and myself had to get involved to show the other countries we could not be treated as an inferior nation.

After a briefing by the master and COMSCO, Phil, I was told I had ten minutes to pack. I packed my working clothes and flashlight with extra batteries and at midnight departed the ship with the other MSC volunteers. Upon arrival at the airport and after brief wait I walked out to the aircraft and saw approximately 200 Marines being loaded on a C-141. While we were waiting to board I heard that there was no more room on

Oiler Epifanio Rodriguez. Sealift Magazine.

the aircraft and started to return to the terminal where arrangements would be made for another flight. No more than a minute later I was told to return to the aircraft and we would be squeezed on board. Squeezed we were — I felt like I had been drafted since all you could see the length of the aircraft were Marines. Throughout the flight I kept thinking of the SS *Mayaguez* and how important this mission would be and how proud I felt to be part of it.[6]

Oiler Herminio Rivera:

I was sleeping aboard the ship and was almost ready to wake up and go on my assigned watch duties. I was awakened by the second assistant engineer, Mr. Saltwick, and was asked if I would volunteer to go on a mission. I asked him what type of mission and he informed me that a select crew was being asked to board the SS *Mayaguez* and sail her to a safe harbor. I was also told the names of the other men who had volunteered and was requested to think it over carefully since it was to be a very dangerous mission.

I volunteered because I don't think it was right for a Communist country to take an American ship and take thirty-nine of my fellow merchant sailors and put their lives in jeopardy. I was then requested to see the master who again asked if I still wanted to volunteer. I

Oiler Herminio Riviera. Sealift Magazine.

told him yes, and was shown a message regarding the SS *Mayaguez*.

I departed the ship after packing my work clothes and flashlight and boarded a pickup truck for Cubi Point, NAS. Upon arrival at the aircraft I was a little scared since I had never seen so many military men with full packs and rifles at so close a range. I talked with my friend Mr. Rodriguez and told him I had a family and knew that this would be a dangerous mission that I might not return from. Mr. Rodriguez calmed me as he stated, "You only die once and what better way than to die for your country." I didn't want to die but if it was to be I knew my family would be proud of me. As the plane progressed on towards Thailand my fears were subsiding. At no time though, did I want to back out of the mission. I knew the men of the SS *Mayaguez* and my country depended on me.[7]

15

U-Tapao Air Base

First Officer Clinton Harriman had the unenviable task ahead of commanding the other five volunteers in re-boarding the ship. It was nerve wracking for this group of six who had never encountered the possibility of military action. They had boarded a plane loaded with Marines ready for combat; many of whom would be experiencing combat for the first time themselves.

During the ride countless questions ran through their minds. Pre-eminent was what it would be like aboard the *Mayaguez*. Was all hell going to break loose when they landed? Word was passed down that between fifteen and forty armed Cambodian soldiers were aboard the *Mayaguez*. Also, while flying to the *Mayaguez* it still hadn't been determined whether they would land on the ship or on another naval vessel.[1]

Finally, it was difficult enough to bring a ship back on line in so short a time period. But if anyone could do it, the six merchant marine volunteers were able — a testament to how well merchant mariners work with so few crew involved in operating a ship.

Clinton Harriman:

> We arrived at U-Tapao Air Force Base in Thailand around 0500 and were taken right out to the runway and were to get underway directly after a briefing that myself and the senior Marine officer were to attend. They had a couple pictures of the *Mayaguez* taken right off Koh Tang Island the day before.
>
> As I was the only one present at the briefing with a shipping background, they asked me if I thought she was underway. I expressed my doubts on this as the port anchor was down and the chain leading slightly forward. Also they were concerned over fighting their way down into the engine room and intelligence reports indicated that there were forty to fifty very hostile members of the Cambodian armed forces aboard.
>
> I pointed out the approximate location of the shaft alley entrance that could be used as an additional means of access to the engine room. Also, that all the engine room skylights were open, giving them a fine opportunity to drop tear gas grenades or concussion grenades down into the engine room with very little exposure to themselves.
>
> At that point the plan was to land the choppers on the topmost containers of the SS *Mayaguez*. We were to go in on the first chopper and as soon as the bridge and engine room was secured, we were to get the ship underway while at the same time the remainder of the Marines in the group were to fan out over the rest of the ship and mop up any other resistance. At the close of the briefing the colonel in charge informed us that the operation had been postponed until noon of that day.
>
> Postponements and rebriefings continued on until 0330. At the last briefing it was decided that the original tactic of landing directly on the SS *Mayaguez* was to be discarded and instead we would be placed aboard the USS *Holt*. The *Holt* was to embark the Marines and ourselves aboard the SS *Mayaguez*.
>
> At approximately 0400 we departed U-Tapao for a rendezvous with the USS *Holt* in the vicinity of Koh Tang Island. We were given flak jackets, helmets and gas masks on the chopper and instructed how to adjust them, etc.

The Mayaguez *with a full load of containers.* William F. Hultgren.

After about an hour-and-a-half in the air we arrived at our destination. Enemy gunfire from Koh Tang was intense. There was a lot of air cover from the Navy and Air Force but the firing from Koh Tang was taking its toll. One chopper got a direct hit and went to pieces in a ball of fire. Out of eleven or twelve choppers, five were either shot down or crippled on the beach at Koh Tang.

Our chopper hovered over the small flight deck of the *Holt* and we all jumped aboard. My group and all the Marines were directed to the hangar deck in anticipation of an aerial gas attack upon the *Mayaguez*. As for myself, I went directly to the bridge and reported my presence to the captain and also the number of men with me and the objective of our mission.

When we were about a mile and a half away from the *Mayaguez* (directly after it had been gassed by the jet fighters) the C.O. of the *Holt* mentioned to me that if I knew something about getting alongside the *Mayaguez* that he didn't know, he would be open to suggestions from myself. I told him I had been a harbor and docking pilot for seven years and would assist him in any way possible and then proceeded to do so. [2]

Karl Lonsdale:

On a jet loaded with Marines I boarded the plane bringing a laundry bag stuffed with toothbrush, clothes, etc. and a head stuffed with visions of sneaking around a strange dark ship, beaning a stray Cambodian or two with my flashlight on my way to the bow.

The first officer attended a briefing after which we piled into buses and shuttled around from gymnasium to helicopter to hotel and back and forth and back again. Around 0300 the next day it became apparent that we would be used. My job would be to heave the anchor or slip the chain if necessary (if she was at anchor) and tend to the navigation.

As our ride to the *Mayaguez* lifted off the airfield I watched the land lights through the after door until they disappeared from sight.[3]

We all sat on our helmets. That was my biggest fear during the whole affair; bullets coming up through the fuselage. Harriman was hooked up with a headset and had a much better idea of what was going on. The door gunner did some shooting. I don't know what that was all about out, but probably just test firing. Harriman had heard of a couple of helicopters going down from his headset and Griffin may have seen one which was confirmed by a hand signal from the gunner. I myself didn't see much of anything except the lights on the ground from Thailand as we left.[4]

Michael Saltwick:

While standing by at the gym I conferred at some length with my two assistants in regards to what problems we might face, what to look for, such as lining up F.O. [Fuel Oil] Systems, Feed Water Systems, preparing the boilers for lighting off, etc.

I stressed the fact of using extreme care as the ship may have been rigged with explosive charges. All machinery would have to be carefully checked over to determine if it had been damaged in any way. We also looked at some pictures of the ship noting that the skylights were open and that the plant was probably secured as the ship was dead in the water.

During the course of the evening I discussed with Mr. Rivera and Mr. Rodriguez possible courses of operation which may be open to us once on the job. Starting the emergency generator would be the first order of business after boarding. Then ventilate the engine spaces and proceed to check the plant. I also stressed the need for flexibility as all plans may have to be changed from moment to moment once on board the ship.

I was issued a gas mask, helmet and flak jacket which the Marines were quick to help one so unfamiliar with the accoutrements of combat, to make adjustments of snaps, zippers, helmet liners, leg bands, etc., and very soon I was properly rigged out and airborne now en route to the landing area. As I lay back trying to relax I couldn't help thinking that if one has to enter a combat area you couldn't do it any better than in the company of the U.S. Marines.[5]

Robert A. Griffin:

During midmorning a Marine major and an entourage of other military officers arrived with aerial recon photos of the SS *Mayaguez*. One of the military plans was to saturate the bridge of the SS *Mayaguez* with gunfire and anti-personnel gas. Mr. Harriman and myself requested that the gunfire be kept to a minimum in the bridge area because of the need for the compass and the danger of destroying the radar and ship's wheel. (I did have a military field compass with me for just that reason.) The MSC engineering volunteers also briefed the military officers on the procedures for effective dispersal of tear gas and the engine room if necessary.

At 0400 we departed. While orbiting near Koh Tang I was watching one of the helicopters to the rear of us. Suddenly a brilliant flash appeared which I thought was a flare. It was then I saw the gesture of the Airman in the rear of the chopper and realized the helicopter I had been watching was shot down. I was surprised that I wasn't scared — maybe I was just too tired to be scared — but the one thought in my mind was getting to the *Mayaguez* and sailing her away.[6]

Epifanio Rodriquez:

At approximately 1000 the Marine major who was leading the Marine assault force came to me with aerial recon photos of the SS *Mayaguez*. He wanted to know how best to blanket the engine room with tear gas. Since I had sailed previously with Sea Land before on the same type of ships I advised them that the best way was to drop the gas canisters down the skylight. I rechecked the photos and pointed out to him that the skylight was open and there should be no problem in reaching it. I was also familiar with the loading cranes installed on this type of ship and offered suggestion on how the *Mayaguez* could be boarded directly by chopper.

After a two hour wait it was learned that the mission would be delayed while government diplomacy was tried. Mr. Harriman informed us that arrangements were made for us to stay at a hotel where we could get hot food and comfortable facilities. Upon arriving at the hotel I had my first hot meal in over twenty-four hours and after eating went to sleep for the first time in over thirty-six hours.

At 0300 we boarded the buses and returned to our helicopter where Mr. Harriman was waiting for us. I was very anxious to get underway and hoped that this would be the real thing. At 0400 we took off and I was happy we were really on our way. I was a little nervous and scared when after an hour in the flight the air crew tested their mini-guns. My thoughts turned to my family but I then realized my country depended on me and my actions.[7]

Herminio Rivera:

Upon arrival at Thailand we boarded buses for the mess hall where arrangements were made for breakfast. My eggs were cooked to perfection and as I sat down to eat my first meal since 1630 the previous day, orders were passed to leave the food and board the buses. We were moving out right away.

Upon arrival back at the runway we stayed in a group while Mr. Harriman was called away for a briefing. Upon his return approximately one hour later we were told we wouldn't be going until noon. At 1000 we received box lunches and it tasted better than the steak. I saw the aerial recon photos of the SS *Mayaguez* and with Mr. Rodriguez discussed plans on how to best disperse gas throughout the engine room.

The mission was postponed until 0400 the next day. Since we were tired and knew that we would be on duty twenty-four hours once we boarded the SS *Mayaguez,* our OIC [Officer In Charge] Mr. Harriman requested permission for us to be billeted in quarters other than the base gymnasium. Permission was granted and at 1500 we departed for a hotel which was just outside the air base. Transportation was provided by Air Force buses and upon arrival at the hotel, I cleaned up and went to bed.

I was called at 2100 by Mr. Rodriguez and was surprised to find out we were leaving so early. Upon return to the holding area at the base gymnasium, I was told that I could stay at the gymnasium or return to the hotel. Since we were trying to remain together it was considered best to return to the hotel. The gymnasium was crowded and it would have been impossible to keep us all together where we could move as a group. I informed Mr. Harriman that I was so tired that if I fell asleep I might not hear anyone moving out and be separated from the group. At 0030 we departed the hotel for the second time and reported back to the gymnasium, I sat on the grass outside the gymnasium and had a meal of cold C-Rations. At 0300 the buses arrived and departed for the helicopter to take us to the SS *Mayaguez.*[8]

Thomas K. Noble, Jr., was a petty officer first class serving on the destroyer USS *Henry B. Wilson:*

On the night of 12 May 1975 the *Wilson* was steaming south from Kaohsiung, Republic of China, en route to the US Naval Base at Subic Bay, Republic of the Philippines, when we received the messages that a U.S. merchant ship, the SS *Mayaguez* had been seized in international waters by the Cambodian Navy. Early morning on 13 May, *Henry B. Wilson's* Commanding Officer, Captain J. Michael Rodgers informed his superiors and after fueling, turned the ship south west toward Koh Tang Island with all four boilers online, at best possible speed. Koh Tang Island was approximately one thousand miles from *Wilson's* position. The ship maintained 31-plus knots for a day-and-a-half arriving at Koh Tang at daybreak on 15 May.[9]

16

ASSAULT ON

KOH TANG

Between 0609 to 0715 eight helicopters in the first wave began arriving at Koh Tang. Three of these helicopters were shot down, two became disabled while the other three were undamaged. Six helicopters were supposed to land in the eastern landing zone and the other two in the western zone. They were subject to intense ground fire and only about 109 of the 175 Marines were landed. Sixty of the 109 were deposited at Point (A). (See map, west side), twenty-nine at Point (B) – (west side) and twenty plus five Air Force personnel were isolated in the east beach (C). With the realization that reinforcements wouldn't be landed for another four hours, an attempt to link up was in order for the Marines.[1] Initial plans of swinging north from the east beach, capturing the village and northern tip, and finally swinging south with the west beach group blocking the Khmer Rouge retreat had gone up in smoke.

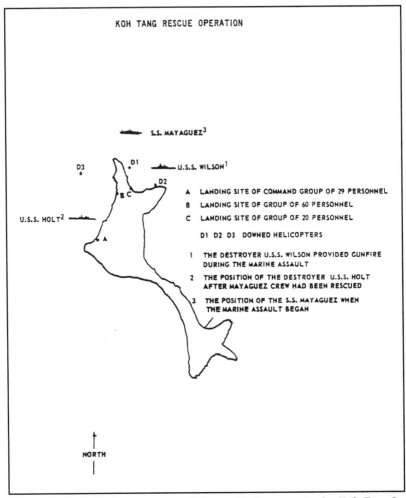

Location of the landing parties and downed helicopters in the Koh Tang Island assault. U.S. House of Representatives.

Lt. Col. Randall Austin was the ground commander. He was supposed to land on the east beach and set up a helicopter landing zone but was forced to change his plans because of heavy Khmer Rouge fire. His helicopter then flew on to west beach but here again he couldn't land at point (B) but was forced to land about a half mile away at point (A). A group of (B) Marines tried to fight their way south to Lt. Col. Austen but were halted by the enemy. Lt. Col. Austin's group finally did link up with group

(A) but only after an assist force led by Second Lt. Hoffman went out to eliminate enemy positions and cleared the bunker between the command element and perimeter. The second wave of helicopters containing Echo Company Marines was now able to land at about 1230.

Meanwhile, the twenty Marines plus five Air Force men on the east beach would be the only successful insertion on that beach, including recovery, made during the entire operation. The east beach was better to land on but the group was surrounded by the enemy. They had the water to their backs and the dense jungle filled with the enemy in front of them and on their flanks as they were in a cove. The west beach was much narrower and the helicopters had to back up to a beach sloping upwards to unload their Marines. The Khmer Rouge used the surrounding jungle and coastlines to their defensive strategy. They were well-entrenched on both beaches with 12.7mm/.50 caliber, heavy machine guns and antiaircraft weapons. They also had gunboats. One gunboat was put out of commission off the east beach but was capable of firing antiaircraft at the incoming helicopters.

From 0725 to 0822 the USS *Harold E. Holt* placed the Marine boarding party with the six Military Sealift volunteers aboard

East and West Beaches of Koh Tang Island. U.S. Air Force.

the *Mayaguez*. Prior to the boarding, U.S. aircraft dropped riot control agents aboard the *Mayaguez* to subdue the Khmer Rouge. The ship was declared vacant and secure at 0922.

At 0815 the White House announced that it had sent the following urgent message to Cambodian authorities:

> We have heard a radio broadcast that you are prepared to release the S.S. *Mayaguez*. We welcome this development, if true. As you know, we have seized the ship. As soon as you issue a statement that you are prepared to release the crew members you hold unconditionally and immediately, we will promptly cease military operations.[2]

Between 0745 and 1100 the Cambodian mainland was the subject of air attacks. A total of fifteen attacks occurred in three cycles. The second cycle "struck Ream Airfield about 9:57 A.M. The runway was cratered, numerous aircraft were destroyed or damaged, and hangars were damaged. About 10:50 A.M., the third and final cycle struck the naval base at Ream, damaging the barracks area. Naval facilities in Kompong Som, including the fuel storage area, were also struck, damaging two warehouses in the port and scoring a direct hit on a large building in the marshalling yard."[3]

In May of 1975 Dan Hoffman was a Marine 2nd Lieutenant in the 2nd Battalion 9th Marine Regiment which at the time was the Air Alert Battalion of the 3rd Marine Division in Okinawa, Japan. He had been an officer a little over a year having graduated from Officer Candidate School after college.

Second Lieutenant Dan Hoffman:

> Most of the Marines under my command were between eighteen and twenty years old. They were well-trained but without combat experience. I was assigned Platoon Commander in Company G as I actually volunteered at the last minute to go. I was the Battalion Motor Transport Officer at the time and would have been left back in Okinawa.
>
> The mission became a sketchy and hastily drawn up plan to rescue a ship's crew held on an island by about eighteen to twenty

people with few weapons. Apparently, the U.S. government did not want another "*Pueblo* Incident" on their hands.

We were flown to U-Tapao Air Base arriving there in the afternoon. Later that afternoon we were issued live ammo and hand grenades. This was serious. In the evening we slept on the airfield tarmac and were on ready alert notice. My helicopter was to land with the main force on east side of Koh Tang Island. Three helicopters lifted off at 5:20 A.M. for the island. (Three to land on the *Holt*, then *Mayaguez*. The rest of the force was the 2/9 for the Koh Tang assault.)

There was very little recon information, magazine articles, photographs etc. concerning the island. All they had was a hand drawn map. Whatever plane photos available were inconclusive because of the height involved.

We were supposed to arrive at sunrise but their helicopter arrived late to the island at about 6:30 A.M.. The enemy could clearly hear and see our arrival. Our orders were to prep the beach and perimeter and to be careful not to kill the merchant crew. They were suppose to land on the east beach with the battalion command group but the first two helicopters were shot down. Plans were changed and we landed with the second helicopter at 7:00 A.M. on west beach.

[The helicopters] were air search and rescue and were called Jolly Green Giants. They were armed with mini-guns vs. the M-60s aboard the USMC CH-53s (Call sign Knife). Most importantly, the HH -53s had self-sealing fuel tanks which the CH-53s didn't. This

A Marine and Air Force pararescuemen run for an Air Force helicopter during the assault on Koh Tang Island. U.S. Air Force.

U.S. Marine Corps soldiers deploy on Koh Tang Island from a CH-53 helicopter. U.S. Air Force.

was a major reason the Knives got shot up so badly. Additionally the USAF HH-53s had a fuel pod pointing up front and could be re-fueled in mid-air.

The helo I landed in (Jolly 42) was shot up very badly and limped back to Thailand. It was unable to fly again that day due to extensive damage. Most importantly it couldn't participate in bringing in the second wave of Marines or help later with the extraction.

According to our intelligence, which proved to be very inaccurate, there was only supposed to be eighteen to twenty Khmer Rouge with light weapons on the island. They were firing heavy weapons because they were knocking down the helicopters. It was very noisy on the helicopter with the rotor and blades spinning and made worse when you heard the enemy rounds hitting around you. You knew you were being shot at!

When my helicopter landed the water was behind us and green trees were in front. Fire and tracer rounds were coming right at us. As I was leaving the helicopter I was carrying a 81mm mortar round that was handed to me just before departure. We were all loaded down with as much ammo as we could carry. The only problem I had was I was issued an extra 81mm round. It was a white phosphorus round which will explode and burn uncontrollably if hit. I tossed it off to the side almost immediately as I left the chopper, to retrieve it later.

A Marine right behind me by the name of David Fowler was wounded. I had to take care of this Marine under heavy gunfire. His arm was wounded and he was bleeding pretty badly. This was the first time I had seen someone shot. I then let a Corpsman take care of the wounded Marine who was later extracted via helicopter.

I was excited and gung ho and really looking forward to the fight. I was like a machine, well-trained, knew what to do command-wise and it was like clockwork, with heavy fire coming at us. Most of the Marines killed were in the first hour. The poor guys never had a chance. The enemy waited for the helicopters to land and we had the hell shot out of us.

It wasn't hot on the beach and the section where they were in was about 700 yards wide and they were in a horseshoe position. When they were fired upon they returned fire at the enemy positions. Lance Corporal Loney was killed here on his first patrol with Second Lt. James McDaniel in command as Golf Company's executive officer at this time.

Lieutenant Dick Keith was tied down on the radios. Communication were really messed up as too many higher ranking officers were trying to find out what was going on.

At 9:30 A.M. the third helicopter was trying to land and made several attempts. The problem was exacerbated by poor communications in that there was no forward air control reconnaissance except on the planes. The pilots had no point of reference because they didn't know where the U.S. or Khmer Rouge positions were.[4]

(In a letter to this author, PFC Allen Bailey stated that he was one of eight Marines assigned to this patrol that was sent out to meet up with, and to escort the battalion commander, Lt. Col. Austin back to the defensive perimeter. The patrol was attacked in a very dense jungle.)

The Khmer Rouge knew where we were but we couldn't see them. A right envelopment was made to link up but when we moved in, all of a sudden, grenades started going off in all directions. A grenade hit the other side of a tree knocking me out. I caught some shrapnel from the grenade, causing a concussion that made me disoriented. Their attack wounded several Marines and killed one.)[5]

Lance Corporal Larry Barnett turned eighteen in boot camp. He was subsequently ordered to Okinawa for an eighteen-month tour. At this point he had become a Platoon Guide in Company G. He was on field maneuvers when Gunny Sgt. Lester A. McNemar *"came running through camp saying, a ship had been seized, get to your barracks and stuff your bags."*

The attitude of the men around him at the time was one of:

> … dismay and shock. After all, the Vietnam War was over and they didn't have to worry about going to war. The men that I was with were the finest people you wanted to meet in your life. During the eighteen-month tour of duty the maturity level of these young men was amazing.

Second Lieutenant Michael Cicere was his platoon leader and all they were told was that they had to make a beach assault rescue via helicopters, that the opposition was no more than fifteen to thirty with small arms and possible snipers, and that the merchant marine crew was suspected to be on the island. They were to assault the east and west beaches and subsequently link up. There were eleven helicopters; three were to land on the USS *Harold E. Holt*, four were to land on the east beach and four were to land on the west beach. "It was sobering to say the least when we were handed ammo, grenades, etc."

Barnett had a full bandoleer on and they were well-stocked with ammo. They were prepped by 2 A.M. and flown out at about 3:30 to 4 A.M.. "We were like, man let's go get this thing over with."

Barnett was on helicopter Knife 23 along with half of Lt. Cicere's platoon of twenty Marines and five Air Force personnel. "Reality began to set in when the helicopter's rotors began to start up. I got that funny feeling in my stomach."

They were in the air for about an hour when the mini guns were tested.

The objective was to get there before sunrise but they were late coming in. Larry Barnett: "While still aboard Knife 23, I saw Knife 31 get hit and was engulfed in a huge ball of flames."[6]

Survivors of the helicopter crash being pulled from the water. W.K. Stewart, courtesy of Tom Noble, Jr.

(*Knife 31* crashed into the sea. The co-pilot Richard Van de Geer was killed by enemy fire. Avoiding enemy fire, twelve of the occupants swam or were assisted out to sea where they were rescued by the Navy. Eleven Marines were reported missing along with two Navy men).

Petty Officer Thomas Noble Jr. aboard the USS *Henry B. Wilson*:

> As we approached the northern tip of Koh Tang the officer of the deck on the bridge noticed several heads bobbing in the water. It was determined that these were U.S. Marines and Air Force personnel who had been shot down in the first landing attempts on Koh Tang. The Cambodian forces were entrenched in the tree line and hostile fire was being directed at the Americans in the water. Capt. Rodgers made the decision to lower the ships captain's "gig" in the water. (The gig is a twenty-six foot boat used for ferrying the captain to and from shore while the ship is at anchor and needless to say it was not designed for combat operations). I, along with seven others, manned the gig and in less than an hour had picked up thirteen Marine and Air Force personnel. After recovering the gig and attending to the wounded, (several were burned), the ship headed toward the USS *Harold E. Holt* which was along side the SS *Mayaguez*, 2,000 yards away, to see if assistance was needed.[7]

LCpl Barnett:

> My helicopter got hit in the tail section as we were beginning to back into the east beach. The tail section just cracked and fell off.

The helicopter began to spin but that pilot was so good he set that open tail right down on the beach and I never got my boots wet. However, I thought I was going to die.

Lt. Cicere, with no combat experience, stood up and ordered everybody to get out the back of the helicopter and follow him to the tree line. The men followed him and when he hit the ground, the nineteen men and five Air Force personnel went down on top of him. Lieutenant Cicere then whispered to me to get these people spread out. I yelled they know we are here – so let's set up. We set up with about ten to fifteen yards between each man and that's where we stayed all day.

(Knife 23 with its twenty-five men safely ashore would be the only force to land on east beach. They bravely held their position).

We were outmanned and against superior firepower. The possible reasons according to Barnett was that we were helicopter bait. We were worth more alive than dead because as soon as a helicopter would try to land the Khmer Rouge would just open fire.[8]

Private First Class Fred Morris was only out of boot camp a couple of weeks when his company went on alert because of the *Mayaguez* incident. Part of his company (Golf 2/9) had been involved in the evacuation of Saigon just a few weeks earlier.

Three days after arriving at Okinawa, we were training in the NTA (Northern Training Area) practicing war tactics. We went on alert, boarded the deuce and a halfs back to Camp Schwab where we were told to re-pack our gear, then boarded the cattle cars for the long trip to Kadena Air Force Base. We then loaded onto transport planes which took us to Thailand. The whole company G was pretty green; maybe sixty days together.

Up to this point, Morris hadn't even had a chance to fire his M-16 rifle.

I was pretty numb by this point, we had been on the move for over forty-eight hours with very little opportunity to sleep. I was issued an M-16 as we were leaving Camp Schwab that looked like a civil war relic and had no chance of sighting it in or a chance to test fire it, still not knowing what we were doing or where we were going, I was thinking, "I hope this thing works ..."

We were briefed by our platoon sergeant that the enemy consisted of about twenty irregulars with light weapons. He tried

Staging in Thailand. Courtesy of Fred Morris and the Koh Tang Beach Club.

to put us at ease and said they didn't think they would put up much resistance with our show of force and he thought that we would be back by noon. After all an entire company of US Marines was going up against about twenty fisherman/farmers militia, what kind of chance did they have? He instructed us to go get ammo. From what I know now, depending on what platoon and what squad you were in the instructions were different. Some were told to grab everything they could carry. I was told to fill both magazines and pick up one Willie peter round for the 3.5 rocket launcher, and a couple of grenades. When I got to the crate full of grenades it all of a sudden started to get very real coming straight from boot camp, I kept looking around expecting to see the Drill Instructor jumping out and yelling "what the hell you doing touching those grenades, maggot!" As we would discover later, we had no idea of what we really were getting into.

After getting the ammo we were told try to get some sleep. Not very easy outside on the tarmac in front of a huge hanger. After a couple of hours, somewhere about 4 A.M. we were to board the CH-53s. On the way into the island, it goes without saying I was pretty stressed. It was pitch black and I was sitting about five feet from the helicopter side gunner when suddenly without warning he decided to test his mini-gun. Having never seen or heard one before, I didn't know what had happened. It was terrifying until I figured out what it was, and then was I just glad that he was on our side...

Fred Morris:

As the CH-53 came in to land, we could see there was a very small area on which to land. The pilot had to come to a hover and spin around so the rear loading ramp was facing the island so we could get off. It seemed to take forever to get turned around and as he did the bullets started hitting the helicopter, hundreds of them... I couldn't hear the gun fire due to the sound of the helicopter but you could hear pop-pop-pop as the rounds came through the fuselage – you knew it was for real. The Marine inside you wanted to go out and play John Wayne but the rounds going pop-pop-pop right thru the helicopter purged that idea real fast. It was hell out there and the side gunner motioned for us to get out. I thought to myself, are you nuts?!! About this time a round came through and hit a fuel or hydraulic line and started to spray liquid all over the inside of the helicopter. We had no choice but to get out or die. The helicopter touched down and we ran out into the tall elephant grass.

The helicopter took off but was so shot up it only made it a about thousand yards before it went down and sank.

After the CH-53 left Sergeant Bernel got up and started shouting commands to start to secure the LZ for the next helos. He was pointing here and there but about forty yards away there was a hooch with two Khmer Rouge shooting at him. These were not the irregulars, the fisherman militia that we were expecting. I realized he didn't see them and stood up and fired. This is when I found out the M-16 I had didn't work... It shot once but the bullet would not eject. Every time I shot I had to manually pry the round out of the chamber and then re-load before I could shoot again. It was real distracting because you had to take your eyes off the action. The Gulf Company Commander, Capt. Davis' helicopter was right behind us and they tried to land but every time they tried to come in the jungle came alive and chased them off. I was put on the left perimeter and there was a cliff above us that the Khmer Rouge had a machine gun on that made our M-60 sound like a pop gun. It was shredding and rejecting everything that came near the LZ (landing zone).

It was obvious to me that someone had blown the intelligence report. I knew we had lots more than twenty Khmer Rouge defending our side of the island and we could hear lots of action elsewhere on the island too. Plan A was to come in with eight helos, join up, sweep the island, rescue the *Mayaguez* crew and be home by noon ... I hoped there was a plan B and it kicked in real soon. They had only two Lieutenants and one Staff Sgt. for officers. We had ... about twenty Marines trying to hold an area about the size of two football

A CH-53 downed in mainland Thailand. Jim Davis and the Koh Tang Beach Club.

fields. I wondered where the other seven helicopters were that were supposed to help us. After what seemed like hours another CH-53 made it into the LZ and helped reinforce our defensive perimeter.[9]

Second Lieutenant Hoffman:

By about 10 A.M. all of the first wave of helicopters that would get in to off-load Marines had done so. The helicopter that contained Capt. James Davis, the Golf Company Commander, was shot up badly and after several attempts to land was damaged so badly it attempted to return to U-Tapao. It was forced to land just inside the Thailand border where it was destroyed to avoid capture. The Marines and air crew were picked up by another helicopter and taken to Thailand where Capt. Davis immediately got on to another chopper which contained Echo Company marines. The second wave force eventually got back to Koh Tang about 12:30.

After all the first wave had been off-loaded, the Marines were separated into three groups. Lt. Cicere with about twenty people was pinned down on the east beach. The main force on the west beach commanded by First Lt. Keith, the Golf Company XO, had about sixty Marines including me. About 1,500 yards south of this position and separated with the enemy between them were the Marines of the Battalion Commander's helicopter. It contained about twenty

Mortars on the Beach. Fred Morris and the Koh Tang Beach Club.

Marines of the command element. They had been forced to land south of the main element on west beach as their helicopter was taking too much fire and landed as close as they could at the time.

Other than obviously being separated from the main combat force, the Battalion Command Element's problem was that they were supposed to land with a large group and not by themselves. Their helicopter contained the Battalion Commander, S-3, doctor, forward air controllers and several radio operators and two sections of the battalion's 81mm mortars with ammunition. There were only three Marines armed with M-16 rifles on the helicopter. It was very hard to fire and maneuver a combat unit with only .45 caliber pistols and three riflemen.

Initially they could only hold a defensive position. They eventually started to move north up the beach utilizing what arms they had and effectively using air cover provided by Navy fighter pilots. Second Lt. Joe McMenamin effectively used his 81 mortar tubes firing up the beach.

Somewhere around 11:00 A.M. after I had spent some time re-supplying the southern sector of the line, I went to First Lt. Keith seeing something needed to be done. I started grabbing guys to man an assault force. I got the company First Sgt., a Staff Sgt., a radioman, an M-60 machine gun team and five Marine riflemen and went to the perimeter and took this force south. To my knowledge this is the only force that ever left our perimeter defense position.

Originally I had ten Marines in a wedge formation with me at point. We advanced fifty to 100 yards into the jungle. We were not receiving any fire and it became so thick that the jungle could not be penetrated without a lot of noise and chopping of foliage. I motioned my unit to head west to the beach. It was rocky and uneven terrain with several outcroppings but at least we could maneuver. We slowly headed south with the jungle to our left and the ocean to our right.

As we were slowly moving south Navy fighters were being directed to drop their ordnance on the enemy positions to my front which was between me and the command element. I found myself having to direct these F-4 phantom jets I assumed were from the USS *Coral Sea*. Here I was laying in the sand on a radio directing the Navy pilots where to drop their ordnance. On several passes they were right over us and I had to instruct them to abort their runs. I later learned as I was directing these Navy jets to bomb further south from me, our forward air controller with the command element was trying to direct them closer to us and away from them. We were in the tight position. About this time we also started to come under heavy mortar fire which I determined was from our own 81mm mortars and I had them stop firing.

As we continued south attempting to link up with the command element, we came upon a point of the island. There was a heavy log bunker with overhead cover. We were taking fire from it. At this point I told my Marines that I was going to throw my last hand grenade and that we would assault the bunker after the grenade went off so we spread out. I threw the grenade which went into the bunker and exploded. I stood up and charged, firing my M-16. All the Marines with me charged right up into and around the bunker and set up a defensive perimeter. With the exception of the two staff NCO's, these Marines were young troops with no combat experience. They behaved magnificently that day.

In the bunker I found three dead bodies (the only KIA's) I saw that day. In the bunker facing down the beach was a 90mm U.S. Army recoilless rifle. It was obviously captured as it had U.S. writing and a U.S. serial number on it. (Incidentally various reports later said this was a 57mm rifle. I know it was a 90mm because the Engineer Lt. we had attached to us inserted a thermite grenade down the barrel later that day when we destroyed it before extraction.)

Also in the bunker was a very nice pair of U.S. Army binoculars with leather case and a U.S. radio that was turned to the frequency we were using. There was also a large quantity of ammunition and three AK-47s and two M-16s.

At about 12:30 two things happened almost simultaneously. The command element came up the beach after we captured the bunker and the helicopters of the second wave started to come. I know this was after I captured the bunker as I ended up using the captured radio to identify to the lead helicopter pilot that the landing zone was secure. Where I got the balls to do that I don't really know. We desperately needed the reinforcements. But why was a lowly second lieutenant saying the landing zone was secure while all of the officers senior to me remained quiet.

After the command element passed through our position we followed them back down the beach into our perimeter. Two of the Marines who assaulted the bunker with me thought they knew where the body of Lance Corporal Ashton Loney was at. He had been killed early in the morning while advancing with 2nd Lt. McDaniel's initial group. I sent six Marines to get his body which they did.

We had sort of a parade single file as we walked up the beach. I had instructed several Marines to bring the 90mm recoilless rifle back into the perimeter with us. I'll never forget walking back to our position lugging the heavy weapon and the body of a fallen Marine.[10]

LCpl. Barnett:

Sometime after Knife 31 crashed I heard the Khmer Rouge firing at the Marines in the water. Later in the day one of the bodies was floating near where the helicopter crashed. I watched as a Khmer Rouge turned over the Marine's body and went through the pockets. A Marine nearby fired his rifle three times at the Khmer Rouge but the rifle hadn't been battle-tested and sighted at that point. When the Khmer Rouge was finished he just trotted off toward the tree line.

Marines on beach with body of LCPL Ashton Loney. Fred Morris and the Koh Tang Beach Club.

We stayed and held a semicircle perimeter all day. They were caught in a crossfire with the jungle in front and the sea behind them. They had a radio but it didn't work. One of the Air Force personnel had an emergency radio but he was unable to find out what was going on.

Eventually, the USS *Holt* sent a gig in an attempt to pick up half of the platoon. Lt. Cicere told me that I had to stay with the remaining ten men. I didn't want to stay but I gave him my thumbs up. Cicere then ordered me to select ten men to stay with him. I told the men, we've been through a lot today, don't make me pick you. One by one they raised their hands to volunteer and stay behind. I didn't have to pick one man.

As the day wore on, I thought I was going to die, but I wasn't going to die with my tail between my legs — I was going to take out one of those tough little bastards with me. They tried to insert more Marines later in the afternoon but the Khmer Rouge just opened up on the helicopters, driving them away just as they did the *Holt*'s gig.

Barnett had only a can of peaches all day, but the real problem was thirst. It was terribly hot and you had a full battle pack on. At one point I had to take a leak. So with full gear on I stood near a tree to take the leak. I was ordered to get down. Just as I finished a sniper bullet tore into a tree limb above my helmet. I never stood again, I did it on my knees.

As darkness began to fall, there was a sense of urgency. Let's do something; they had been there all day! By evening I had gone around to each man and told them that if nothing happened by evening, they were going to move north to swing around the tip of the island and link up with Capt. Davis and the main force on the west beach. It was a good thing we didn't move north because we would have walked right into the Khmer Rouge.

Barnett had a terrified Marine who told him he was preparing to charge the jungle and when he did, he was going to lose his mind. I told the Marine, you can charge but you're not going to lose your mind until I tell you, you can. What you're really going to do is stay right here and you're going to watch that tree line. With that, I slammed the Marine's head down and told him, we're still here, we're still alive — keep going, doing your job. I had to do something because the young marine was about to lose his sanity.

We knew there was a hell of a fire fight going on the other side of the island. We also had no idea how they were doing. The left hand didn't know what the right hand was doing. We had to do something![11]

PFC Fred Morris:

About midday the action lightened up. Captain Davis' helo finally got there somewhere around noon along with several others. We finally had enough men to properly defend the LZ and those of us that had been there from the beginning were able to take it down a notch. Some of the wounded were getting taken off the island and things were looking up from my view anyway. Not knowing whether or not we were going to get off the island anytime soon, we improved our fighting positions. This turned out to be a very good thing. Someone decided to drop the mother of all bombs on the island. I could not tell how close they dropped it but the bomb shock wave was phenomenal. It rained dirt and debris on us for quite a while. I later learned it was the largest non-nuclear bomb in the U.S. arsenal, a 15,000 lb. BLU-82 Daisy Cutter. The island and the Khmer Rouge got dead quiet after that. A few more helicopters finally made it in and we were able to stand up and walk around without getting shot at. I reached for a cigarette and forgot that I had a small 110 camera in my flack jacket. I walked around and took some tourist type pictures of what was happening at the moment.

I ended up back where I started on the north end of west beach. Now that we could explore a bit, there was a weapons cache carved into the side of the hill we were defending. Staff Sgt. Tuitele entered it and found every kind of a ammo imaginable; bandoliers of ammo for grenade launchers, lots of U.S. weapons and ammo. We took photos with some of the weapons he found. After we took the pictures we were standing there on the beach with loud breaking waves crashing in. I was looking at the sand and it looked like there

Fred Morris, with glasses and rifle, and fellow Marine on Koh Tang Island. Fred Morris and the Koh Tang Beach Club.

was some type of critter flinging up the sand. I asked Sgt. Hoyle and S.Sgt. Tuitele what kind of critter would do that. We watched whatever it was for a bit and then curiosity got the best of me. I waited until it happened again and then took my rifle butt and dug where I saw it happen and what I found was a bullet! I hollered, "SHIT, they are shooting at us."

We couldn't hear the report of the guns but as we looked around across the bay about 400 yards away could see the muzzle flashes. The Khmer Rouge had gotten out on a little jetty behind our lines and were shooting at us. With a M-79 Grenade launcher that we had just captured from the weapons cache we started to lob grenades at them but were just coming up just short of reaching them. We had an M-60 team that was with us turn their weapon around and take care of them.

As more helicopters started to come in, the Khmer Rouge started to regroup and fire at them with that big gun again. S.Sgt. Tuitele was going out on a solo recon to try to find where this gun was. We were ordered not to fire into the jungle until he was back. There was this towering old tree about 150 yards away on top of the hill that we were at the base of. I spotted a Khmer Rouge sniper scaling this tree with a rifle. From that tree he would be able to pick off any of us and I tried to get permission to fire at him before he got into the main body were we couldn't see him. No one would allow me to fire. I finally convinced them of what I saw and they had the M-60 gun team start raking the tree where I saw him last. I don't know if they hit him but if they didn't the fifty-foot fall ruined his day.[12]

17

RECAPTURE OF THE

SS *MAYAGUEZ*

Karl P. Lonsdale:

        … I was awakened by Mr. Harriman who motioned to-wards the forward door. Glancing in that direction I observed Marines jumping out. I got in line and hopped off onto the deck of the USS *Holt*. Mr. Harriman proceeded to the bridge. The rest of us took cover in the hangar at the call to General Quarters. Gas masks in place, we waited.[1]

    All or some of the Marine assault team also waited in the space. Then there was the Call to Battle Stations with the "This is not a drill part," too. That was pretty exciting. I was not fearful of my own safety as I wouldn't be going on until all was clear. I looked at the Marines and thought if I was one of them I think I would be scared. They were the ones that might be killed. There are a lot of places to hide on a ship, and with containers, a lot more. So there was the possibility someone could later pop out of hiding and try to kill you … [2]

Clinton Harriman:

U.S. Marines preparing to board the Mayaguez *as USS* Harold E. Holt *pulls alongside.* U.S. Air Force.

Armed with rifles, U.S. Marines search the Mayaguez *for Cambodian soldiers.* Sealift.

The Cambodians had left recently, their food was still warm. U.S. Navy.

First Officer Clinton H. Harriman of the Greenville Victory *discusses the boarding operation with Cdr. Robert A. Peterson of USS* Harold E. Holt. *At right is 2nd Engineer Michael A. Saltwick.* Sealift.

The *Holt* handled like a canoe in a mill pond. She slid along the *Mayaguez* so close, the line handlers just had to step aboard the *Mayaguez* to make her fast.

Gas was still very heavy in the area and all were wearing gas masks when we made fast. Mind you, this landing was not accomplished under the most ideal conditions as we expected large bursts of gunfire from the *Mayaguez* as soon as we were alongside.

As soon as we were tied up, I would judge about seventy-five percent of the Marines went aboard and commenced their search. The remainder remained aboard the *Holt* as a backup. The search for hostiles took about fifteen or twenty minutes during which time I consulted with both the C.O. of the *Holt* and the Commodore aboard relative to the procedures of getting the *Mayaguez* underway. I explained that if the plant were dead it would take about three hours (under our ideal conditions) to get her going. I suggested that if this was the case the best thing to do would be to slip the anchor and have the *Holt* take us in tow to get out of range of the gun emplacements at Koh Tang. Captain Peterson's towing experience was fairly sketchy but he was game for anything and most helpful and cooperative in every way. Having had the eight months inter-island towing experience myself, I wasn't long in convincing Captain Peterson that, handled properly, the risk of damage to take out the ship would be nil.[3]

Michael A. Saltwick:

By the time Mr. Harriman and I disembarked from the helicopter it was but a short step down onto the landing pad of the USS *Holt*. Although the chopper was too big to land on the *Holt* the pilot set down on a part of the landing pad and held the chopper as steady as a rock. The performance of the airman was superb. Mr. Harriman

The American flag is again raised on the SS Mayaguez *after she was successfully reboarded and recovered by U.S. Marines.* U.S. Navy.

proceeded to the bridge of the USS *Holt* and the rest of us were directed into the destroyer's helicopter hangar so as to be safe from any hostile fire and the effects of nausea gas that would be used prior to boarding the *Mayaguez*.[4]

At 0755 MSC personnel began boarding the *Mayaguez* to check equipment and the ship's seaworthiness. They quickly discovered the ship was surprisingly vacant. However, it hadn't been vacant for long as some of the food left on board was still warm.

At 0820 the American flag was raised on the *Mayaguez*. She was back in American hands and now the volunteer mission could begin. With large amounts of gas remaining in pockets, the crew had to work in gas masks. Flak vests and helmets were also to be worn since extremely heavy action was in progress on Koh Tang Island, located approximately one mile off the port side of the *Mayaguez*. Despite the heavy equipment and burning skin from the gas, the emergency diesel generator was started by MSC personnel in five minutes.[5]

Karl P. Lonsdale:

> The Bos'n Mate arrived at the hangar and informed me the vessel would be taken in tow. He gave me a list of whistle signals used

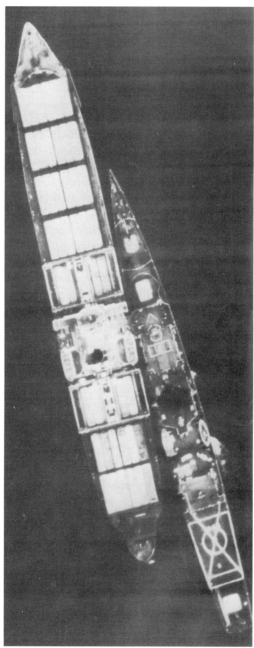

Photographed from an Air Force plane, USS Holt is shown maneuvering alongside the Mayaguez. U.S. Navy.

in towing operations and we reviewed the procedures of rigging the anchor chain for towing. Later, all MSC personnel were called to the bridge. At this time the *Holt* was made fast alongside the *Mayaguez* and the Marines had boarded and done what they were to do.[6]

Clinton Harriman:

At this point, while the Marines were completing their search for Cambodian troops aboard the *Mayaguez*, I went aboard, carrying a .45 automatic borrowed from the X.O. As soon as I got on the deck I asked the X.O. of the *Holt* to pass me an American flag to run up. He got one out of the wheelhouse and threw it to me and I proceeded to the bridge area to run the flag up one of the halyards of the *Mayaguez*. At this point I encountered a Marine major who was pretty insistent about getting a flag detail together and running up the flag ceremoniously. I had more to think about at this point than waiting for a flag detail so I gave him the ensign and went about my business.

First I went to the wheelhouse. The gyro, radar and all equipment was dead. I checked the chronometer (it was a 56 hour chronometer, the first I'd ever seen) and it had almost run out and I wound it for future use. About this time the rest of my gang were aboard and I had Mr. Saltwick and his engineers check the engine room. I wasn't long in finding out the plant was dead as a haddock. Towing her was the order of the day. I went down on the boat deck and talked to Capt. Peterson, appraising him of the situation.

Meanwhile, Mr. Saltwick was working on the emergency generator so as to get the lights on and the blowers going to gas free the engine room. I told Capt. Peterson that I was going up to the bow and see if I couldn't jury rig a towing bridal and asked for a couple of men to give Mr. Lonsdale and myself a hand. He very quickly assigned me three sailors and a very savvy chief bos'n mate.

We made our way up to the bow and found the anchor windlass in gear and no way to disengage it or to heave the anchor home, for lack of power. Fortunately they had some good nylon mooring lines on deck and I instructed the chief to run out a bight or an eye from the two mooring lines, one from each chock and shackle them together and take plenty of turns on the bitts. I then left and went back midships and asked Capt. Peterson for a portable cutting torch to cut the anchor chain. This was supplied right away and sent up to the bow. It was imperative for Capt. Peterson and myself to stay in close communication with one another during the operation so he sent over a radio pack for this purpose.[7]

Flanked by U.S. Marines aboard the Mayaguez *are First Officer Clinton H. Harriman, without a helmet, and to his right, Second Assistant Engineer Michael A. Saltwick.* U.S. Navy.

Karl P. Lonsdale:

From the bridge deck of the *Holt* we boarded the *Mayaguez*. After the flag raising, Mr. Harriman, the bos'n from the *Holt* and I proceeded to the bow to assess the situation:

    a. The anchor ball had been hoisted.

    b. Vessel was anchored with what appeared to be five shots at the water's edge leading to the port anchor. Port anchor was engaged.

    c. Starboard anchor disengaged, however the chain on deck was slack and jammed against the riding pawl with which was supporting the starboard anchor in the hawse.

    d. Getting power to the windless in the near future was doubtful.

    e. Acetylene torch and operator would be readily available courtesy of the USS *Holt*.

    f. Two decent mooring lines were on deck in a disorderly fashion.

After checking the port break to ensure it was tight, I inserted the lever bar in one of the slots and attempted to disengage the wildcat. The bar promptly slipped out of the slot and hit me on the head. Luckily I was wearing my Marine Corps issue ship chapeau and escaped injury. The corners of the bar were rounded with age and wear. Another attempt and I managed to budge it but not enough to disengage it. The devils claw was then applied and the turnbuckle tightened in hopes of taking off the strain. I again tried but to no avail.[8]

Michael A. Saltwick:

After the USS *Holt* had been moored to the *Mayaguez* I made my way to the bridge of the ship and met the commodore, captain, X.O. and various other officers of the ship. The Marines were already aboard the *Mayaguez*. Capt. Peterson asked me if I needed any more men and I replied that there were only three of us which would be spreading our forces a little thin. Capt. Peterson directed his X.O. to take me to the wardroom to meet the men he could give us for the job ahead.

In the wardroom over a very welcomed cup of coffee the X.O. introduced me to the chief machinist mate and his assistants so we could get together on what had to be done on boarding the *Mayaguez*.

Upon returning to the bridge I found Mr. Harriman had boarded the *Mayaguez* and had assumed command of the SS *Mayaguez*. After the flag raising ceremony I boarded the SS *Mayaguez* with the rest of the engineering personnel.

Upon boarding the *Mayaguez* I reported directly to Mr. Harriman on the bridge. We held a brief conference during which he asked how long it would take me to have the plant on the line. I answered three to four hours minimum. Since the ship was anchored within easy range of shore batteries he directed me to put aside all previous plans and directed me to go to the bow to check the condition of the anchor windlass and see what could be done about slipping the anchor chain or if necessary have the Portable Burning Unit tested and ready for instant use.

Upon leaving the bridge I directed Mr. Rivera and Mr. Rodriguez to see to the location of the emergency generator and report to me on the bow. On the bow I found the anchor windlass to be in good order.

Upon testing the burning outfit, when ignited the whole burner was a mass of flames. After disassembling the burning torch, cleaning and reassembling the torch it was relit and proved to be in good order and ready for use. The decision was made after careful examination that the anchor and or chain could not be slipped. The next step was deciding where the cut of the chain would be made in the safest possible manner.

On returning to the house, Mr. Rivera reported the location of the emergency generator. My request for an electrician from the

Capt. of the USS *Holt* was quickly filled and the batteries tested and found to have sufficient charge for starting the diesel generator. With gas masks on, entry was made into the generator room and the switchboard carefully checked and cleared prior to starting. Mr. Rodriguez and I, after some initial confusion due in part to the masks and lack of good communication, started the generator providing emergency lights for the ship. Once the ship had lights the engineering group headed for the engine room.

Since I was the only one armed in our group, I entered first with the rest of the detail close behind. Once in the engine room, the vent fans were started and it quickly became apparent that we would not be able to function or talk with one another so the masks had to be removed. After cleaning the main electrical board, a careful check was made of all machinery for possible damage. None was found, so I asked Mr. Rivera and Mr. Rodriguez to start checking out the F.O. System and making up burners for lighting off the boilers. I requested the Navy Chief to have all his men check out the diesel oil piping to the emergency generator so we could we fill the tank before it would run dry.

Mr. Harriman had asked me to check very carefully to see if there wasn't some possible way of providing power to the anchor windlass with the emergency generator. After many trips from the engine room to the bow and back I reported to Mr. Harriman that there was no possible way to run the windlass from the emergency generator. The tow line had been now made fast from the *Holt* to the *Mayaguez* and the cutting torch was used to cut the anchor chain.[9]

Robert A. Griffin:

At 0755 I boarded the *Mayaguez* but was stopped by a Marine Major who ordered me to return to the USS *Holt* since the ship had not been completely checked out yet. I tried to inform the major of my duties and intentions but he could not or would not listen to me since it is very difficult to talk and be heard while wearing a gas mask. I tried to get Mr. Harriman's attention so he would know where I was but to no avail. Rather than jeopardize our position as civilian mariners I returned to the bridge of the USS *Holt*.

Immediately after the flag raising ceremony I was allowed to reboard the SS *Mayaguez*. I reported directly to Mr. Harriman on the bridge. I checked the wheel and found it intact and ready for use when power was restored. I then proceeded to the bow to assist Mr. Lonsdale in readying the tow lines.

While flaking out one of the lines I came in contact with a pocket of gas. My hands, arms and neck started to burn but getting the ship ready was of primary importance. Although hostile action was intense on Koh Tang and undispersed pockets of gas were still on the ship; flak jackets, helmets and gas masks had to be removed in order to work easier and faster. At any moment we expected firing directed towards the *Mayaguez*. There was nothing between us and the island to stop the enemy from zeroing in and we were only about a mile from shore where two helicopters were burning on the beach. The anti-personnel gas was lying in pockets under the mooring lines and every time I moved one, more gas would escape and burn the exposed parts of my body. (Next time I'll be sure to bring long sleeve shirts.)

After the line was flaked out Mr. Lonsdale had the situation in hand in making up the bridal so I reported back to the bridge to offer further assistance to Mr. Harriman. Prior to reporting I washed down my face, neck, hands and arms with fresh water to relieve the burning. I was also starting to feel a little nauseous.

Upon reporting to the bridge Mr. Harriman requested I try to find the Bridge Log Book. I searched the bridge area and finally found it in the corner in the chart room. I inspected the pages and found none torn out or missing. The chart used by the *Mayaguez* at the time of boarding was still on the chart table but since we were going to use it I left it there. I took the Bridge Log and locked it in my suitcase to prevent any unauthorized party from confiscating it.

I then went down to the radio shack to familiarize myself with the equipment on board. The radio appeared undamaged and a hand key and speed key were still in place and connected. If necessary, when full power was restored the radio could be used. I was unfamiliar with the switchover procedures to emergency batteries so I left that alone. Prior to leaving the radio shack I secured the Radio Log and some scraps of paper which appeared to have Cambodian or Thai hand lettering on them and locked them in my suitcase.

Upon returning to the bridge I commenced in keeping our own Log. On the bridge I found the Aldis Lamp and the battery. I was concerned about that since I found no other signal lights on the bridge.

While the tow line was being passed to us from the USS *Holt* I assisted Mr. Harriman on the bridge by keeping in touch with the bow by sound-powered telephone. The bow was completely out of sight of the bridge due to the height of the containers on deck and was one of the ways of coordinating the hookup. I also found the Dangerous Cargo Manifest and brought it to the attention of Mr. Harriman. Plans by the USS *Holt* were to tow the SS *Mayaguez* under the noses of the Cambodians. Once the nature of the cargo was known (cotton, paint, naptha and assorted gasses) it was deemed advisable to get the *Mayaguez* out of the range of Koh Tang and enemy gunfire A.S.A.P. If we were hit we would have burned like a Zippo lighter. We were still approximately one mile from shore.[10]

Epifanio Rodriguez:

As soon as ordered to board the *Mayaguez*, I was instructed by Mr. Saltwick to find the emergency generator and put it on the line. Mr. Rivera found the generator and requested the USS *Holt* to send an electrician over to check the batteries. After the electrician from the *Holt* gave his O.K., Mr. Saltwick and I started the generator.

Once the emergency generator was on the line, I went down below to the engine room and started checking the plants and machinery. I was subjected to a lot of gas and found it hard at first to move around. It was very hot and my gas mask was more of a hindrance than a help.

After becoming acclimatized to the surroundings I was surprised to find everything in good shape. I then began to prepare the boilers for lighting off. I also found the Engine Room Log Book and brought it up to Mr. Harriman. Mr. Saltwick and I checked the last readings used on the *Mayaguez*. I requested a sounding tape and took soundings to ensure that the settling tanks were safe to use. I found the readings in the Log Book to be true.

After taking the soundings I again continued to ready the plant for operation. However, due to the heavy pockets of gas remaining in the engine room and the loss of power of the emergency generator which started overheating, I went topside and informed Mr. Saltwick that I would be unable to start the plant until power was restored or most of the gas had been dispersed.

The plant was ready to go but as a safety factor and since we were already under tow it was considered best to wait… Once under tow the gas began to disperse and we estimated that we would be able to be under our own power in approximately one to two hours (1200-1300). At one point I felt nauseous from the gas and Mr. Saltwick advised me not to return to the engine room until more of the gas was dispersed…[11]

Herminio Rivera:

Mr. Saltwick gave me orders to go below to the engine room with him and Mr. Rodriguez. I reminded him that the emergency generator had to be started first in order to provide lighting and ventilation to disperse the gas in the engine room. I then went to the emergency generator with him and Mr. Rodriguez and when we found it and opened the door it was too filled with gas to enter immediately. We attached our gas masks and entered to check it out before starting. I asked the captain of the USS *Holt* to send an electrician to test the batteries. The chief electrician from the USS *Holt* came over and when Mr. Saltwick returned from the bow we started the emergency generator.

I then went down to the engine room and found everything in place but the plant was dead. I tried to put the burners in place but the holes were blocked with carbon. I cleared away the carbon and then placed the burner tips in. From the Engine Room Log of the SS *Mayaguez* we were able to determine what size tips to use. I then reported at approximately 0930 that the boilers were ready to be lit off. At that moment the emergency generator overheated blacking out the engine room. I then went to the emergency generator with Mr. Rodriguez and we determined that the fuel tank was empty. I went back to the engine room with my flashlight to find the diesel fuel line which runs to the emergency generator. I then felt a large explosion which shook the ship. Thinking that it might have been an act of sabotage somewhere on the ship I went topside to investigate. All the time this was happening the engine room was in complete darkness with much gas still there. Upon reporting topside I saw a helicopter crash in on the beach — shot down by enemy gunfire. This was probably the explosion I heard. I reported to my engineer and started to work with him on the emergency generator.[12]

Clinton H. Harriman:

It was time for the hookup. I had them run a messenger from the towing line on their stern to our bow and for them to cast off and slowly pull ahead of us while we took up the slack on the messenger and heave up the tow line to shackle on to our bridal. As they were doing so the messenger fetched up somewhere on the *Holt* and parted, but no matter. They fired a shot line over and the towing line was made fast to the shackle. I asked Capt. Peterson to pay out about six hundred feet and take up a very light strain, which he did. The critical part of this was the fact that the tow line was six inch braided nylon and the *Mayaguez* was in excess of 10,000 tons. I gave the order to burn off the chain. This was accomplished in less than a minute and we were free from the ground. The anchor ball was hauled down and I advised Capt. Peterson to get off to a very slow start. The tow line and bridal were taking the strain very well and we were underway. As our momentum increased I would ask the *Holt* for a few more turns at a time, until we got up to almost five knots. We were under way for almost an hour and well clear of Koh

Tang when Mr. Saltwick informed me that he would be lighting off the boilers in about ten minutes.[13]

Karl P. Lonsdale:

The mooring lines were straightened out and an eye of each passed through the port and starboard chocks and shackled together at the stem. A round turn around the bitts with each line and a bridal was ready.

The bow had become a popular spot. There were about six Marines, four Sailors and the Bos'n mate from the USS *Holt*. With the messenger line from the tow line on the *Holt* passed up to the bow of the *Mayaguez* the USS *Holt* pulled ahead. All hands were required to heave on the messenger. With a few minor difficulties the tow line was connected. Communications were maintained between Mr. Harriman, the focsle and the *Holt* via field radio and sound-powered phone. While the port chain was being cut the bridal was slacked out about 100 feet and made fast with figure eights on the forward bitts, fair-leaded to the after bitts and secured again. With the port chain cut, the anchor ball was lowered. As the USS *Holt* gradually went ahead the strain was evened on the bridal and we preceded undertow. The tow had worked up speed to about four knots when word was received on the bow the *Mayaguez* crew had returned on board. All was in good order on the bow so I departed for the Pilot House.[14]

Michael Saltwick:

We were now under way under tow by the USS *Holt*. When you consider that a destroyer was not designed with the idea of it being used as a sea going tug and we were now moving through the water very smoothly you can well appreciate the expertise of Capt. Peterson and the officers and crew of the USS *Holt*. I was a tin can sailor (*destroyer*) for three years during the Korean campaign but the officers and crew of the USS *Holt* were far and away the best trained most versatile sailors I have ever run across. Upon returning to the engine room we had to increase the load on the emergency generator to its full limit… After one last check with the engine room personnel I called Mr. Harriman and reported I would be ready to fire the boilers in about ten minutes. Mr. Harriman very readily granted his permission to light the fires. At the time I received a report that the diesel generator was showing signs of excessive electrical load. I left the engine room and climbed to the 04 level and found that the generator was laboring under the load and showing signs of over-heating. The Navy Chief and I shut down the generator deciding to let it cool down for a short while to reduce the electrical load to a bare minimum. Mr. Rodriguez told me he felt sick to his stomach and I advised him to get as much fresh air as possible and rest for a while. I ordered all personnel to remain clear of the engine room until power was restored. I could ill afford to have any of my men overcome with gas once the boilers were fired.[15]

The Mayaguez *is towed out to sea by* USS Holt. U.S. Navy.

18

THE *MAYAGUEZ* CREW

RETURNS

A t 0935 on May 15, a P-3 aircraft was sent to investigate a small craft seen leaving the mainland, proceeding toward Koh Tang Island. Aboard the vessel were approximately thirty Caucasians waving white flags. Twenty minutes later this vessel was intercepted by the USS *Wilson*. Aboard the small vessel was Capt. Miller, his crew and five Thais. The captain and crew were taken aboard the *Wilson*. The Thais were given food and fuel and left the area. Capt. Miller informed the captain of the *Wilson* of his agreement with the Khmer Rouge that the US would stop the bombing upon their release.[1]

Petty Officer Noble:

> As the *Henry B. Wilson* passed close aboard the *Mayaguez*, a Navy P-3 Orion patrol aircraft reported that a Cambodian gunboat was steaming from mainland Cambodia toward the island. *Henry B. Wilson* then proceeded to intercept the gunboat and stop it from

approaching the *Mayaguez*. As the *Henry B. Wilson* aimed all guns at the incoming craft, the P-3 patrol aircraft reported that the craft was actually a fishing boat with Americans aboard. The Officer of the Deck then took the *Henry B. Wilson* alongside the fishing boat for inspection. Capt. Rogers called through the ship's topside loudspeakers and asked, "Are you the crew of the *Mayaguez*?"

"Yes," "Yes," "Yes," came the reply.

Capt. Rogers then asked, "Are you all there?"

Again "Yes," "Yes," "Yes," was the reply.

Captain Rogers then told the fishing boat to "Lay along side, you are safe now."

The forty members of the *Mayaguez* crew were then brought on board the *Henry B. Wilson*... The crew of the *Mayaguez* was then transferred back to the ship by the *Henry B. Wilson*'s gig. The *Henry B. Wilson* then proceeded toward the northern tip of Koh Tang and gave naval gunfire support as directed by an Airborne Command spotter, against several enemy gun emplacements that were firing at the Marines on the beach. Additionally, *Henry B. Wilson* sank one former U.S. Navy Swift boat that had fired on a U.S. Air Force helicopter.[2]

At 1227, President Ford announced that the *Mayaguez* and her crew had been recovered.[3]

President Ford's Letter to the Speaker of the House and the President Pro Tempore of the Senate Reporting on United Sates Actions in the Recovery of the SS *Mayaguez*.

On 12 May 1975, I was advised that the SS *Mayaguez*, a merchant vessel of United States registry on route from Hong Kong to Thailand with a U.S. citizen crew, was fired upon, stopped, boarded and seized by Cambodian naval patrol boats of the armed forces of Cambodia in international waters in the vicinity of Poulo Wai Island. The seized vessel was then forced to proceed to Koh Tang Island, where it was required to anchor. This hostile act was in clear violation of international law.

In view of this illegal and dangerous act, I ordered, as you have been previously advised, United States military forces to conduct the necessary reconnaissance and to be ready to respond if diplomatic efforts to secure the return of the vessel and its personnel were not successful. Two United States reconnaissance aircraft in the course of locating the *Mayaquez* sustained minimal damage from small firearms. Appropriate demands for the return of the *Mayaquez* and its crews were made, both publicly and privately, without success.

In accordance with my desire that the Congress be informed on this matter and taking note of Section 4 (A)(1) of the War Powers Resolution, I wish to report to you that at about 6:20 A.M., 13 May, pursuant to my instructions to prevent the movement of the *Mayaquez* into a mainland port, U.S. aircraft fired warning shots across the bow of the ship and gave visual signals to small craft approaching the ship. Subsequently, in order to stabilize the situation and in an attempt to preclude removal of the American crew of the *Mayaquez* to the mainland, where their rescue would be more difficult, I directed the United States armed forces to isolate the island and interdict any movement between the ship or the island and the mainland, and to prevent movement of the ship itself, while still taking all possible care to prevent loss of life or injury to the U.S. captives. During the evening of 13 May, a Cambodian patrol boat attempting to leave the island disregarded aircraft warning and was sunk. Thereafter, two other Cambodian patrol craft were destroyed and four others were damaged and immobilized. One boat, suspected of having some U.S. captives aboard, succeeded in reaching Kompong Som after efforts to turn it around without injury to the passengers failed.

Our continued objective in this operation was the rescue of the captured American crew along with the retaking of the ship *Mayaguez*. For that purpose I ordered late this afternoon an assault by United States marines on the Koh Tang to search out and rescue such Americans as might still be there, and I ordered retaking of the *Mayaguez* by other marines boarding from the destroyer escort *Holt*. In addition to continued fighter and gunship coverage of the Koh Tang area, these Marines activities were supported by tactical aircraft from the *Coral Sea*, striking the military airfield at Ream and other military targets in the Kompong Som area in order to prevent reinforcement or support from the mainland of the Cambodian forces detaining the American vessel and crew.

At approximately 9 P.M.. E.S.T. on 14 May, the *Mayaguez* was retaken by United States forces. At approximately 11:30 P.M. the entire crew of the *Mayaguez* was taken aboard the *Wilson*. U.S. forces had begun the process of disengagement and withdrawal.

This operation was ordered and conducted pursuant to the President's constitutional executive power and his authority as Commander-in-Chief of the United States Armed Forces.

Once aboard the USS *Wilson,* Capt. Miller was debriefed by Navy Intelligence.

Capt. Charles T. Miller:

They wanted to know why they [Khmer Rouge] released me. Why they seized me. I informed them [the Khmer Rouge] that if they released me, I was going to call off the military attack and the aircraft over the land. I requested this from Cdr. Rogers, and he said, "Captain, you were about three hours too late." He said the Marines were landed on Koh Tang Island at daybreak. At 8:00 o'clock in the morning our jets had started bombing Kompong Som, not the city of Kompong Som, the military installation, the refinery, the POL oil dock and their commercial pier.

The reason that the Marines were landed on Koh Tang Island was that the recon plane saw two fishing boats go in and only one leave. They figured half the prisoners were held on Koh Tang, and they were going to get half of them, and the other half was held at Kompong Som.

I believe, and the thirty-nine other crew members with me believe, the military action taken by our forces, the Air Force, the Navy, and the Marines was necessary to get our release. If I didn't have the promise of removing the aircraft over Cambodian soil, I don't think they would have released us. I think we would have been held as hostages for ransom, that is to get the 125 aircraft that were flown into U-Tapao Air Base and all the Navy aircraft that was sailed out of South Vietnam into neutral ports, such as Sattahip, Subic Bay, Guam, Okinawa, Singapore. I believe that was one of their intentions, that they were going to use us to ransom off for something the Cambodians wanted…

The officer that debriefed me on the *Wilson*, requested how I negotiated my agreement. I told him it was negotiated with the Cambodian Supreme Commander in Phnom Penh, that they were deathly afraid of the aircraft that was over the area where we are being held. The only reason I could talk to these men, the only reason I think that they took me into an area where I could speak to this man that spoke English and who could understand English was after the aircraft had reached the area.

Up to that point nobody was interested in talking to me. They were just holding me as a spy ship, They wanted me to go into wharf No.2. They wanted me to discharge the cargo on the dock. I figured once I got the cargo on the dock, I wouldn't get it back.

I could have taken the ship in but I absolutely refused to go into the mainland of Cambodia. If there was a rescue effort to be made, it would be a lot easier where we were held, where the ship was. That was my opinion at all times, to keep the ship out of the Cambodian hands. They would never get the ship. I knew our aircraft would blow it up before they would leave it to in the hands of the Cambodians.

… I was in the debriefing room about twenty minutes the first time, then they took me down to see if I needed any medical aid for the gas burns on my body. They wanted to check to see my eyes were not injured with the gas they dropped on the Thai boat. They wanted to give me something to eat. What I needed most was a pack of cigarettes.

I told them the agreement that I had, which I negotiated with the commanders, that we would call the aircraft away when my crew was safe. In the meantime my crew was in the mess deck, they made them sign a paper, everybody signed their name and rating, whether they were an engineer, AB, mess boy. Some of the men were in the sick bay with the doctor. They didn't get their names, and that was the reason when they counted the names on the paper they put the information out as only thirty of us were brought back to the ship. I informed them all thirty-nine of my crew were aboard the ship. I am not a crew member. I am the man that signs the agreement with the crew that I will live up to certain regulations of the maritime law with the crew, that they get so much food a day, they are entitled to so much money at every port. I am on the official crew list of the ship, but I am not a member. They start the chief engineer as the number one officer right on down the line.

… I was logged aboard my vessel by the six volunteers that came out to rescue the *Mayaguez*. They were deck officers, engineering officers, and a couple of storekeepers off the *Greenville Victory*. She is a U.S. ship operated by civilian crews, civil service employees…[4]

Capt. Ray Iacobacci of the *Greenville Victory* reported, "At 1130 hours a small fishing boat was seen approaching the SS *Mayaguez* with a white flag flying. At 1140 hours the master of the SS *Mayaguez* came onboard with some of his crew members and reported that all crew members would be returned. At 1205 hours all SS *Mayaguez* crew members were onboard safely."[5]

Capt. Charles T. Miller:

When I boarded the *Mayaguez* the vessel was under tow by the *Holt*. The six MSC men off the *Greenville Victory* had already used two of our mooring lines to make a bridal and the *Holt* used one of their lines as a tow rope. They burned the anchor chain with an acetylene torch and left five and-a-half shots of chain in the harbor of Kompong Som. The MSC men had been up most of the night traveling by chopper, boarding the ship at 8:00 A.M. and working — it was heavy work to bring up the towing bridal and cutting the anchor chain.

All my crew didn't come aboard with me at the same time. The captain's gig they put off the side from the *Wilson* would hold only about twenty of us. So there were two trips made… I wanted to get the engine started and they had enough steam up by 1:30 that I could go on slow bell but the didn't want to cut me loose until they towed me outside the twelve-mile limit and away from any gunboat that would be in the area.[6]

Meanwhile the inevitable meeting of the two mariner crews took place. Yeoman-Storekeeper Griffin from the *Greenville Victory* described the humorous encounter:

At about 1120, Mr. Rodriguez, one of the volunteers from the engine department came to me for assistance in finding the source of a tank near the emergency generator. I took him to the chief engineer's office where I presumed the blueprints would be kept. I found the plans and was handing them to Mr. Rodriguez when a man in civilian clothes came up behind me and said, "Who the hell are you"?

I think I jumped about six feet in the air and then replied, "Who the hell are YOU?"

After my shock and initial greeting I met the chief engineer of the SS *Mayaguez*. He informed me the full crew would be returning and they would take over from here. I stayed with him while Mr. Rodriguez went to the bridge to inform them. After all he could have been a round-eyed Cambodian. After verification I reported back to the bridge and met Mr. Miller, master of the SS *Mayaguez* who was engaged in discussion with Mr. Harriman. I informed Mr. Miller I was keeping a log of activities since boarding and turned it over to his mate on watch. I also returned the Ship's Log and Radio Log upon advice from Mr. Harriman. I then offered to remain on duty and assist the crew of the *Mayaguez* in any way I could so I remained on the bridge until approximately 1400 assisting the watch officer.[7]

Epifanio Rodriquez:

After I felt a little better I returned to check on the emergency generator which had ceased operation. I noticed a foreign fishing boat flying a white flag heading for the *Mayaguez*. I told Mr. Rivera who was with me to take over and I ran to the bridge to inform Mr. Harriman. At that point I was very suspicious since it could have been a trick for the Cambodians to get close to the *Mayaguez* to destroy it. Mr. Harriman informed me that the crew of the *Mayaguez* was allegedly on the fishing boat but that the Marines were ready in case it was a trick. I then asked Mr. Griffin if he could assist me to find the blueprints on the emergency generator to identify a tank located inside the generator room. I went with Mr. Griffin to the Chief Engineer's office where we started going through the blueprints. Right after he had pulled the correct blueprints a man came in the room and wanted to know who we were. Mr. Griffin asked him the same question since we were very suspicious of anyone on board. He identified himself as the chief engineer of the SS *Mayaguez*. I introduced myself and went to tell Mr. Saltwick that a man was on the ship who claimed he was the chief engineer of the *Mayaguez* while Mr. Griffin remained with him as a security precaution. Mr. Saltwick returned with me to meet the chief engineer.

We offered our services to continue working and briefed him on what we had accomplished up to that point. The chief thanked us but said he had a full crew returning and they would take over. I was a little disappointed that the six MSC volunteers would not be sailing the ship but at the same time very happy that the crew had been returned safely.

I then went down to the main deck and assisted the rest of the crew on board. I greeted them and they were very happy to have returned and see their ship in American hands. I was very happy also to see the United States take such action to defend her rights to International Waters.

After being relieved of duties on the *Mayaguez* the chief steward set us up with some spare mattresses on the deck and prepared cold cuts and salad for us to eat. We were also issued towels and soap for showers when the water was able to be turned back on again. After hot showers (needed to wash off the gas we had all been covered with), we were fed a hot meal in the Officer's Salon at 1900. While eating we were informed a tug was coming alongside to take us back to Thailand. At 1930 we boarded a tug boat for a return trip to Thailand.

All the men of the *Mayaguez* we talked to were very appreciative of what we had risked to save them and their ship and I must say I left with a profound sense of accomplishment for a job well done by all concerned. If a similar situation calls for my services I will be willing to go and defend the rights of the United States.[8]

Herminio Rivera:

A short time later I saw a small fishing boat approaching. We took cover not knowing if it were friendly or hostile. It turned out to be the crew of the SS *Mayaguez* returning. I went to the ladder and started helping the men aboard and greeting them. They were very happy to see an American face since some men were actually crying. When the chief engineer of the SS *Mayaguez* (Clifford Harrington) came aboard he immediately started to work. I offered my continued assistance to him but he said he had a full crew and for me to relax, they would take care of everything.[9]

First Officer Clinton Harriman of the USNS *Greenville Victory* said that Capt. Miller came up on the bridge and thanked him profusely for having gotten the ship underway. I stayed on the bridge until towing operations were completed at about 1400 at which time the bridal was severed by two sharp blows from an axe.[10]

Third Officer Karl Lonsdale said the crew members appeared to be in good health and no more bedraggled than anyone else. They were happy to be back and very grateful that the U.S. government had taken action.[11]

Second Assistant Engineer Michael A. Saltwick commented on the rescue and the outcome. His praise of the U.S. Marine detachment, and that of his own crew, especially the competent work of Rodriquez and Rivera, was "of the highest order."

Michael Saltwick:

The engineering officers again thanked us for the work we had done and I've ordered the engine room team up on deck for some much needed rest and fresh air. We remained aboard the *Mayaguez* the remainder of the day and at 1900 hours, some twelve hours after boarding the ship we left aboard the ATS seagoing tug which arrived at Sattahip at noon the following day.

I might mention in closing that working conditions aboard the *Mayaguez* were pretty good except for the gas pockets which were everywhere and seemed to linger for so long I was positive it was stuck on the paint. I well realize the need for the use of gas and can imagine how effective it must be, for hours after we boarded pockets of gas could still be found which stung the eyes causing them to run and any exposed skin on face, neck, arms, etc. felt like mild acid had been applied. In the engine spaces it made working for those below very trying and difficult.

The military personnel observed were all well-trained competent people from the MAC flight crews of the 141s, who did a great job and extended all courtesies possible to the helicopter flight crew which was top notch.

Capt. Peterson and his officers and crew were truly a well trained, well-organized unit. Because of their tremendous effort our job was made much easier. My personal thanks are gratefully extended to all members of the USS *Holt*, a ship the Navy can truly be proud of.

The U.S. Marines pretty much speak for themselves. They are surely the finest fighting outfit in the world and they too extended many courtesies and much help which will never be forgotten. I now realize why one can be proud to be a U.S. Marine. The special detail from the *Holt* working below with the MSC crew deserves special thanks for their splendid work, their quickness to adopt to a type of ship they had never seen before and the magnificent cooperation they extended to me.

Mr. Rivera and Mr. Rodriguez; one cannot say enough about these two. Their competence is of the highest order. They knew what had to be done, how it had to be done and they set about the job at hand with very few orders from me. Their devotion to their duty under trying conditions, the great effort and endless desire to see the job through makes them an invaluable part of any engine room team. With these two men you could go to hell and back and they would be with you every step of the way. My personal thanks to Mr. Rodriguez and Mr. Rivera for a job well done.

The MSC deck division are true professionals and they had the situation under their complete control at all times. Mr. Harriman, the OIC of the MSC unit, was a pleasure to work with and inspired confidence in all of us with the calm cool manner with which he conducted himself. His efforts to see to our comfort and well being far after the mission was completed were greatly appreciated.

Should such a problem arise in the future I would most certainly volunteer my services, especially so with the crew I was so fortunate to be a part of.[12]

Capt. Charles T. Miller:

So around three we cut the tow line of the *Holt*. The *Holt* had to go back to the island of Koh Tang. They were making an evacuation of the Marines off the island of Koh Tang. As soon as we were rescued, the evacuation of the Marines that had already been landed was commenced again off the island. They didn't want to have any more fighting on the island seeing the crew was all safe.

The Marines were pinned down on the beach by small arms fire from the jungle and surrounded the beach of Koh Tang. They couldn't get them off until following morning.

We could see some of the military action taking place. The jets were flying over and shooting rockets into the jungle. I didn't see any bombing of the port of Kompong Som. We were too far away. I did see some of the bombing of Koh Tang Island. *Wilson* was there, she didn't use any rockets, she used the 5-inch and 3-inch guns she had aboard. We were not close enough to see any of the people that were on the beach. All we saw were the aircraft flying over the island letting the rockets go.

I decided to cut the lines rather than take them in and get them tangled up in the *Holt*. I told Cdr. Peterson when I cut the lines I would let him know over the VHO and he could speed up and not get them caught in his propellers. I had the crew cut them off with a fire axe and I had about six or seven yards off until he was clear and could proceed back to the island.

I requested that they remove the nineteen Marines and six Navy men and six MSC men but he said he didn't have enough time so I proceeded to take them into Sattahip with me.

We prepared berthing areas for the nineteen Marines, seven Navy men and six MSC's. We made arrangements to sleep all the men.

About 1900, two big LT tugs from Sattahip contacted me on my VHF and wanted to know my position. They were going to come alongside to remove the military personnel and they had been informed before they left Sattahip to divert my vessel and instead of going to Sattahip to proceed to Singapore.

I think it was 1930 when we had all the military off and the two large tugs and I issued some fresh fruit that was still on the ship to the crew of the tug. They don't sleep on the tugs when they are in Sattahip. They have quarters ashore so they had no food outside of K-rations they threw on board the tugs when they left Sattahip. So I gave them about ten cartons of cigarettes each on the tugboats and fresh fruit and then departed and steamed on my way to Singapore.

All the time that we steamed down the coast of Cambodia and Malaysia, there was a big Marine recon plane that followed us to within eight hours prior to my arrival at Jahor Baharu in to the Joho Baharu, which was my arrival point in Singapore. Then it turned around and flew back to Subic Bay.

[After the ship arrived in Singapore] my cargo was open for inspection but I don't think any of the press looked at the cargo. We opened the containers to show them what was there, it was getting dark, the press conference lasted from around 3:30 to close to 1900. They didn't want to go aboard. But when I got back in to Hong

Kong and I discharged all the Sattahip cargo on the dock in Hong Kong, it was inspected there. The company was willing to open up any van that they wanted to look into and I think they only looked in about seven or eight ...

The company opened the invitation to anybody that wanted to look at the cargo to show them that they were not carrying small arms, ammunition, or bombs, or rifles or anything else.

The Singapore authorities requested the manifest of the cargo. I think the press was issued a manifest of the cargo, the military attaché to the Embassy a copy of the manifest. Our consul also got a copy of the manifest.[13]

[When we first came aboard I saw] they tore open all the rooms that were locked. None of the containers were opened. They stole $5,000 of company money. They stole $250 of my money plus around ninety Hong Kong dollars, and about $44.15 that belonged to the slop chest on the ship. They stole everything they thought was useful. The radio room was intact, but it struck me unusual they did not put a rifle butt in my receivers, transmitters and my telephones. I figured after they removed us from the ship that they had no use for it. I couldn't use it. I wasn't there. We had no electricity to operate it. Why destroy the ship?[14]

In his final report to COMSC, Washington DC, dated 20 May 1975, the captain of the USNS *Greenville Victory*, Ray Iacobacci, was highly complimentary of the U.S Navy personnel of the USS *Harold E. Holt*. The amount of assistance provided to his six volunteers and the subsequent teamwork made for a successful operation.[15]

Stephen Zarley:

We sailed on for the next two days. I was wondering what kind of welcome we would get once we arrived in Singapore. When we sailed into the harbor on Saturday morning, we were greeted by helicopters and small watercraft. This was the press. We didn't go through the usual immigration quarantine check and when we reached our berth, the press was out in force taking pictures and asking questions. The dock was set up for a press conference which we had been told was going to take place after we tied up.

The crew was looked upon as heroes, but none of us felt that way. We had done nothing heroic. Of course, we were the cause of the hullabaloo so I guess we deserved some attention. We were treated quite well. The company was giving us a thousand dollar bonus and free transportation home from Singapore for anyone who wish to sign-off. I requested a mutual sign-off Friday, so this was good news.

Toll free telephones had been set up in the company office on the dock for our use and there was a party being given at the Mandarin Hotel, in downtown Singapore, in our honor, along with free accommodations for the night.

There were eighteen of us signing off the ship and when our replacements came, we had to leave the ship and were put up at the Ramada Inn for the rest of Sunday. Monday morning we signed-off at the U.S. Embassy and made reservations home…

I arrived home about five. Shirley was playing outside and when she saw me in the taxi, and she ran to our apartment to get her mother. "Mama, mama. Papa's here!"

It was good to be back. It was my birthday![16]

19

Koh Tang Island

May 15, 1975

S oon after President Ford's announcement, the Joint Chiefs of Staff, at 1155, ordered all offensive operations to cease and withdrawal of all forces from the operational area as soon as possible consistent with safety and self-defense.[1]

As the afternoon in Cambodia commenced, a string of events unfolded with the Marines still under fire:

1. At noon an F-4 aircraft sank a large Cambodian barge north of Koh Tang Island.
2. At 1230 a second wave of approximately 100 Marines were successfully landed on Koh Tang Island.
3. A 1245 two small craft were sunk south of Koh Tang Island.
4. A BLU-82 15,000 pound bomb was dropped on the Island.[2]

Petty Officer Thomas K. Noble, Jr.:

The recovery of the crew of the *Mayaguez* added a whole new twist to the operation since it was believed that they were being held on Koh Tang Island. The 219 Marines that had been inserted on Koh Tang at first light were under heavy fire and we had lost three CH-53 helicopters as well as several Marines and Air Force personnel. These Marines had been engaged in close combat all day with the enemy. As with any major military operation many things went extremely well and many things did not. One of the things that was very bad from the beginning was the absence of any correct military intelligence. As stated previously, the crew of the *Mayaguez* was believed to be on the island and the enemy was more experienced and in much greater numbers than we had been told. The Marines were not equipped for a prolonged engagement.

So after realizing all these facts everyone knew that the situation had completely changed. We had our Marines and Air Force crewmen on the island and had to find a way to get them off. We also realized that these folks had no food and very little water.

The photograph is of Koh Tang Island with the USS *Henry B. Wilson* in the foreground. You're looking at the picture from the north and the Marines were pinned down on the east and west side of the point where the smoke is visible. The Marines on the east beach were particularly more vulnerable because of the proximity of the enemy. So our first effort was to concentrate on those folks.

The USS *Wilson* was firing its guns and Air Force helicopters made a series of attempts to land in the vicinity of the Marines on the east beach but were driven off by extremely heavy gunfire.

In mid-afternoon it was determined that a massive effort would be made to recover forces from the island. After dark it would be very difficult to direct fire from the Navy and Air Force units. The friendly and enemy lines were exceptionally close to each other. Capt. Rodgers made the decision to arm our gig and have it proceed as close to the recovery area as possible, to draw fire away from

USS Henry B. Wilson *Shelling Koh Tang Island.* U.S. Navy Photograph.

the recovery helicopters, suppress hostile fire, and rescue anyone who made a dash for the water. Eight sailors, including myself were picked to man this gig because of our familiarity with small weapons and our prior experience in Vietnam.[3]

Extraction efforts began in earnest in the afternoon. These efforts would continue for the next six hours. At 1430 initial efforts were concentrated on extracting the twenty-two isolated personnel. The main body of this marine force with approximately 213 personnel was unable to reach the twenty-two Marines. It was felt that there would be considerable risk to the twenty-two men if they were left there overnight.[4]

"These Marines were not picked up until well after sunset. In an all-out effort, the three remaining helicopters made repeated landings on the beach while fire support was provided by the helicopters themselves, small boats from the USS *Holt* and *Wilson,* an airborne forward controller, USAF fighters, and a gunship."[5]

On the east beach, two attempts were made to extract the twenty-five personnel there. The Khmer Rouge severely damaged the first helicopter attempting to land, forcing it back to USS *Coral Sea.* The second attempt was successful under tremendous fire from the Khmer Rouge.

Lance Cpl. Barnett: (East Beach)

> One boat and two helicopters tried to extract us. Finally, the third helicopter, Jolly 11 came in as the sun was setting and again the tree line opened up with fire from the Khmer Rouge. The helicopter was shot up like Swiss cheese. The pilot later said, he knew he was the last train out of Dodge. If they hadn't been extracted, they would've been left there. The pilot landed the helicopter between the rocks and the beach.
>
> As we ran to the helicopter we had to grab the runners on the helicopter which was going up and down. You had to hang on and be pulled up and into the helicopter. I landed face down on the bottom of the helicopter. Lieutenant Ciceri was the first man on the East Beach and he was the last to leave.
>
> On the helicopter we were exhausted and relieved to be alive. We were shocked that we actually made it off the island. The bullets

were still hitting the helicopter as we flew away and we were jumping up and down with joy. We ended up going to one of the ships which I don't remember the name of (USS *Coral Sea*). I had a case of shell shock. If someone banged the door I thought they were bombing the ship. It took three days before I got over the shock and started to settle down. The Navy men laid out a great spread of food for us and I must've slept for eighteen hours after the extraction.[6]

USS *Henry B. Wilson* provided offshore support by sailing a course up and down the east beach about a mile off-shore. She also "provided naval gunfire support. Her crew fired a total of 157 rounds of 5-inch shells at enemy positions while covering the Marine extraction."[7] At about 1640 USS *Henry B. Wilson* sank a Cambodian patrol craft north of Koh Tang Island.

Petty Officer Thomas K. Noble, Jr.:

At approximately 1500 the gig headed for east beach. Once we arrived on station, the Air Force laid down a barrage of fire and two CH-53s flew over us into the landing zone. We on the gig were trying to determine where the friendly and enemy lines were and we had started taking fire at this time. Fire from the enemy machine guns and recoilless rifles from this jungle was extremely intense. I had been in more than my share of fire fights in Vietnam and this one was right up there. While this heavy fire was going on, Air Force Lt. Donald Backlund flew his helicopter within fifty yards of that enemy fire and set it down to take the Marines aboard. He then started receiving even heavier fire from three different directions. We on the gig opened up on the position to the west of the CH-53 and then two of the three enemy positions opened up on the gig.

After this action was completed the gig proceeded to the west side of the island and repeated the action of running cover fire for the CH-53 helicopters that were extracting Marines on that side of the island. The last CH-53 left the island at approximately 2100. The gig was then ordered to return to the *Henry B. Wilson* and we pulled alongside at approximately 2130 and were brought back aboard. All the Marines that were extracted were taken to the USS *Harold E. Holt* or the USS *Coral Sea*. The *Henry B. Wilson* had thirteen Marines and Air Force personnel on board that were picked out of the water that morning from one of the CH-53s. We were told that all the people that were alive had been extracted from the island. Capt. Rogers patrolled the coast of Koh Tang looking for any sign of Americans who might've been left on the island but none were sighted.[8]

An Air Force CH-53 helicopter landing on USS Harold E. Holt. U.S. Air Force.

Late in the afternoon at around 1715 USS *Harold E. Holt* and USS *Henry B. Wilson* commenced efforts to approach the beaches. This effort failed because of the Khmer Rouge continued to use ground fire driving the rescuers away. A combined effort involving tactical aircraft and naval gunfire began to extract the remaining Marines which continued into darkness.[9]

An Air Force perspective of the operation was provided by Maj. A.J.C. Lavalle:

A damaged CH-53 helicoptor on USS Coral Sea *undergoing repairs.* Fred Morris and the Koh Tang Beach Club.

A Spectre gunship. Note the weapons protruding on the port side. Kowabunga. org.

There were no available helicopters left for extraction. Knife 51 piloted by Lt. Richard C. Brims flew back immediately after off-loading on the *Coral Sea*.

To provide defensive support a Spectre gunship fired down at the Khmer Rouge behind the defensive perimeter. To complicate matters the remaining Marines were down below in pitch black darkness.

However *Nail 69*, a OV-10 FAC (Forward Air Controller) had just come upon the scene. The FAC was circling above the Marines at 1,000 feet and switching its lights off and on to help Knife 51 land. As soon as its lights were turned on the Khmer Rouge would fire up at the plane and the Spectre gunship would then return the fire.

Am OV-10FAC used for air control of combat situations. Flying-leathernecks.org.

Because of light conditions, not being able to use the landing lights, smoke and haze, high tide conditions, and returning enemy gunfire, Lt. Brims was forced to abort his landing three times. While attempting to land a fourth time the Marines waved off the helicopter because they considered the beach unsafe, but Brims pressed into the landing zone. While the wounded were being taken on, the rest of the Marines set up suppressive fire, the Nail FAC delivered his rockets, the Spectre gunship laid down a continuous barrage, and Knife 51 added the firepower of its mini guns. The visual effects of the battle were like a scene from a science fiction movie: the bright tracers from the mini guns created a pulsing corridor of fire which surged from the helicopter and burned itself out in the jungle. In the face of this pummeling, enemy effectiveness was substantially diminished. Even so, some hostile fire was still being received, and sniper fire was observed coming from the beach itself."[10]

Before the final liftoff a last check of the beach area was conducted by Capt. Davis, his Gunnery Sgt. and U.S.A.F. T.Sgt.. Wayne Fisk who had bravely volunteered to go out and search.

PFC Fred Morris: (West Beach)

The worst part of the whole day was during the extraction that evening. Gunny Mac came over to my area and said they were going to change things, getting ready to get off the island. He put me with a M-60 gun team and moved us out to the farthest northeast position in our perimeter. It was in the heavy foliage part of the jungle down a trail about forty to fifty yards from the main trail that went over to the other side of the island. Where he put us it was pretty dark when the sun was up and as the sun went down, dark turned into total blackness. We could see absolutely nothing until a chopper would come in and then you could get your bearings from the muzzle flashes. A few times they shot some illumination rounds and then your night vision was shot and the shadows made everything look alive.

In between choppers it was really quiet, to the point that you would swear the trees were moving around. I could hear the Khmer creeping in closer and closer and every time they pulled someone else out for the extraction the gaps in our lines got bigger. After every chopper, Gunny or a runner he sent around would come and tell us exactly what was going on, and who would be leaving on the next bird. Finally Gunny came out before the last chopper and told us this is it, the last bird out so be ready. He said wait till you can hear the pitch of the blades change so you'd know the bird was on the ground, give a quick burst into the jungle to get their heads down, and get the hell on that helicopter. It was a good twenty minutes before that last bird came in and as spent as I was, at the same time I was so wired listening to every little sound as they crept closer and closer, my mind was playing tricks too, making it worse. It was so dark I had visions of not being able to find the trail and missing that helicopter, I knew I had about thirty-five steps to get to the main trail, and from there could just run to the sound, because we had a direct shot to the bird from the main trail. As the chopper came in, it seemed like it took forever to touchdown but when we could hear the blade pitch change the gunner let it rip into the jungle as instructed and that gun team was gone with me close behind. After about three steps there was an explosion to my right front that knocked me off my feet, the blast shattered the hand guards on my gun along with cutting up my hand but I was so focused on getting off that Godforsaken island, I knew I had to get up to get off. To say I was dazed would be an understatement but I got up and continued on toward the sound, the blast still echoing in my ears. By the time I reached the helo I was at a dead run. Because of the blast I wasn't hearing very well, and the helo had no exterior lights on. As I arrived my left foot found the loading ramp but my right one missed it and I went head first into the right door bulkhead and fell outside the bird. Gunny and someone else picked me up and got me onboard the already overflowing helo. I can still hear gunny swearing as he was hauling me back inside. We tried to take off almost immediately, and that bird shook so bad I thought the walls were going to collapse. As we started to lift off, one of the chopper crewmen started to slide out the back of the chopper because the ramp wasn't secure and went down as we were leaving. Someone grabbed him and literally threw him back on board right on my lap. After about thirty seconds when we knew we were airborne and out of range, everyone hugged each other and let out a huge sigh of relief. The trip to the *Coral Sea* took about twenty minutes but I had no idea where I was heading or that there was an aircraft carrier near. The helicopter was still vibrating very badly and it didn't look like we were very high off the water. The vibrations were getting a lot worse and I could tell we were slowing down. Just as I thought something was terribly wrong, I saw a bright red light. (A landing light) For a second I thought it was a tracer as he set it down on the aircraft carrier *Coral Sea*.

We had a memorial service on the *Coral Sea* for our Fallen Brothers. At that point I really did not know how many men we had

Marines' memorial service held on USS Coral Sea *for their fallen comrades.* Fred Morris and the Koh Tang Beach Club.

lost. Some Marines were taken to the *Holt* and some to the *Wilson* in addition to the *Coral Sea*. We lined up in front of the ceremonial helmets and M-16s where marines should be standing. There were 14 sets lined up, that was a eye opener... I went to Boot Camp with Pvt. James Jacques who was lost in Knife 31 on the East beach. I really didn't find out who all had died till we got back to Okinawa. Lots of open bunks, lots of hurting families and memories that haunt me still today.

Thinking back, we were young Marines with the bravado of "Let's go, let's go, kick butt and get that ship back!"

If you've never seen battle, talk is cheap. When you're 100 Marines against twenty farmer/fishermen on the island — you're invincible, you are pumped! They were originally told there were only twenty defenders on the island. However, the after action reports and others believe it was actually between 200-400 Khmer Rouge.

While on the island for the first hour, we were obviously outnumbered, I had an M-16 that don't work, all the other helos are being shot up and turned away by an overwhelming firepower. A bit overwhelming... Thanks to our training, adapt, improvise, overcome, the leadership of our entire command staff, the support of the Air Force and the Navy during the day and the brass balls of the helo crews from the Jollies and the Knives that night for the extraction, I'm still here to tell my story. Capt. Davis had flown in an airplane with a 35mm camera to take intelligence photos. All we knew there were two beaches. Later they received more detailed photos but we had already taken off and it was too late. The photos showed gun emplacements, etc. This was no twenty-man enemy![11]

After being safely extracted and back on the ship, Lt. Hoffman said in his interview that, "he was pretty shook up and reiterated again that the poor guys never had a chance![12]

By 2015 the Marine force had been extracted from Koh Tang Island. All military operations subsequently ceased.

Unfortunately, all the Marines weren't extracted. PFC Gary C. Hall, LCpl. Joseph N. Hargrove and Private Danny G. Marshall were left behind and when last seen were alive. In addition, LCpl. Ashton N. Loney's body was never recovered.

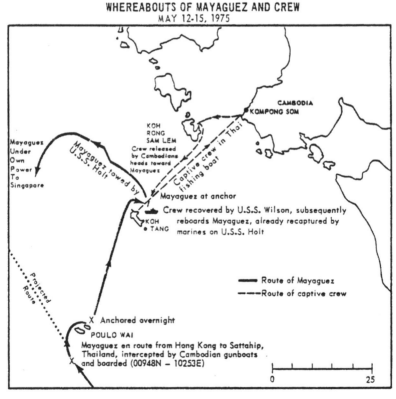

This map details in the capture and recovery of the Mayaguez. U.S. House of Representative, Seizure of the *Mayaguez*, Part IV.

20

CELEBRATION

The six MSC volunteers from the *Greenville Victory* and the *Mayaguez* crew did indeed have reason to celebrate. Their survival without any casualties was remarkable. Additionally, following so closely after the less than successful end of the Vietnam War, America's prestige was given a much needed boost by the successful outcome of the *Mayaguez* incident. The outcome was also timely, coming at one of the most critical points in American history involving the Cold War.

The General Accounting Office in its analysis pointed out that the SS *Mayaguez* and all crew members were recovered in just over three days. Other U.S. officials pointed out that through prompt military response they not only achieved these specific objectives but also accomplished two other goals. First, another *Pueblo* incident, with protracted and somewhat humiliating negotiations to recover crew members, was avoided. Second, the United States showed its resolve to other countries in the

A happy group of MSC Mayaguez *Rescue Crew Volunteers: left to right, Robert A. Griffin, Epifanio Rodriquez, Michael A. Saltwick, Herminio Rivera, Clinton H. Harriman and Karl P. Lonsdale.* US Navy Photograph.

context of the recent fall of the governments of Cambodia and South Vietnam and decreased U.S. influence in Southeast Asia.[1]

The GAO singled out the following points of praise:

1. The publicly stated aim of the U.S. actions — release of the ship and crew was achieved.
2. U.S. Naval, Marine and Air Force assets were generally assembled effectively and efficiently.
3. Command and control of our communications between the multiservice assets applied, was applied expeditiously.
4. The willingness of members of the Armed Forces to perform assigned missions despite the personal risks involved was inspiring as was the valor and prowess with which the missions were performed.[2]

The six MSC volunteers were honored as heroes and rightly so. Never in history had such a group been selected for a mission so fraught with danger. No one could anticipate the situation aboard the *Mayaguez*. They might easily have been airlifted into a mob of belligerent, armed, soldiers. Luckily, this was not what happened. The dropping of riot control agents in all likelihood prevented a real battle aboard the ship because the Khmer Rouge quickly departed, possibly fearing something worse than the tear gas that was dropped.

The USNS *Greenville Victory* received several accolades for her participation in the refugee evacuations and for the work of the six MSC volunteers. On May 20, 1975 Capt. Iacobacci was sent the following communication concerning the *Mayaguez*:

> To: Master USNS *Greenville Victory*
> Express my congratulations to the six crew members participating in Subj. Mission. I and all MSC are extremely proud of the accomplishment. I am initiating action to assure suitable recognition.
>
> RADM. S.H. Moore, Commander, Military Sealift Sends.[3]

On 23 May Secretary of the Navy J.W. Middendorf II sent the following communication to these ships; USNS *Miller,* USNS *Greenville Victory*, USNS *Kimbro* regarding their evacuation achievements:

> Outstanding Performance
> 1. Please accept my heartiest congratulations and gratitude for the outstanding performance you and your ship's crew demonstrated during the evacuation of South Vietnam. As they have time and time again during the past 25 years, U.S. Navy Civil Service employees who man ships operated by Military Sealift Command have demonstrated great professional skill and equally admirable human qualities in a time of need.
> 2. The officers and men of your ship can be very proud of the contributions they have made to the welfare of their fellow men, and to the reputation of both Military Sealift Command and the U.S. Navy.
> 3. Skill, courage, compassion, dedication to a cause and a willingness to exert effort far above that normally expected in the line of duty are but a few of the characteristics which typified their performance throughout the evacuation effort.
> 4. Thousands of South Vietnamese owe their futures, and, in many cases, their lives, to the men serving aboard your ship and on the other vessels that took part in the overall operation.

5. Please convey to them both my personal appreciation and the regard of the uniformed Navy men whom they so ably supported and
were worked with in this humanitarian undertaking.[4]

After returning to the *Greenville Victory,* Third Mate Karl
Lonsdale said:

> I had heard that day it was the B-52s that finally convinced
> the Khmers to release the crew. I was happy with the successful
> outcome of the mission, but I don't think I was aware except for
> maybe a crashed chopper, that quite a few Marines had been killed
> in combat.
>
> At some point back on the *Greenville*, Capt. Ray told us that
> someone higher up wanted to know if we perhaps would accept
> some cash for our services or would rather get an award or a medal. I
> wanted the cash, but was outvoted 5 to 1. The others thought awards
> would be more valuable than cash in furthering their careers. I did
> not think that I had done anything heroic. The operation would have
> been successful without me... And so we were asked to submit in-
> dividual reports about our experience. We did and that was that until
> ceremonies in Mobile, Alabama and Washington, D.C. I bought a
> suit at Sears in Mobile to wear in Washington, D.C.[5]

In Mobile, Alabama on July 11, 1975 in a Welcoming
Home Ceremony, the USNS *Greenville Victory* and her crew
received the Navy Award of Merit for Group Achievement for
humanitarian achievement.

The letter from Secretary of the Navy J. William Middendorf
II read:

> 1. It is with great personal pleasure that I inform you that the master,
> officers and crewmen of Military Sealift Command's USNS *Green-
> ville Victory* has been awarded the Navy Award of Merit for Group
> Achievement. This award honors your significant humanitarian
> achievements during the recent evacuation of refugees from South
> Vietnam, and the subsequent transport of many of those refugees to
> safe havens, as indicated by the following citation:
>
> Between April 2 and May 4, 1975, USNS *Greenville Victory*
> lifted more than 10,000 South Vietnamese refuges to safety as
> part of the Department of State directed request to aid citizens of
> that country. Converting the troop compartment of your ship to a

hospital, crewmen of the USNS *Greenville Victory* worked literally around the clock, to help assure the well-being and future freedom of your passengers. Throughout this operation, the entire crew of USNS *Greenville Victory* demonstrated a degree of courage, compassion and professionalism which made each of you an outstanding representative of both the U.S. Navy and the United States Government.

2. I am very proud of your accomplishments, and on behalf of the U.S. Navy wish you the greatest possible success in your future seafaring career. We are happy to have you on the Navy team.[6]

Speaking at the ceremony, RADM Sam H. Moore said:

Among the greatest sources of pride and satisfaction to me as Commander of Military Sealift Command are the accomplishments of those who sail MSC ships. The crew of the USNS *Greenville Victory* is an outstanding example.

In transporting more than 10,000 South Vietnamese refugees to safety, you once again demonstrated qualities of courage, of compassion, of professional seafaring skills which have earned the respect of your fellow mariners, and those you transported to safety.

The *Greenville Victory* crewmen who volunteered to assist in the recapture of the SS *Mayaguez* added new luster to your reputation, and helped write another bright chapter in the history of U.S. Merchant Marine. I am proud to serve with you as a member of the U.S. Navy's Military Sealift Command, and wish you continued success in the future.[7]

RADM Frank B. Guest, Jr., Commander Military Sealift Command Atlantic, added:

The outstanding performance displayed by you, the officers and crew of USNS *Greenville Victory*, during the recently completed South Vietnamese refugee evacuation was and is a source of pride and admiration for all of us in the Military Sealift Command, Atlantic.

You demonstrated professional skill and showed a genuine human compassion during the arduous refugee evacuation which exemplified the patriotism of U.S. Navy Civil Service seamen and the ships operated by the Military Sealift Command.

The high caliber of men serving on *Greenville Victory* was manifested again when volunteers from the ship participated in the recovery operation of the SS *Mayaguez*. The bravery and dedication exhibited by *Greenville Victory* crewmen was in the highest traditions of seafaring men. Well done to all of you from me and your fellow seamen everywhere.[8]

And Raymond Iacobacci, master of the *Greenville Victory* had these comments:

1. Ships of war and ships of trade must be a part of the nation dependent on commerce. They complement each other. The USNS *Greenville Victory* has the proud distinction of serving both factions. As a cargo ship we have transported many diversified categories of freight but none more important than the human cargo we carried during the Vietnamese refugee evacuation.
2. Whether one agrees or disagrees with foreign policies the timely humanitarian efforts were the only rays of sunshine through the dark clouds of despair of the South Vietnamese people.
3. This ship was involved in refugee evacuations for almost two months and carried an estimated total on her trips of 15,000 refugees. Many of these are in the United States now.
4. We saw several cities under the onslaught of the communist

The Greenville Victory *volunteers line up with MSC Commander Rear Adm. Sam H. Moore after the award ceremony in Mobile. Left to right, Michael A. Saltwick, Herminio Rivera, Clinton H. Harriman, Ray Iacobacci, Adm. Moore, Epifanio Rodriquez, Karl P. Lonsdale and Robert A. Griffin.* Sealift.

troops and were frustrated several times in our efforts by enemy action, but, in the final count when you saw the grateful faces of those who were able to be saved it was well worth it.

5. We have heard many reports that said the refugees were forced to come aboard the ships. Nothing could be farther from the truth…

6. While the vessel was in Subic Bay, Philippines, storing for further refugee operations, the SS *Mayaguez* was seized. At the request of RADM. Moore, six crewmen from this ship volunteered and boarded the *Mayaguez* and were vital factors to its successful recapture. These men are a credit to the Military Sealift Command and the country they serve. I am proud to have them aboard then USNS *Greenville Victory*.

7. On behalf of myself, the officers and crew we thank you for this award. I also wish to thank all involved for the efforts put forth in providing the officers and men with this Welcome Home Ceremony. We are glad to be home and ready to continue to serve the needs of our nation.[9]

On 24 July 1975 Captain Miller of the *Mayaguez* and the six volunteers from *Greenville Victory* were invited to an Awards Ceremony at the Department of Commerce in Washington,

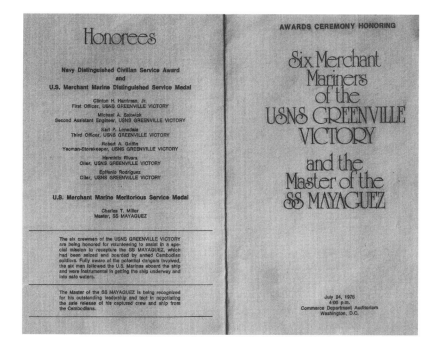

DC. The honorees are named in the program at the bottom of the previous page. The highlight of the ceremony was meeting President Gerald Ford.

Eifanio Rodriguez, oiler, steps forward to receive his U.S. Merchant Marine Distinguished Service Medal. Sealift.

Captain Miller, to left of President Ford, presented him with the ship's wheel from the Mayaguez. The White House photo courtesy of Ray Iacobacci..

President Ford congratulating Karl Lonsdale. The White House.

President Ford congratulating Herminio Rivera. The White House.

UNITED STATES DEPARTMENT OF COMMERCE
The Assistant Secretary for Maritime Affairs
Washington, D.C. 20230

July 24, 1975

It is my privilege to present the MERCHANT MARINE DISTINGUISHED SERVICE MEDAL, authorized by the Secretary of Commerce, to

H E R M I N I O   R I V E R A
Oiler
USNS GREENVILLE VICTORY

in recognition of his heroic action as cited below:

At Subic Bay, Philippines, May 13, 1975, Oiler Herminio Rivera, with five fellow crew members of the USNS GREENVILLE VICTORY volunteered to assist in a special mission to recapture the SS MAYAGUEZ, which had been seized and boarded by armed Cambodian soldiers. Fully aware of the possibility of combat, the team accompanied the contingent of United States Marines spearheading the mission. On May 15, they were flown by helicopters to the USS HOLT, a Navy destroyer in the area of the SS MAYAGUEZ. En route, enemy fire downed one helicopter. At dawn, the group landed on board the USS HOLT, while American planes launched a gas attack against the MAYAGUEZ to incapacitate reported armed forces aboard. After the USS HOLT was brought alongside and made fast, the six seamen followed the Marines over the side to the seized ship moored offshore Kach Tang Island where heavy battle action was in progress. The vessel was deserted but within range of enemy guns. Large pockets of gas remained on board. The GREENVILLE VICTORY team, encumbered by gas masks, flak vests and helmets, worked at top speed checking deck and engine equipment to assure the seaworthiness of the vessel. In less than an hour, with the American flag raised, the emergency diesel generator in operation, the anchor cut away, and lines secured, the MAYAGUEZ was ready to be towed by the USS HOLT to safer waters until the main plant could be started. About 1130 a small fishing vessel approached carrying the Master of the MAYAGUEZ with some of his crew, who boarded the vessel and assumed control. The GREENVILLE VICTORY volunteers continued their support until 1930, when they departed aboard an ATC tugboat. Their dauntless courage, competence and teamwork displayed throughout this hazardous mission are in keeping with the highest traditions of the United States Merchant Marine.

A copy of this commendation for DISTINGUISHED SERVICE has been made a part of Herminio Rivera's official service record.

ROBERT J. BLACKWELL
Assistant Secretary
for Maritime Affairs

Herminio Rivera's certificate which accompanied his Merchant Marine Distinguished Service Medal. Courtesy of Herminio Rivera.

21

AFTERMATH

It is common in military and government circles to analyze the results of an action and summarize those results under the heading of "Lessons Learned." The purpose of this is so the next time a similar situation occurs the end result can be achieved more effectively, more efficiently, and with fewer casualties. The General Accounting Office (GAO) published an investigative report on the *Mayaguez* incident. Their findings included:

1. The United States did not warn its merchant ships after the *Mayaguez* was seized, despite increasing evidence that Cambodian forces were asserting historical claims to offshore islands and that Cambodia had greatly extended its territorial limit and was seizing ships entering these waters....
2. A significant time elapsed before reconnaissance aircraft were launched to locate the *Mayaguez* ....
3. Some valuable assets were not used to obtain better evidence of the location of the crew. Defense indicated that with the limited resources available, their inherent limitations, and the

227

rapid tactical situation, it is difficult to see what more could
have been done....

4. Some important details on the possible location of the crew did
not reach decision makers. Reports prepared in Washington
and Hawaii on the number of Caucasians taken away from Koh
Tang Island to the mainland were inaccurate;...

5. While the United States undertook a number of diplomatic
initiatives to secure the release of the *Mayaquez* and its crew,
little weight appears to have been given to indications that the
Cambodians might be working on a political solution. Among
these indications was a report received more than 14 hours
before the marine assault was initiated which indicated that a
foreign government was using its influence with Cambodia to
seek an early release of the *Mayaquez* and expected it to be
released soon ....

6. Marine assault forces planned and carried out the assault on
Koh Tang with inaccurate estimates of Cambodia strength on
the island. GAO was unable to determine why the available
more accurate intelligence estimates did not reach the task
group and assault commanders....

7. The degree to which relative military risks were assessed is not
clear. The risks involved in the Marine assault on Koh Tang
— even without the traditional pre-softening of the Island by
bombardment and with a relatively slow Marine buildup rate —
were deemed acceptable. On the other hand, the risk of having
an aircraft carrying the marine assault commander fly below a
6,000 foot altitude restriction to obtain first-hand information
on Koh Tang, was deemed unacceptable. Defense officials said
all risks were appropriately evaluated but GAO was unable
to ascertain whether the President or other NSC participants
requested or received information concerning relative risks
involved.

8. In retrospect, the final Marine assault and the bombing of the
Cambodian mainland did not influence the Cambodian decision
to release the crew. However, certain U.S. actions probably did
influence that decision; for example, the sinking of gunboats and
the U.S. air activity in the area. Defense stated that the decision
to assault Koh Tang was reasonable in lieu of information at
the time and that the mainland was bombed since Cambodia
had the capability to interfere with the operation. GAO does
not question the purpose of either the assault or the mainland
bombing.[1]

It is one thing to make an urgent decision; with the world watching and assessing American response, with the negative aspects of the *Pueblo* incident in recent memory, and having just pulled out from the long, drawnout war in Vietnam. It is quite another to, after the fact, take the attitude that those responsible for decision-making should have acted differently. Nevertheless, the GAO investigative report leaves questions and concerns, involving four aspects of the seizure: haste, intelligence, communication, and command structure.

First and foremost, was haste necessary and was it responsible for the deaths, wounded and "Missing in Action" of our military personnel? The casualty rate of forty-one killed was tragic:

USMC, USAF, USN
Eighteen Killed in Action.
Fifty-two Wounded.
Twenty-three Air Force Security killed en route to U-Tapao.
Four Marines Missing in Action (three left on the island, one killed and left on the island).
Eighteen total MIAs.

Haste overshadowed the entire operation. This was evident in the discussions held in the National Security Council. The safety of the military men involved was secondary to the outcome of rescue and regained prestige, although the argument could be made that that is the nature, the risk, of being in the military. The seizure of the *Mayaquez* came at a time when it became necessary to show the world that an American ship could not be seized at sea in an act of piracy.

Intelligence and communication were vital to the outcome of this mission. The Marine assault might be questioned as being based on poor intelligence. There were no maps, photographs, site preparation or solid intelligence of how many Khmer Rouge were on the island. The location of the *Mayaguez* crew was unknown. Planning objectives didn't reach the ground forces because of poor communication. Objectives came from

Washington, D.C., when decisions should have been made between the ground commanders and headquarters.

Glenn T. Starnes in a report to the Naval War College faculty wrote the following analysis:

1. Numerous problems existed at the operational level in command and leadership.
2. An ad hoc command organization whose operational staff was purely Air Force led to tremendous problems in unity of command as well planning, coordination, and execution.
3. The lack of Marine and Navy representation on the USSAG/7th AF operational staff magnified these problems.
4. Advanced communications technology and ineffective operational leadership enabled decision makers at the strategic level (NSC, JCS and CinCPac) to adversely affect the tactical and operational execution of the mission.
5. Possibly the greatest operational failure was the inability at the operational level to translate strategic intent into operational/tactical planning and execution.[2]

Starnes cites an article by Peter J. Kelly's entitled, "Raids and National Command: Mutually Exclusive!"

Kelly wrote, "Once the decision to use force is made — planning and execution should be the responsibility of the operational/tactical commander. The President cannot become a tactical commander. The JCS cannot solve operational problems. Neither the NSC nor the JCS should allow Washington to function as a super tactical operations center*, greatly increasing the risk of failure and unnecessary casualties."[3]

Starnes finally cautions the reader that "in the *Mayaguez* incident, the failures in operational command and leadership could have led to mission failure.+"[4]

In a later interview, Fred Morris said they:

---

* Despite Kelly's criticism, what could have happened was not actually what did happen. Ed.

+ However, they did not. The mission was not a failure. Ed.

... didn't talk much about the mission after the war. Apparently, a lot of people didn't want to discuss it. It wasn't one of our proudest moments. The intelligence was terrible. Getting off the island was great but it wasn't one of the shining moments for our armed services. The public perception was one of victory because the crew had been rescued, but they were never aware of how many were killed and how many helicopters crashed.[5]

Larry Barnett said that he:

... hoped our leaders learned a lesson from what happened. The heroics of the Knives and Jollies are the reason why many of us are here today. We would have been wiped out on the east beach if it hadn't been the helicopter pilots' bravery, dedication and honor. I hope the politicians learn to stay out of wars. Let the generals run the war. A lot of men and women will stay alive if the public stays out of future wars. Furthermore, common sense dictates that you can't assault a beach in a helicopter. This was the only time in history that an assault was executed using helicopters on a beach. Hopefully it'll be the last time.

The island had been contested by the Khmer Rouge and Vietnamese. For the U.S. government to believe that only fifteen to thirty people were on the island was just irresponsible to me. The operation was put up so quickly and people did their absolute best. But if you're going into battle you have to know what the playground is like. We had no intelligence and no cover fire. These are basic rules of engagement which we didn't have. The mission was an absolute success and the intelligence was an absolute failure.[6]

Capt. Miller was in disagreement concerning GAO's view that the bombing of the mainland did not influence the release of the *Mayaguez* and crew. He testified that,

In my judgment, I'm not a military man, but I believe, and the thirty-nine other crew members with me believe, the military action taken by our forces, the Air Force, the Navy, and the Marines was necessary to get our release. If I didn't have the promise of removing the aircraft over Cambodian soil, I don't think they would have released us. I think we would have been held as hostages for ransom...

On October 6, 1976 Capt. Miller flew to San Francisco, at

President Ford's invitation, to support Ford in a debate with Jimmy Carter during that presidential campaign. Capt. Miller was thankful for President Ford's actions of sending the Marines and Air Force in to rescue them. At the press conference afterward, he reiterated, "If our military hadn't been on the scene, we would have been taken inland to a military prison. I was able to negotiate with them for four days with a gun at my back or my head at all times until the Cambodians decided they had been bombed and attacked enough."[7]

In a 2006 reunion of the *Mayaguez* and Koh Tang Island Veterans, President Ford honored this group with the following

GERALD R. FORD

May 13, 2006

To the Mayaguez and Koh Tang Island Veterans:

I was extremely pleased to hear that you are gathering this weekend in Washington, D.C., to remember the events surrounding the seizure of the U.S.-flag containership Mayaguez and the illegal detention of her crew in the Cambodian jungle.

Thirty-one years ago this week, you fought bravely to defend America's honor and protect American lives in a remote and dangerous part of the world. For those of you gathered tonight to commemorate that battle, I say, as I have many times before, 'Thank you." The forty Americans who were freed as a result of your heroic actions have thanked you through the years as well. Captain Charles Miller, Master of the Mayaguez at the time, told me on several occasions that without the quick and determined action of U.S. military forces, he and his crew would likely have met a far different fate at the hands of the Khmer Rouge.

To the families and friends of your comrades who gave their lives during this brief but critical conflict, we again express our deep sadness for their loss. You who returned and those who died sent a powerful message to the world at a critical time – that the United States will defend and protect its citizens under threat wherever they may be.

I wish you all well as you remember this short but important chapter in our country's military history.

With continuing gratitude,

Gerald R. Ford

22

MISSING
IN
ACTION

An investigation into the circumstances surrounding the three missing Marines was conducted on June 7, 1975. The results were published in, *Investigation to Inquire into the Circumstances Surrounding the Missing in Action Status in the Case of Private First Class Gary C. Hall USMC, Lance Corporal Joseph N. Hargrove USMC and Private Danny G. Marshall USMC.* This unclassified document was also used in a two-part series CBS news report entitled *Dead or Alive?: Fate of 3 Marines Lost On Koh Tang Island Still Unknown* by News Correspondent Vince Gonzales on January 25, 2001. The Investigation was conducted by Major Peter C. Brown, USMC.

In the Preliminary Statement the points were as follows:

1. In accordance with the Commanding General, 3rd Marine Division appointing order of 24 May 1975, which appears as enclosure and, the detailed investigation into the events surrounding the missing in action status of those three Marines

cited in the subject, above, and hereinafter referred to as Hall, Hargrove and Marshall was conducted. The results of this investigation are as set forth in the remainder of this investigative report.

2. … These three Marines, members of Company "E," Second Battalion, Ninth Marine Regiment, were part of the Marine force which made a helicopter borne assault on Koh Tang Island during the morning of 15 May 1975.

3. Koh Tang Island is forest covered, has no mountains, is 5 miles long and 1 mile wide. Beaches are sandy on the North East side of the island and more rocky on the North West side. All approaches to the island have deep water.

4. The area of Koh Tang Island in which the Marine force operations took place was characterized by normal tropical foliage which included dense jungle forest broken by an area without trees but in which grass ranging from 4 to 6 feet in height was present. Visibility in the general area of operations where Hall, Hargrove and Marshall were last seen was limited during daylight hours and nonexistent during darkness. The beach area where all personnel were extracted was clear.

5. Combat operations against the enemy forces continued throughout the daylight hours with extraction of the Marine forces effected during the hours of darkness on 15 May 1975. Hall, Hargrove and Marshall were present and participated in combat operations throughout the day as indicated in the findings of fact, below. None of the three Marines were injured or wounded prior to their disappearance. None of the three men were seen subsequent to the final extraction of the Marine force from Koh Tang Island which occurred about 2200, 15 May 1975 …

9. The service records of Hall, Hargrove and Marshall disclosed that Hall and Hargrove were unqualified swimmers and that Marshall was a Third Class Swimmer.[1]

The Findings of Fact:

1. Hall, Hargrove and Marshall landed on Koh Tang Island, Cambodia at 1230 on 15 May 1975.

2. Hall, Hargrove and Marshall comprised an M-60 machine gun team which was attached to the 3rd Platoon, Company "E", 2nd Battalion, Ninth Marines.

3. The machine gun team formed by these three Marines was positioned on the extreme right flank of a 180° defensive

perimeter, of which the right portion consisted of 3rd Platoon of Company "E."

4. The 180 degree defensive perimeter extended a maximum of 300 meters from the beach at its farthest point inland.

5. The machine gun position occupied by Hall, Hargrove and Marshall was located not more than 25 meters from the beach.

6. Hall, Hargrove and Marshall were located about 5 meters forward of a position co-occupied by Sergeant Carl C. Anderson, 3rd Platoon right guard and Private First Class Fernando A. Rios.

7. During the daylight hours of 15 May 1975 Hall, Hargrove and Marshall were observed in their defensive position by several members of Company "E".

8. Between 1830 and 1900 a prearranged signal was sounded initiating withdrawal of the defensive perimeter toward the beach, to execute the extraction of all Marine forces from Koh Tang Island.

9. Prior to initiation of the preplanned withdrawal Hall, Hargrove and Marshall had been briefed on the sequence of events which would culminate with the extraction of all Marine forces from Koh Tang Island.

10. When the signal was sounded to begin withdrawing toward the beach area, PFC Rios, who was located about 5 meters from Hall, Hargrove and Marshall, shouted to the three Marines telling them to pull back, whereupon Rios withdrew and did not see the three men again.

11. The first phase of the withdrawal was executed as planned and a perimeter defense was reestablished.

12. Near darkness prevailed when the signal to commence withdrawal was sounded and the action was executed.

13. Upon reestablishment of the perimeter defense Hall, Hargrove and Marshall were observed by Sgt. Anderson to be nervous and in a confused state. Furthermore, upon questioning the three men Sgt. Anderson determined their supply of machine gun ammunition was completely expended.

14. Upon determining Hall, Hargrove and Marshall were ineffective as a machine gun team, Sgt. Anderson ordered them to move to a new position which was located to the left of the position occupied by Captain James H. Davis, Commanding Officer, Company "G" who was then in charge of all Marine forces remaining on Koh Tang Island, and then to board the next helicopter which was extracting Marines from the island.

15. Sgt. Anderson was the last member of the Marine force to see Hall, Hargrove and Marshall and that the time was about 2000.

16. Capt. Davis' position was located about 25 meters from the point where Sgt. Anderson directed Hall, Hargrove and Marshall to withdraw from the reestablished defensive perimeter.
17. Hall, Hargrove and Marshal did not report to Capt. Davis.
18. During the approximate time when Hall, Hargrove and Marshall should have reported to Capt. Davis, a state of confusion existed in and about the beach area.
19. When the 5th of 6 helicopters landed, incoming enemy small arms fire was received as well as incoming enemy grenades and the execution of a final protective fire was ordered by Capt. Davis.
20. After the 5th of 6 helicopters lifted off, a 30-40 minute period of quiet prevailed at the Koh Tang Island extraction site. At this time no sounds were heard outside the Marine defensive perimeter.
21. About 10 minutes after the 5th of 6 helicopters lifted off Koh Tang Island an aerial illumination flare was ignited which lighted the entire area in and around the Marine defensive perimeter. At this time no movement was observed outside the perimeter.
22. Before lift-off of the final helicopter a check of the beach area was made by Capt. Davis, his gunnery sergeant and the Air Force helicopter crew chief and so no personnel remained in the beach area.
23. Darkness prevailed when the last extraction of Marine force personnel was made from Koh Tang Island.
24. Subsequent to the extraction of Marine forces from Koh Tang Island a search for serialized equipment known to be in the possession of Hall, Hargrove and Marshall was directed by Capt. Stahl resulting in negative findings.
25. A physical search of Koh Tang Island was not made after Hall, Hargrove and Marshall were discovered missing as the conduct of such a search was not authorized.[2]

Statement of LCpl. John S. Standfast:

My squad was assigned the right flank of the defensive perimeter around the LZ. At about 1500 we were setting defense positions. Hall and Marshall were attached to my squad with Hall the gunner on an M-60 machine gun and Marshall claiming to be the [sic] gunner. About thirty minutes later Hargrove came to me and said he was the assistant gunner. I moved Hargrove into the position with Hall and I moved Marshall about five feet to the right. This put Marshall on the extreme right flank of the perimeter with

Hall and Hargrove in the next position with their M-60 machine gun. Sergeant Anderson and PFC Rios, a grenadier were about ten feet to the rear of the M-60 position. During the afternoon there was no incoming fire and Hargrove, Hall and Marshall were in good physical condition with their mental condition appearing average. About 1700 I had a meeting with the Platoon Commander, 2d Lt. Davis, and was designated as rear security when the perimeter was to pull back into consolidated positions on the beach. I asked Sergeant Anderson if he would make sure all the people got off the line and back to the beach when the signal was given. Sergeant Anderson said he would. About one hour after dark the signal to pull back to the beach was given and as Sergeant Anderson passed my position as rear security I asked him if that was everybody and he said it was. After the fourth helicopter departed somebody shouted that everyone to the left of a particular fighting hole was to get on the next helicopter. I was centered on the hole so I moved to the right so as to get on the last helicopter. At this time I looked to my right and saw PFC Piechna and ten feet to his right was PFC Hall. I did not see Hargrove or Marshall on the beach. I don't remember if he had his M-60 with him. When the next helicopter came in those on the left moved out to board. Somebody grabbed my leg and told me to get on the helicopter. However it tilted before I could board. I returned to the beach and did not see Hall again. The word was passed that everyone was to get on the next helicopter. When it came in I got on. We landed on the USS *Coral Sea*.[3]

Statement of PFC Andrew F. Piechna:

I was on the defensive perimeter around the LZ and saw PFC Hall on the right hand corner of the perimeter. When the word came to pull back to the beach into a consolidated perimeter defense I moved back and got down into a fighting position. Someone said all those on the left of the particular fighting hole were to get on the next helicopter. I was on the right side of the hole. To my right was LCpl Standfast and about 1 meter to his right was PFC Hall. When the next helicopter came in the people to the left moved to board it. Somebody grabbed my leg and told me to get on that helicopter. I got up and ran to it. There were about five people in front of me when the helicopter lifted off. I don't know if anybody was behind me. As the helicopter lifted off the group moved back on to the beach and took up fighting positions.

About ten minutes later the last helicopter landed and everyone got on. The last time I saw PFC Hall was just before I got up to attempt to board the second to last helicopter. I don't know if he attempted to board it. I do not know Hargrove or Marshall and don't recall seeing them at all.[4]

Statement of PFC David M. Wagner:

During the evacuation phase of the operation and after the defensive perimeter had been pulled back to consolidated positions on the beach I was dug in on the beach. I was responsible for putting the wounded on one of the evacuation helicopters. PFC Hall was also on the beach with his M-60 machine gun. He was supposed to provide cover for us. When the helicopter landed we started to get on. I heard Hall yell for ammo so I gave him mine. Then I got on the helicopter. I did not see Hargrove or Marshall and did not see Hall again after I boarded the helicopter.[5]

Statement of Private Mario R.M. Gutierrez:

During the evacuation phase of the operation and after the defensive perimeter had been pulled back to consolidated positions on the beach PFC Wagner and I were dug in on the beach. We were responsible for putting wounded on the first helicopter that came in. PFC Hall was also dug in on the beach with his M-60 machine gun. He was supposed to provide cover for us. When the helicopter landed I got on. I heard PFC Hall yelling for more ammo. I did not see Hargrove and Marshall and did not see Hall after I boarded the helicopter.[6]

The Opinions put forth by the Investigation were as follows:

1. That all Marine force personnel exercising authority over Hall, Hargrove and Marshall performed their duties in a satisfactory manner.
2. That Hall, Hargrove and Marshall did not obey the order issued by Sergeant Anderson to report to Captain Davis' position and moved elsewhere.
3. That Hall, Hargrove and Marshall were not in the helicopter landing site area after lift-off of the fifth of six extraction helicopters.
4. That Hall, Hargrove and Marshall were not in the helicopter landing site area when the sixth and final extraction helicopter landed.

5. That if Hall, Hargrove and Marshall had been in the general vicinity of helicopter landing site area they would have attempted to board either the 5th or 6th helicopter unless there were unconscious, incapacitated because of wounds, or were dead.
6. That if Hall, Hargrove and Marshall had been conscious and or/were wounded or separated from the Marines remaining in the helicopter landing site area, they would have called for help during the 30-40 minute period of quiet which prevailed after the 5th of 6 helicopters lifted off.
7. Data.
8. That Hall and Hargrove would not have attempted to swim from Koh Tang Island because they were unqualified swimmers.
9. That Marshall could have attempted to swim to safety from Koh Tang Island.
10. That Hall, Hargrove and Marshall could have been fatally wounded subsequent to the time that they were last seen by Sgt. Anderson at about 2000 and the time when the final helicopter lifted off, since there was firing by both enemy forces and Marines awaiting extraction from Koh Tang Island.[7]

Recommendation
1. That the status of Hall, Hargrove and Marshall be changed from missing in action to killed in action (body not recovered).[8]
Peter C. Brown

In declassified radio traffic action tapes, the following conversations between the Air Force pilots and Capt. Davis indicates the dire situation the group was in as the extraction entered its final stages.

Capt. Davis: "They're all around us. What can you do for us? Over?"

Pilot: "We're coming man! We're coming! We're coming! Do you have all your men on the beach?..."

Capt. Davis: "I just don't know. It's dark out here and I don't know who's going and who's here. I'm just going to have to do the best I can."

During the extraction flights, pilot to pilot:
Pilot: "Soon as you're a safe distance away from the island I want you to get hold of a guy (Capt. Davis) whose call sign

should be "Bingo Shoes 06." Ask him if he's got everybody out that needs to be out."

Pilot: "According to Capt. Davis he has everybody out on the last load."

Pilot: "Outstanding."[9]

However, Capt. Davis was unaware of the Marines being left behind on the island because they were not in his unit, nor had they ever reported to him when they were ordered to, nor was he told there were men left behind as they were leaving after a visual search had been made.

Capt. Mike E. Stahl was Hall, Hargrove and Marshall's company commander. He had issued orders to reconstitute the beach perimeter after it had been breached by the Khmer Rouge. Orders had been given to the three Marines to pull back and move to the center of the zone for extraction.

According to Capt. Stahl there was no logical reason why they didn't reach the extraction zone. When the 5th helicopter landed Capt. Stahl was helping wounded Marines onto the helicopter. Before he had a chance to leave, the helicopter lifted off.

On board the ship they searched for weapons and treated the wounded. They tried to put events into sequence to see how many were aboard. They discussed a possible return to the island next morning with a Navy Seal team to search for bodies in the wreckage of the two helicopters that were shot down, and to look for the three Marines who were MIA. Captain Stahl volunteered to go with the team but the mission was cancelled.[10]

Further transmission between the pilots:

Pilot 1: "Some of the Marines on board say there are still Marines on the island at this time."

Pilot 2: "OK there are still Marines on the island, in the LZ? Is that affirmative?"

Pilot 1: "That's affirmative. That's what was passed on to us by Marines on the chopper at this time."

Pilot 2: "OK, find out if they were in the LZ or whether they were maintaining our perimeter defense position?"

Pilot 1: "Sir, we are told by the people in here that there are more Marines on the beach."[11]

When *Knife 51* returned to the *Coral Sea* the Admiral summoned Capt. Davis to his wardroom. Capt. Davis told the Admiral, "To the best of his knowledge we didn't have anybody left on the beach."

And in this interview, "Still as far as I'm concerned to the best of my knowledge nobody was left alive on the beach."[12]

Petty Officer Thomas K. Noble Jr.:

> The night of 15 May *Henry B. Wilson* moved further to sea and fueled from the USS *Coral Sea*. After fueling was completed *Henry B. Wilson* steamed back to the vicinity of Koh Tang and at first light made as close as possible observation run on the island with many people looking through high power binoculars. I cannot remember for sure but I believe we also hailed to anyone who could hear over the ship's topside loudspeakers. No Americans were sighted. After completing the observation run we on loaded all the Marines from the *Harold Holt* (approximately eighty-five) on board the *Henry B. Wilson* and steamed toward Subic Bay in the Republic of the Philippines.[13]

23

THIRTY-FIVE

YEARS LATER

In 1973, the Central Identification Laboratory (CIL) was
formed in Thailand to help identify the remains of U.S. military lost. Three years later a CIL was set up in Hawaii "to
search for, recover, and identify missing Americans from all previous conflicts."[1] In 1992, a new organization was formed, Joint
Task Force-Full Accounting (JTF-FA) "to focus on achieving
the fullest possible accounting of Americans missing as a result
of the Vietnam War."[2] In October 2003 JTF-FA and the Central
Identification Lab in Hawaii were combined to form JPAC.

The mission of the Joint POW/MIA Accounting Command
(JPAC):

> ... is to achieve the fullest possible accounting of all Americans
> missing as a result of the nation's past conflicts. The highest priority
> of the organization is the return of any living Americans that remain
> prisoners of war. To date, the U.S. government has not found
> evidence that there are still American POWs in captivity from past
> U.S. conflicts.[3]

244 AN ACT OF PIRACY

There are 1,800 MIAs associated with the Vietnam War. Every year JPAC "conducts at least five recovery missions associated with the Korean War, ten missions in Southeast Asia for Vietnam War cases, and ten missions in other areas ... To date, over 1,400 Americans have been identified. The Central Identification Laboratory identifies, on average, about six individuals a month."[4]

Reports surfaced concerning the deaths of the three Marines, and even a fourth, after the extraction of the *Mayaguez* rescue troops from Koh Tang Island. One of the refugee reports was issued in April 1983 by the Joint Casualty Resolution Center entitled, "Sighting of Two Skeletons: *Mayaguez* Related Death." The report was taken from a former Democratic Kampuchean Khmer Rouge soldier who had been sent to Koh Tang Island for several days training to repair naval engines. In September 1981 he defected from his unit. At the time this report was issued, the source hadn't been interviewed by the JCRC personnel.

The information in the soldier's report reads:

Around September-October 1975 (about 4 to 5 months following the *Mayaguez* Incident), two skeletons were seen lying in the sand at the waterline on the northeastern end of Koh Tang Island. The skeletons were located near wreckage of a U.S. helicopter (with four rotor blades). The helicopter had been destroyed during the fighting between Democratic Kampuchean (DK) forces/U.S. troops during the *Mayaguez* incident.

Apparently no effort had been made to bury the skeletons, which were believed to be those of U.S. soldiers killed in the fighting. According to soldiers of the 408 Battalion 21st Regiment 3rd— DK Division who were assigned to defend the island and participated in the *Mayaguez* fighting, one American soldier was left behind on Koh Tang Island when U.S. forces withdrew following the incident. The soldiers stated that the American hid in the hills on the island for fifteen days before DK forces found him. The American was killed when he resisted DK efforts to capture him.

Paul D. Mather
Lieutenant Colonel, USA F
JCRC Liaison Officer[5]

"In 1988, the communist government of Cambodia announced that it wished to return the remains of several dozen Americans to the United States. However, because the U.S. did not officially recognize the Cambodian government, it refused to respond directly to the Cambodians regarding the remains offered."[6] This attitude radically changed in the 1990s. "Between 1991-99, U.S. and Cambodian investigators conducted seven joint investigations, led by the Joint Task Force-Full Accounting."[7]

In 1995, the first of three teams from the Joint Task Force for Full Accounting (JTFFA) was allowed onto Koh Tang Island to search for the remains of the eighteen Americans who lost their lives or were listed Missing in Action in Operation *Mayaguez*. As part of the JTFFA contingent, a salvage crew from the USS *Brunswick*, the first US military vessel allowed to penetrate Cambodian waters since the end of the war, began pulling pieces of *Knife 31* to the shore. Over the recovery site, the team placed eight feet by sixteen feet open boxes made of steel plates to stabilize the search area and to prevent outside sand and other material from backfilling the recovery site.

On the surface two work boats containing diesel engines connected to ten-inch suction hoses drew layer of debris from beneath the steel boxes and deposited the material onto screening tables set up on makeshift barges. From inside and under sections of the helicopter came teeth along with arm, leg, finger, rib and jaw bones — 161 specimens in all, plus 144 personal items

USS Brunswick *(AS-3) was launched on October 14, 1969 and delivered to the Norfolk Naval Shipyard. She was decommissioned in 1996.* U.S. Navy.

and 101 pieces of equipment mixed in with live and exploded ammunition.

One recovered thigh bone had shattered six inches below the hip and the injury occurred before or at the time of death. According to JTFFA members, that single bone forcefully and painfully brought home the level of suffering these men endured in the last moments before *Knife 31* slipped below the shallow water just off the east beach landing zone.[8]

A further unclassified report issued in June 1996 involved interviews with witnesses. The report "is based on field analysis only and is not intended to provide final analytical conclusions."

> … Both witnesses heard of one American who survived a couple days or weeks after the attack, but was captured and executed while stealing food on the eastern side of the island. Witness one was told the American was white and had a mustache. Both witnesses could not provide any other information about the American. Neither witness knew where the American was buried.
>
> Witness two said an American was buried at the end of the jungle in a cultivated area of the Khmer Rouge camp on the eastern side of the island. He was shown some 1975 aerial photos of the island which showed the old Khmer Rouge compound. Witness two said the area had changed too much in twenty years for him to pinpoint the alleged grave site.
>
> Mr. Eik said during his tenure on Tang Island, he saw three alleged American bodies in a cave. Both witnesses heard from troops stationed on the island with the 410th Battalion that approximately one month after the American attack on the island, members of the 410th BN were patrolling on the northwestern end of the island when they encountered three American troops who were hiding in a cave on the north end of the island. They fought with the Americans for over two hours before the Americans were killed. Both witnesses said the Khmer Rouge did not bother to bury the bodies, but left them, their equipment, and shell casings in the cave. Mr. Eik said he saw the site while he was off duty and walking on the northwestern side of the island. He described the cave as a sort of trench approximately forty meters from the shoreline, on the northwestern side of the island. He described the Americans as wearing U.S. type uniforms. He could not remember anything else about the Americans…

Summary of the Investigation:

From 21 April 1996 to April 1996, Investigation Element One (IE1) and Recovery Element One (RE1) interviewed two witnesses who were in the Khmer Rouge and stationed on Koh Tang Island from September 1975 to June 1977. Both witnesses stayed on Koh Tang Island for seven days to locate the site where they allegedly saw the bodies of three Americans who evaded capture from the Khmer Rouge for two months before being (killed in a fire fight) on the west side of Koh Tang Island. RE1 interviewed one other witness who reported one possible burial location of Americans on the eastern shore of Koh Tang Island. The teams dug test pits at all reported burial locations, and did not find any remains or personal effects...[9]

Analysis of DNA, dental records and personal effects led to the announcement on May 8, 2000, that the remains of the following Marines from *Knife 31*; Lynn Blessing, Walter Boyd, Gregory Copenhaver, Andres Garcia, Antonio Sandoval and Kelton Turner had been identified. On June 23, 2000 it was announced that Richard Van de Geer (co-pilot), Bernard Gause and Ronald Manning, the two Navy corpsmen were identified.[10]

October 27, 2000 – Air Force Pilot 2nd Lt. Richard Van de Geer is buried at Arlington National Cemetery. Koh Tang Beach Club.

From January to March 2008 JPAC had an investigative team searching "for Americans lost during combat operations along the Cambodian coast." The Koh Tang Beach Club Veterans Organization received an email from Monte Marchant, Quartermaster of VFW 11575 Post in Cambodia, on February 23, 2008. Marchant wrote:

> I recently went with the JPAC (Joint POW/KIA Accounting Command) out to Koh Tang and I have some updates. Most importantly, there has been a recovery on the Island. There will be a repatriation ceremony on March 1st at the Phnom Penh airport. *Mayaquez* memorial Post members will be attending and participating in the ceremony ...

One of the dig sites on the West Beach at Koh Tang Island. JPAC photo courtesy of Koh Tang Beach Club.

Another excavation site on West Beach at Koh Tang Island. JPAC photo courtesy of the Koh Tang Beach Club.

The team is only eight members this time but without a doubt the best group I have met over the years here. They are very dedicated and from day one had that positive persona that made you think they would be successful. Our thanks to them and their dedication.[11]

On March 10, 2008, the Joint POW/MIA Accounting Command issued the following press release from their Public Affairs Office:

Release No. #08-02
JPAC Arrival Ceremony Set For March 14, 2008
Hickam Air Force Base, Hawaii

The Joint POW/MIA Accounting Command will conduct an Arrival Ceremony at 9 a.m., Friday in Hangar 35, Hickam AFB, to honor fallen U.S. military personnel whose identities remain unknown.

There will be three flag-draped transfer cases. Two of them are associated with the Vietnam War: one from the Lao People's Democratic Republic and one from the Kingdom of Cambodia. The remaining case is associated with a World War II loss in Palau.

Following the ceremony, the remains of these fallen service members will be transported to the Joint POW/MIA Accounting Command Central Identification Laboratory where the forensic identification process begins.

Once identifications are established, the names will be announced following the notification of next-of-kin …

Major Brian DeSantis:[12]

According to the Koh Tang Beach Club Veteran's website, "As of 1/30/09 we still have no definite word on what they found on the dig. The last word we got was they did recover some very small samples, but what they had were not the good enough quality to get DNA from."[13]

The *Mayaguez* incident is over but not forgotten. The outcome has been examined and continues to be studied. There are still brave men unaccounted for in the conflict. There are still families grieving over the results of those four days. There are still merchant ships being pirated in international waters.

The questions raised in the capture and recovery of the *Mayaguez* should be answered and those answers applied to similar future conflicts and events. Those four days in May 1975 took place during a time of turmoil and defeat. But even in defeat, in Vietnam the U.S. Merchant Marine was true to its motto, "In Peace and War." Captains Miller and Iacobacci, and the crews of the SS *Mayaguez* and USNS *Greenville Victory* were equal to, and, in fact, above the task.

It is a deep tragedy that our military men were killed, wounded or left behind. One can see, read and hear the angst expressed by the Marines involved in their correspondence and the audio-tapes of the veterans in the Koh Tang Beach Club Veterans Organization. However, *Semper Fi* exists and is stronger than ever.

This author has a profound respect for the Marine Code of Brothers, and for all the military men and mariners involved in the *Mayaguez* incident. There were a very special group of heroes.

APPENDICES

ENDNOTES

ABOUT THE AUTHOR

BIBLIOGRAPHY

INDEX

APPENDIX A

THE VIETNAM WAR

The Vietnam War consisted of two stages involving two opponents engaged in civil war. To the north was the Communist Democratic Republic of North Vietnam supported by the North Vietnamese Army (NVA) and its ally the National Liberation Front (NLF, also called the Vietcong). In the south was the Republic of Vietnam with its military, the Army of the Republic of South Vietnam (ARVN). Assisting South Vietnam in the Second Phase were approximately forty nations for which the United States provided most of the munitions and troops. The other countries involved were Australia, New Zealand, Philippines, South Korea and Thailand. North Vietnam was supported by China and Russia through financing and military aid. North Korea provided supplies.

The First Stage of the Vietnam War, more commonly known as the Indochina War occurred between 1946 and 1954. This stage was an outgrowth of French colonization which began in the mid-1800s. During World War II, French Vichy forces cooperated with the Japanese Imperial Military forces during their occupation of Vietnam, Cambodia and Laos. Toward the end of the war, Japan forced out the French colonial government and took control of Vietnam. Later that year a famine occurred in Hanoi, killing millions of people and resulting in political turmoil and revolt. Ho Chin Minh took advantage of the tragedy and became the government opposition's leader.

The Potsdam Conference, held on July 16, 1945, was attended by the big three powers with President Roosevelt, Premier Stalin and Prime Ministers Churchill and Atlee. They discussed a multitude of issues, including the future of Europe, and the unconditional surrender of the Japanese. They also decided on the ultimate division of Vietnam with the Chinese nationalists in the north and the British controlling the southern half. France, however, successfully convinced Britain, Russia and the United States to return the colonies she had before World War II — Cambodia, Laos and Vietnam.

After Japan surrendered, Ho Chi Minh's supporters occupied Hanoi. On September 2, 1945, Minh delivered his famous speech before a million people in Hanoi Square borrowing lines from the U.S. Declaration of Independence. It began:

> All men are created equal. They are endowed by their Creator with certain unalienable rights, among them are Life, Liberty, and the pursuit of Happiness. This immortal statement was made in the Declaration of Independence of the United States of America in 1776.
> In a broader sense, this means: All the peoples of the earth are equal from birth, all the peoples have a right to live, to be happy and free.
> The Declaration of the French Revolution made in 1791 on the Rights of man and the citizen, also states: "All men are born free and with equal rights, and must always remain free and have equal rights." Those are undeniable truths.

Although Ho Chi Minh tried to sound democratic, in reality he was a Communist. As a result, the First Stage of the Vietnam War, also called the First Indochina War, was set. It began with France taking control of her pre-war colonies: Cambodia, Laos and Vietnam. In an attempt to ease relations with these countries, France bestowed upon them a provisional form of sovereignty making them "associated" states of the French Union. It would take nine years for Ho Chi Minh and the Vietnamese nationalist army combined with the Viet Minh (League for the Independence of Vietnam) to fully dislodge France from their Vietnam.

America's foreign policy during that era, known as the Cold War, was fashioned from the Truman Doctrine. That is, an American presence was needed in Southeast Asia to prevent the spread of Communism. Furthermore, this policy was adopted by the succeeding Presidents: Eisenhower, Kennedy and Johnson. It was Eisenhower who coined the expression the "Domino Effect." If one country fell to the communists, the others would follow suit just like in the game of dominoes. The U.S. began to supply these three "associated states" with economic aid, military aid and training advisors via France.

As war broke out in 1946 between France and the Viet Minh, several key developments took place. In November both forces battled each other and the French proceeded to bomb Haiphong harbor. By doing so, the French were able to occupy Hanoi. Ho Chi Minh and his supporters were forced to flee into the jungle and surrounding areas. Toward the end of December, the Viet Minh launched their first large counterattack under the genius of Four Star General Vo Nguyen Giap. Giap had developed a method of attack that would be the cornerstone of his military strategy for the Second stage of the Vietnam War, ultimately achieving victory. His strategy was three-fold. First his forces would conduct guerilla and terrorist activities to control the population. Once the population was controlled and sympathetic to his cause, they would then be used to attack the fringe areas of the population. Larger military units then could be established to gain total control and support from all the people.

The First Indochina War came to an end by a brilliant maneuver conducted by Giap and his troops. The French were stationed in their garrison in the valley of Dien Bien Phu. General Giap, not caring how long it would take nor how many lives would be sacrificed was confident that he could hold out. He rallied his troops to total commitment. Rather then being caught in head-to-head battle on the valley plain, Giap moved his troops and armor over the mountainous terrain and surrounded the garrison from above. After a fifty-five-day battle, the French surrendered in May of 1954.

Two months later, France and the Viet Minh met in Geneva to sign a peace agreement. The Geneva Accords stated that Vietnam would be divided into two temporary zones: North and South divided by the 17th parallel. National elections would be held the following year.

Meanwhile, Ngo Dinh Diem was selected Prime Minister of the Southern Vietnam Republic, and Ho Chi Minh was installed as Communist leader of the north with Hanoi as its capital. With the departure of the French and the Geneva Peace Accord, the U.S. began to immediately support the South Vietnamese army with military aid and advisors to train their military. Interestingly, neither the U.S. nor South Vietnam agreed to the peace plan but didn't they do anything to impede it, either.

Fearing a well-developed Communist party, popular support for it and possible election fraud, national elections were stalled by Diem with U.S. support. The U.S. was slowly being dragged deeper into a political quagmire by sending more advisors. Meanwhile, with the communist's inability to gain more support via national elections, they again began to resort to military and terrorism campaigns to seek victory. Thus the two sides were drawn: one to prevent the spread of communism in Vietnam and the rest of Southeast Asia, and the other to rid the area of foreign colonial intervention and aggression. The Second Phase of the Vietnam War had begun.

During 1957, many of the Vietcong living in South Vietnam began moving northward to join the National Vietnamese Army (NVA). After being re-supplied and trained they infiltrated back into South Vietnam. These guerillas now called themselves the National Liberation Front (NLF). Philosophically speaking, the (NLF) were still Southern Vietnamese and wanted their own form of government, but one with a communist philosophy. They weren't interested in joining the northern part of Vietnam. Even so, further finances and supplies came from Hanoi.

The guerilla attacks escalated especially with the use of the Ho Chin Minh Trail (see page 5). This "trail" was an ingenious system of bicycle and walking paths that wound its way though mountainous and jungle roads stretching from North Vietnam through Cambodia, Laos and into South Vietnam.

Comprising more than 12,000 miles of roads and paths through some of the world's harshest geography, it was a vital gateway linking a divided nation … The road network extended from Mu Gia pass in the north, southward along the heavily forested western slopes of Laos, before entering South Vietnam at the northwestern end of the Plei Trap Valley – "the "Valley of Tears" – and points south. It was kept in good condition by 300,000 full-time workers and almost as many part-time farmers…[1]

The trail was the primary conduit that funneled arms, supplies, and troops to the North Vietnamese and Vietcong. A major problem for South Vietnam and its allies was, that according to the Geneva Accords, Laos and Cambodia were neutral countries and were not supposed to be involved in the conflict.

Travel on the trail was slow in the beginning of the war.

> "It took six months to travel from North Vietnam to Saigon … But the more people who traveled along the route the easier it became. By 1970, fit and experienced soldiers could make the journey in six weeks… As many as 20,000 soldiers a month came from Hanoi in this way."[2]
>
> "The number of soldiers and military specialists sent to southern battlefields rose according to the increasingly fierce features of the war. In 1960, more than 1,200 people went south. By 1974, the number reached nearly 296,200. Over the next sixteen-year period, approximately 1,349,000 tonnes of weapons, military equipment and food was transported through the Ho Chi Minh Trail to the front lines."[3]

In 1963, Buddhists made up two thirds of the South Vietnamese population. During this time they began to revolt against the Diem government maintaining that he was practicing religious discrimination against them. Diem countered by ordering their temples burned and many were also arrested. Much of this work was carried out by Diem's brother, Ngo Dinh Nhu. Many monks burned themselves in protest.

Diem ignored President Kennedy's request that he change his policy toward the Buddhists. Kennedy, not seeing his advice followed, sought support of a group of South Vietnamese generals to overthrow Diem. Subsequently, both Diem and his brother were killed in early November 1963, three weeks before Kennedy was killed. With the death of Diem, South Vietnam fell into total chaos which facilitated the infiltration into South Vietnam.

Eventually, a government was established, in 1967, with the election of General Nguyen Van Thieu as President. The newly installed President Lyndon Johnson continued U.S. policy in the area. It was during Johnson's presidency that the American troop involvement escalated from the first marines arriving with 20,000 troops to a total of some 540,000 troops in 1969.

On August 2, 1964, the North Vietnamese fired upon the U.S. destroyer *Maddox*. The U.S.S. *Maddox* had been ordered into the Gulf of Tonkin, and to gather intelligence while cruising the North Vietnamese coast. The "information would support South Vietnamese against North Vietnam."[4]

That afternoon, *Maddox* was sailing in international waters when she was suddenly attacked by three North Vietnamese motor torpedo boats. *Maddox*, with help from air support supplied by the aircraft carrier, USS *Ticonderoga*, thwarted the attack damaging all three boats and setting one on fire.

During the next evening, South Vietnam attacked North Vietnamese installations. The following day, August 4th, *Maddox* was accompanied by the destroyer *Turner C. Joy* as they both patrolled the North Vietnamese coastline. During the evening horrendous weather set in including thunderstorms that severely affected the radar.

On the night of 4 August, the warships reported making contact and then being attacked by several fast craft far out to sea. Officers in the naval chain of command and the U.S. leaders in Washington

USS Maddox (DD-731). U.S. Navy.

were persuaded by interpretation of the special intelligence and reports from the ships that the North Vietnamese naval forces had attacked the two destroyers. More recent analysis of that data and additional information gathered on 4 August episode now makes it clear that North Vietnamese naval forces did not attack *Maddox* and *Turner Joy* that night in the summer of 1964.[5]

The attack on August 2nd actually took place in daylight and was photographed along with the damaged Vietnamese torpedo boats. The evidence of the attack existed. No such evidence existed on the stormy night of August 4 nor was any damage found in the water or on the ships the next day. In an audiotape made later, Admiral U.S. Sharpe, Commander of the Pacific Forces gave the following information to General Burchinal, Air Force General of the Joint Chiefs of Staff, who was eagerly awaiting information to be relayed to Secretary McNamara and President Johnson:

Adm. Sharp: "It does appear now that a lot of these torpedo attacks were torpedoes reported in the water from the sonar man, you see, and probably a lot of them inaccurate because whenever they get keyed up on a thing like this everything they hear on

Sonar is a torpedo."

Gen. Burchinal: "You're pretty sure there was a torpedo attack?"

Adm. Sharp: "No doubt about that, I think."[6]

Furthermore, "Though information obtained well after the fact indicates that there was actually no North Vietnamese attack that night, U.S. authorities were convinced at the time that one had taken place, and reacted by sending planes from the carriers *Ticonderoga* and *Constellation* to hit the North Vietnamese torpedo boats and fuel facilities."[7]

Cdr. James B. Stockdale, while commanding jets off the carrier *Ticonderoga* wrote in a later article and in his memoir:

> There was absolutely no gunfire except our own, no PT boat wakes, not a candle light let alone a burning ship. None could have been there and not have been seen on such a black night ... and I had the best seat in the house from which to detect boats — if there were any. I didn't have to look through the surface haze and spray like the destroyers did, and yet I could see the destroyers' ever more vividly.[8]

An August 28th Top-Secret Report written for President Johnson of the actions that took place on August 4th summarized Capt. John Herrick's actions:

> ... a review of the action makes many recorded contacts and torpedoes fired "appear doubtful." "Freak weather effects" on radar, and "overeager sonarmen" may have accounted for many reports. "No visual sightings" have been reported by *Maddox*, and the Commander suggests that a "complete evaluation" be undertaken before any action.[9]

Thus, the resulting consequences of this alleged attack were enormous. President Johnson and Secretary of Defense Robert McNamara were able to persuade the U.S. Congress to pass a resolution expanding Johnson's powers. In his message to Congress on August 5, 1964, President Johnson said:

These latest actions of the North Vietnamese regime has given a new and grave turn to the already serious situation in southeast Asia...Our commitments in that area are well known to the Congress. They were first made by President Eisenhower. They were further defined in the Southeast Asia Collective Defense Treaty approved by the Senate in February 1955. This treaty with its accompanying protocol obligates the United States and other members to act in accordance with their constitutional processes to meet Communist aggression against any of the parties or protocol states.

Our Policy in southeast Asia has been consistent and unchanged since 1955. I summarized it on June 2nd in four simple propositions:

1. America keeps her word. Here as elsewhere, we must and shall honor our commitments.
2. The issue is the future of southeast Asia as a whole. A threat to any nation in that region is a threat to all, and a threat to us.
3. Our purpose is peace. We have no military, political, or territorial ambitions in the area.
4. This is not a jungle war, but struggle for freedom on every front of human activity. Our military and economic assistance to South Vietnam and Laos in particular has the purpose of helping these countries to repel aggression and strengthen their independence.

The threat to the free nations of southeast Asia has long been clear. The North Vietnamese regime has constantly sought to take over South Vietnam and Laos. This Communist regime has violated the Geneva Accords for Vietnam. It has systematically conducted a campaign of subversion, which includes the direction, training, and supply of personnel and arms for the conduct of guerilla warfare in South Vietnamese territory. In Laos, the North Vietnamese regime has maintained military forces, used Laotian territory for infiltration into South Vietnam, and most recently carried out combat operations - all in direct violation of the Geneva agreements of 1962.

In recent months, the actions of the North Vietnamese regime have become steadily more threatening ...

As President of the United States I have concluded that I should now ask the Congress, on its part, to join it in affirming the national determination that all such attacks will be met, and that the United States will continue in its basic policy of assisting the free nations of the area to defend their freedom.

As I have repeatedly made clear the United States intends no rashness, and seeks no wider war. We must make it clear to all that the United States is united in its determination to bring about the end of Communist subversion and aggression in the area ...

On August 7, 1964 both Houses of Congress approved the Tonkin Gulf Resolution, opening the door and escalating the war in Vietnam. In part, it stated:

Joint Resolution of Congress
H.J. RES 1145 August 7, 1964

... That the Congress approves and supports the determination of the President, as Commander in Chief, to take all necessary measures to repel any armed attack against the forces of the United States and to prevent further aggression ...

Section 3. This resolution shall expire when the President shall determine that the peace and security of the area is reasonably assured by international conditions created by action of the United Nations or otherwise, except that it may be determined earlier by concurrent resolution of Congress.

Late in 1964, the U.S. developed its plan to end the war. The plan was essentially twofold; large scale bombing of the north by the huge B-52s and a military build-up to support the ground warfare in the south. The bombing campaign was known as code name *Operation Rolling Thunder*. The purpose of the bombing was to destroy the North Vietnamese will to fight, their industrial capacity and the Ho Chi Minh Trail preventing the re-supplying of troops, armor and supplies. It was felt that the plan would bring the North Vietnamese quickly to the peace table.

The U.S seriously underestimated the resolve of the North Vietnamese as they decided to fight a long protracted war using guerilla tactics that eventually would wear down the U.S. resolve to continue fighting. The North Vietnamese were correct. Furthermore, by lengthening the war, public opinion was changed in the United States. The American public, for the most part, wanted U.S. troops out of Vietnam.

The U.S. did inflict heavy damage with their bombing raids in the north but Russia and China were able to re-supply the North

Vietnamese. The U.S. was usually the victor concerning ground warfare in the south. But here again, the North Vietnamese and Viet Cong preferred guerilla warfare only to return to the jungle to be refortified and supplied from the Ho Chi Minh Trail.

The war took a dramatic turn in what became known as the Tet Offensive. This took place on January 30, 1968 which was the beginning of the Vietnamese New Year. A series of attacks on South Vietnam was planned by North Vietnamese General Vo Nguyen Giap. Attacks occurred in most of the major southern cities with the goal to incite riots against the U.S. and to overthrow the South Vietnamese government. The fighting was particularly severe in Saigon and Hue. A war that was supposedly being won by South Vietnam and its allies was now seen as a negative in outcome based on the ferocity of the Tet offensive.

On March 31, 1968, President Johnson made two profound announcements; the bombing runs would be halted and he would not run for re-election. By not seeking re-election American policy was now ambiguous at best. The bombing was halted during peace talks that were held that spring. There had been previous peace attempts along with bombing cessations but the bottom line was that the U.S. and other foreign nations had to completely withdraw from the country before negotiations could take place.

The U.S. Army and Marines were also facing a troop shortage that year. During October an involuntary second-term recall was put into effect. This resulted in 25,000 more troops being sent back to Vietnam. By year's end, U.S. troop strength reached its peak of about 536,000.

On October 31st, President Johnson announced another cessation to the war because of progress at the Paris Peace Talks. He said, "…all air, naval, and artillery bombardment of North Vietnam would cease as of 8 A.M., Washington time, Friday morning." The negotiations eventually broke down.

On November 5th, Richard Nixon was elected President.

In March 1969, President Nixon ordered the bombing of Cambodia to begin. A few months later Nixon put forth his new policy which was called "Vietnamization of the War." This policy called for the gradual reduction of U.S. troops beginning with 25,000 in July of 1969. In addition, "Vietnamization" meant that more and more responsibility for the conduct of the war would be transferred over to the South Vietnamese. The training of South Vietnamese forces was increased to support this policy.

In the fall of 1969, Ho Chi Minh died and another 65,000 U.S. troops were brought home. Tremendous anti-war demonstrations also began in Washington, D.C. The American public also learned of the Mai Lai Massacre, which further incited them against the war. Troop strength at the end of 1969 was 475,000.

In April 1970, President Nixon ordered the invasion of Cambodia to shut down the supply centers along the Ho Chi Minh Trail and the renewal of attacks on North Vietnam. This ignited college protests across the United States. One of these riots took place at Kent State University where the National Guard killed several students. Three months after the campaign began Nixon ended it, but he also renewed the bombing of North Vietnam.

During 1971 the South Vietnamese were fulfilling their role in "Vietnamization." They fought the North Vietnamese in the south, in Laos, and in Cambodia. American public opinion became more and more negative toward the war. The situation was complicated by the presidential election held in South Vietnam. Nguyen Van Thieu won another four-year term. During this time, Australia and New Zealand announced that their troops would be withdrawn from Vietnam by the end of 1971. U.S. troop level was now below 200,000.

An American presidential election occurred in 1972. Just before it occurred, Secretary of State Kissinger announced that "peace was at hand." President Nixon thoroughly defeated George McGovern. Following the election, heavy bombing resumed in Hanoi and Haiphong. This shocked and further angered the American people and resulted in another halt in bombing at the end of December 1972.

In mid-January President Nixon called for a total cessation of the war and on January 27, 1973 the Paris Peace Accords were signed. The United States agreed to the following points in the treaty:

1. Withdrawal of all U.S. troops.
2. Release of North Vietnamese prisoners of war.
3. Establishment of an international peace keeping force.
4. The right of the South Vietnamese to govern themselves.
5. The North would be allowed to keep their troops in the South but not to replace them.

Nixon was able to convince the South Vietnamese that their country wouldn't be abandoned by the United States.

The remaining U.S. forces left Vietnam on March 29, 1973. However, the war between North and South Vietnam continued throughout 1973 and into 1974. In January 1975, the North Vietnamese and Vietcong attacked Phuoc Long province, easily defeating the South Vietnamese. This set the final stage as the South Vietnamese retreated from the Central Highlands. Subsequently the North Vietnamese moved on Saigon capturing the city on April 30, 1975. After the surrender, the North Vietnamese announced the country would be reunified and called the Socialist Republic of Vietnam. This became effective on July 2, 1976. In addition Saigon was renamed Ho Chi Minh City.

The Communist-controlled government of North Vietnam was correct in their war philosophy. They had won the fifteen year war of attrition.

APPENDIX B

HISTORY OF THE WARTIME

U.S. MERCHANT MARINE

At the beginning of the War for Independence there were only thirty-one ships in the Continental Navy. In addition, there were privateers. These were privately-owned, commissioned and armed merchant ships. They operated under the authority of a device known as a *Letter of Marque.* This gave a vessel the right to attack an enemy vessel. Congress authorized privateering under Article I, section 8 of the Constitution which gave Congress the power "To declare War, grant Letters of Marque and Reprisal, and make Rules concerning Captures on Land and Water."

One of the outstanding differences between a privateer and a naval ship was the lack of constraint placed on the vessel.

> Privateers were individualists. They liked to do things their own way, and resented regulation. Unlike many vessels, privateers never had to fight anything close to their own size. They could run away if they thought running away the best course. They were not held down by onerous duties, like patrolling or blockading an enemy port.[1]

When the war began, the total number of vessels attributed to the Continental navy and others within the colonies was "…

sixty-four vessels of all descriptions, carrying a total of 1,242 guns and swivels. This force captured 196 vessels. Of the privateers there were 792 carrying more than 13,000 guns and swivels. These vessels captured or destroyed about 600 British vessels."[2]

In addition to lack of constraint American privateers had two other valuable assets. "Although the Americans had no navy as such, they did have a lot of sailors — fishermen and traders who knew how to handle small, fast ships. They also had another big advantage — they were familiar with much of the coastline."[3]

The first sea battle of the Revolutionary War took place in Machias, Maine and involved the privateers *Polly* and *Unity* owned by Captain Ichabod Jones. Under the leadership of patriots Benjamin Foster and Jeremiah O'Brien the British warship, *Margaretta* was captured.[4] In World War II, a Liberty ship was named after the patriot *Jeremiah O'Brien*. Today, the *Jeremiah O'Brien* is a national historic museum located in San Francisco.

The American Revolutionary War was won, thanks in large part, to American Privateers. In "Peace and War," became the motto for the U.S. Merchant Marine.

War of 1812

During the American Revolution, the Continental Congress developed a small navy which, at its peak, totaled sixty-four ships. By war's end only a few remained.[5] This small number was disbanded and forgotten until war broke out in Europe in 1793. At this time the Barbary pirates of North Africa began preying on American commercial ships in the Mediterranean. Seeing a need to protect U.S. interests, Congress passed a Naval Act in March 1794 providing for the construction of six frigates — the forty-four-gun frigates *Constitution*, *United States*, and *President* and the thirty-six-gun frigates *Congress*, *Consolation*, and *Chesapeake*. Successful diplomacy, however, cut short the program.[6] Then, in 1797, Congress established the United States Navy. In 1798 it authorized the first secretary of the Navy, Benjamin Stoddert.

In 1812 the United States declared war against Great Britain for taking seaman off American ships and impressing them into duty on British warships. "Between the years 1808 and 1811, 6,000 bona fide U.S. citizens were impressed. Many were killed in service or died of disease, leaving embittered families back home."[7]

When this war broke out the U.S. Navy had only "seventeen vessels, carrying 442 guns and 5,000 men. Of these only eight, in the first few months of the war, were able to get to sea."[8] Hence a great cry went out once again to include American privateers in the defense of the new country:

> At the first sound of war our merchants hastened to repeat their marvelous achievements on the ocean in the struggle for independence. Every available pilot boat, merchant craft, coasting vessel, and fishing smack was quickly overhauled, mounted with a few guns and sent out with a commission to "burn, sink, and destroy." A newspaper article dated July 1st, 1812, noted: "The people in the Eastern States are laboring almost night and day to fit out privateers ..."[9]

Over 500 privateers eventually would fight in the war of 1812. They "did great damage to the British and they had a great effect on the outcome of the war.... In all, they captured or destroyed about 1,350 British merchantmen, taking home prizes worth $39 million."[10]

The Mexican-American War (1846-1848)

The Mexican-American War was fought for two reasons: America's desire to expand westward (Manifest Destiny) and Mexico's resisting its annexation of Texas after the Texas War of Independence. This war was a new venture for the American army and navy. Never before had such large numbers of troops, supplies, and munitions been required to be shipped to a foreign country.

American privateers at the outset weren't needed because the American Navy was able to blockade the Mexican ports. As the war developed, huge amounts of goods and personnel had to be shipped and the responsibility for shipping fell on the shoulders of Quartermaster General of the Army, Brigadier General Thomas S. Jesup.

In November 1846, a key objective was developed to support General Winfield Scott and his inland attack of Mexico City. In order to do this Veracruz was captured first. But then a logistical nightmare faced General Scott. He

> ... projected that he would need 4,000 regulars, 10,000 volunteers, and 1,000 marines and sailors; 50 transports of 500 to 750 tons to carry the force; and a siege train of 8-inch howitzers, 24-pounders, and 40 to 50 mortars. For the initial landing on the beach, he wanted 140 surf boats that could land 5,000 men and 8 artillery pieces ... For shipment to the theater, they were to be nested within each other aboard the transport.[11]

To transport what was needed, General Scott turned to the privateers of the American merchant marine. In Atlantic ports the Quartermaster's Department obtained fifty-three ships — barks, brigs, and schooners, mostly chartered, which it used for transporting men and supplies southward. On the Gulf Coast, where Jesup personally assumed charge of operations, 163 vessels — all that could be chartered at reasonable rate — were collected at New Orleans, Point Isabel, and Tampico, the second largest Mexican port, which had been seized by the Navy in November.[12]

The result was the successful invasion of Vera Cruz on March 8, 1847. "The Mexican commander chose not to oppose the landing, so over 8,600 men were landed without a single loss in just over four hours. This was an unprecedented military achievement for the time."[13]

The American merchant marine had supplied and operated the transport ships for our country's first overseas expeditionary force.

The American Civil War

As the war began, U.S. commerce ranked second in the world to Great Britain. Ten percent of the tonnage belonged to the Confederacy. This ten percent was quickly destroyed by northern blockade vessels.[14]

The United States Navy had just a few dozen vessels which were inadequate to enforce a blockade. Once again the U.S. merchant marine came forward. "The Navy drew six hundred vessels from the merchant marine, exceeding one million tons, and manned by about 70,000 seamen, for blockades and armed service."[15]

The first campaign objective of the North was the "establishment of a blockade of all Southern seaports, thus cutting off imports of materiél, medical supplies, and household goods. By preventing the sale of cotton abroad in exchange for war materiél, the union blockade changed the balance of power in the war."[16]

The South did use privateers involving the small number of her merchant ships on their side. "This effort was short-lived because of the effectiveness of the blockade, the successful capture of privateers by the North, and their subsequent trials for piracy. Confederate privateers captured forty Yankee ships, but by February 1863 only the schooner *Retribution* remained."[17]

According to Winthrop Marvin:

> … without its great merchant marine of 1861, the United States could never have drawn the relentless cordon of the blockade about the Southern coasts, which in the end, smothered and starved the Confederacy.
>
> More than half of the ships, four-fifths of the officers, five-sixths of the men who performed this vital work came directly from the merchant service.
>
> When the Civil War began, United States Navy contained only thirty steamships of war, with about twice as many obsolete sailing vessels. There were 1,450 officers and 7,600 seamen. Before the war ended, this force had been expanded to 600 steamers, 9,000 officers, and 51,000 seamen.[18]

When the war ended in 1865, the Quartermaster General, "owned or chartered 719 vessels for use in the oceans and lakes, with a total tonnage of 224,984. The Rail and River Transportation division owned ninety-one steamers, 352 barges, and 139 boats."[19]

The American Civil War brought about many changes in how wars were fought and in the maritime industry. Unfortunately, despite the progress in development, American shipbuilding came to a standstill in the later part of the 19th century.

The Spanish-American War

Following the Civil War, America was ready to expand its economy and industry. However, most of the expansion was westward, by land. Building ships had become a low priority.

> The nation that had been a leading maritime and naval power turned away from seaports and rotting ships and concentrated on railroads and industries, which had little visible connection with the sea. Within a decade about the only people who could see any reason for maintaining a Navy were a few senior officers who believed that a fighting fleet was as necessary in keeping the peace as in winning the war.[20]

The attitude began to change as America became more industrialized and recognized the need for commercial ships to compete in worldwide commerce. She also needed a navy to protect these ventures and U.S. interests.

> In 1883 Congress authorized the building of four steam powered, steel-hulled ships: the Cruisers *Atlanta*, *Boston*, and *Chicago* and the small despatch boat *Dolphin*. Painted white, the ships were known as the White Squadron and also as the ABCD ships. Annually, for the next ten years, Congress authorized more new ships. This shipbuilding program, which resulted in improved techniques for steel production and manufacture, reached its height in 1889 when Congress appropriated funds for the Navy's first true battleships ...[21]

Late in the 19th century, America surpassed Britain in coal, iron and steel production. But little of this production was directed toward expanding the merchant fleets.

In 1895, when the Armed Forces again had a great need for oceangoing ships, the Merchant Marine was no longer in a position to supply all the required shipping as it had done in the past, because it had dwindled away to such an extent that American ships carried only ten percent of the exports of the United States. The Army and Navy had to buy foreign vessels and take care of their own ship operating requirements by establishing sea transportation services. At the outbreak of war with Spain the Quartermaster had only ten small harbor boats and was unprepared for a large overseas movement. The Navy was well-equipped with warships to fight a war with a weak country like Spain, but they lacked supply ships and coaling facilities both at home and abroad.[22]

The Navy had to spend approximately $5 million in five Navy yards to prepare auxiliary merchant vessels for warfare. Private shipyards also assisted employing some 6,000 men. These merchant vessels were strengthened to withstand gunfire, wood removed, batteries installed, engines updated, and fully outfitted. Every possible merchant ship was used.[23]

This was the first war that America fought abroad, reaching as far as the Philippines. Ocean transportation was obviously essential to carry out the war plans. The army had no previous experience in transporting soldiers and munitions except during the Mexican-American war.

Even before the war was declared, the Quartermaster General, Brigadier General Marshall I. Ludington, began investigating the availability of commercial vessels that could be chartered as transports. Congress [was] opposed to granting U.S. registry to foreign vessels, so for the Cuba expedition the army was limited to chartering U.S. vessels involved in the Atlantic and Gulf coastal trade. By 1 July, the Quartermaster Department had chartered forty-three transports, four water boats, three steam lighters, two ocean tugs, and three decked barges for Cuba; another fourteen transports were charted on the Pacific Coast for the Philippine expeditions. More were charted in July and August. When enough vessels could not be chartered, the Army purchased fourteen steam ships and quickly outfitted them to carry troops to Cuba and Puerto Rico.[24]

Although the Spanish-American War was of a short duration, glaring weaknesses in America's preparedness became evident.

The U.S. Merchant Marine was not prepared to assist in the event of a future war.

World War I

At the beginning of World War I, the American merchant marine was in dire shape. So much so, that the United States found itself in the precarious situation of having to depend upon foreign nations to export its troops and war materiels.

The obvious went unheeded until 1914 when the country was caught dozing in isolation with ninety percent of its overseas commerce in foreign bottoms. Quickly, most of that ninety percent was withdrawn by its owners rather than risk it in war. The United States paid a billion dollar freight bill for what space could be had in the three years to 1917. Mountains of goods piled up.[25]

Once the United States entered the war, the problem of getting the troops and their supplies overseas was magnified because she had no transport ships. "The U.S. merchant fleet in 1917 consisted of a little over 500,000 tons of steam and motor vessels, plus a considerable number of sailing craft."[26]

What was needed was a massive ship construction program. Congress responded with the Shipping Act of 1916. This act established a government agency, the U.S. Shipping Board, which was given the authority to set up The Emergency Fleet Corporation to build ships. That organization built a total of 2,318 vessels from 1918 to 1922. Unfortunately, most of them were delivered after the war was over. In addition, because they were hurriedly designed under emergency conditions, many of these vessels were not suited to peacetime use.[27]

World War I saw a radical increase in merchant mariners killed and ships sunk. "The total of merchant marine ships sunk in World War I was 197 compared to the U.S. Navy's ninety-eight. The number of mariners killed was 629 compared to 1,323 for the Navy."[28]

World War II

Following World War I, ship construction was practically

nonexistent. With the Great Depression shipbuilding came to a standstill. The ships built during World War I and completed after the war were the only tonnage available. Furthermore, a drastic problem developed in the 1930s as these World War I ships became outdated. Their projected life span was only fifteen years. The U.S. merchant fleet fell behind the world powers. According to the Maritime Administration, "In 1936, our merchant marine was fourth among the six leading maritime nations in tonnage, sixth in vessels ten years of age or less, fifth in vessels with speeds of 12 knots or more."[29]

In 1936, the cornerstone of the new U.S. merchant marine was laid by the passage of the Merchant Marine Act of 1936. Passage of this Act came just as war loomed in Europe and Asia. With the passage of the Merchant Marine Act, five hundred ships were to be built over the next ten years. The Act declared a national policy:

> ... to foster the development and encourage the maintenance of a merchant marine sufficient to carry the domestic water-borne commerce and a substantial portion of the foreign commerce of the country in essential trades, capable of serving as a naval and military auxiliary in time of war, owned and operated in so far as practicable by citizens of the United States, and composed of the best equipped, safest, and most suitable type of vessels, constructed in the United States, manned by a trained and efficient citizen personal.
>
> To obtain such a fleet, the Act Provided for construction and operating subsidies to be paid by the government to shipping lines. The subsidies were designed to equal the difference between the cost of building and operating ships under the American flag and the much lower cost of under foreign flags.[30]

The building of ships began, but soon the United States found herself immersed in a global war. Ship construction was inadequate, primarily because of Germany's use of the submarine. With the fall of France in 1940, German U-boats roamed the Atlantic Ocean sinking ships transporting vital supplies to Britain and Russia. When Germany declared war on the U.S. in 1941, Hitler sent his U-boat's off the coast of the United States. They caused terrible havoc and destruction. In 1942 alone, off the East Coast, Caribbean, Gulf and North Atlantic, "378 American ships were sunk or damaged."[31] It wasn't until 1943 that the U.S. was able to turn this tide of affairs by the construction of more ships and by effectively using the convoy system with better defensive measures involving radar and air support. The ship construction program was a massive operation which will never be duplicated again.

Within a year-and-a-half after the United States entered the war, shipyards were building ships faster than the enemy was able to sink them. From 1942 through 1945 United States shipyards built 5,592 merchant ships, of which 2,710 were Liberty ships, 414 were the faster Victory type [used for the longer distances across the Pacific Ocean], 651 were tankers, 417 were standard cargo ships, and the remaining 1,409 were military or minor types.[32]

The Liberty ship became the backbone of the merchant fleet. They were slow but could carry tremendous cargo loads; as much as four railroad trains of seventy cars each. As American shipyards became more efficient the construction time to build a Liberty ship was reduced from five months down to the record time [less than five days] it took to construct the SS *Robert E Peary*. The Liberty ship was so vital to Allied success because it took between seven and fifteen tons of supplies to support one G.I. for a year overseas. "During 1945, the merchant marine delivered 17 million pounds of cargo every hour including ammunition, airplanes, aviation fuel, PT boats, explosives, tanks, Jeeps, trucks, gasoline, medicines, locomotives, boots, and food rations."[33]

To crew these ships, a massive training program involving a huge amount of men, who volunteered their services, was necessary. At the beginning of the war there were only 55,000 trained men available. By war's end, the War Shipping Administration would train 262,474 graduates.[34]

There were three factors why the Allies won the war; the fighting force overseas, the work force at home and the United States Merchant Marine which served as the vital link between the other two. The U.S. Merchant Marine took part in every invasion. They were sworn in as military auxiliaries and assisted the U.S. Navy Armed Guard gunners who protected the ships. In the process, the U. S. merchant marine paid a tremendous price in ships lost and men killed.

"According to the War Shipping Administration, the U.S. Merchant Marine suffered the highest rate of casualties of any service in World War II. Officially, a total of 1,554 ships were sunk due to war conditions, including 733 ships of over 1,000 gross tons. Hundreds of other ships were damaged by torpedoes, shelling, bombs, kamikazes, mines, etc."[35] An update compiled by the American Merchant Marine at War organization as of July 2006, shows "that 8,421 mariners died in World War II. If you include POWs killed plus those who died of wounds ashore, the total then becomes 9,521 or a 1 in 26 ratio."[36]

Many testimonials were given concerning the superlative job that the U.S. Merchant Marine performed during war:

> Every man in the Allied command is quick to express his admiration for the loyalty, courage, and fortitude of the officers and men of the Merchant Marine. ... they have never failed us ... When final victory is ours there is no organization that will share its credit more deservedly than the Merchant Marine.
>
> General Dwight D. Eisenhower

> To you who answered the call of your country and served in its Merchant Marine to bring about the total defeat of the enemy, I extend a heartfelt thanks of the Nation.
>
> President Harry S. Truman

> ... they shared the heaviest enemy fire ... they have suffered in bloodshed and death ... They have contributed tremendously to our success. I hold no branch in higher esteem than the Merchant Marine Services.
>
> General Douglas MacArthur

> ... the Navy has been dependent upon the Merchant Marine to
> supply our far-flung fleet and bases. Without this support the Navy
> could not have accomplished its mission. I take great pleasure in
> expressing the Navy's heartfelt thanks ... to the officers and men
> of the Merchant Marine for their magnificent support during World
> War II ... a job well done.
>
> Fleet Admiral Ernest J. King,
Commander-in-Chief of the U.S. Navy
Chief of Naval Operations

World War II was the defining point of the 20th century. It was also the United States Merchant Marines' finest hour.

Following World War II it became the responsibility of the merchant marine to transport our troops and enemy troops back from overseas.

While action by Japanese units continued in various areas throughout the Pacific, the U.S. Merchant Marine was given the job of transporting the surrendered armies back to Japan. The Merchant Marine also had to return the tired, wounded, and dead U.S. troops home, and to bring replacement forces and supplies for the Occupation. Arms and bombs had to be returned to the U.S. In December 1945, the War Shipping Administration listed 1,200 sailings — 400 more than in the busiest month of the previous four years. Forty-nine U.S. merchant ships were sunk or damaged after V-J Day with at least seven mariners killed and thirty wounded.[37]

On September 1st, 1946 the War Shipping Administration was dissolved. Ship control was given back to the owners as quickly as possible and was completed by the end of 1947. Meanwhile, the surplus vessels were sold according to the Merchant Ships Sales Act of 1946. This Act allowed American companies to purchase the best ships available of those left over from the war. Many of the Liberty ships were also sold to foreign countries to help them recover economically from World War II. In 1951 the act expired. A total of "1,956 ships had been sold, 843 to American and 1,113 to foreign flag operators ..."[38]

Of equal importance to ship sales was the establishment of
a reserve fleet, the National Defense Reserve Fleet (NDRF) for
use during emergencies. These ships were laid up in eight sites
the United States. The total number of the ships in the Reserve
Fleet would reach a maximum of "2,227 ships in 1950."[39]

To eradicate the problems that existed during World War
II whereby four government agencies competed for the use
of American merchant ships, the Secretary of Defense, James
Forrestal declared in December 1948 that, "all military sea
transport including Army transports would be placed under
Navy command."[40] Thus the Military Sea Transportation Service
(MSTS) was created in July 1949.

Korean War

The Korean War began on June 25, 1950 as more than 130,000
North Korean soldiers crossed the 38th parallel and attacked
South Korea. The attack was a complete success because the
South Koreans had only about 35,000 soldiers in their army. The
North Korean army overran most of the country except for the
area around Pusan.

Abiding by her United Nations commitment, the United
States joined other U.N. members to halt the aggressor. Other
large contributors to the U.N effort were Australia, Canada,
Great Britain, and New Zealand.

There were two problems confronting the initial efforts of
the United States: One, mobilizing ships, supplies and troops.
Two, providing coal and food to countries in Europe and Asia
who were suffering from a severe winter. "About 700 ships were
activated from NDRF for services to the Far East. In addition,
a worldwide tonnage shortage shortfall between 1951 and 1953
required reactivation of over 600 ships to lift coal to Northern
Europe and grain to India …[41]

Furthermore, just like in World War II, the "backbone" of
merchant ships crossing the Pacific Ocean provided the Allies
with the necessary supplies and troops for victory.

From just six ships under charter when the war began, this total peaked at 255. According to the Military Sea Transportation Service (MSTS), eighty-five percent of the dry cargo requirements during the Korean War were met through commercial vessels — only five percent were shipped by air. More than $475 million, or seventy-five percent of the MSTS operating budget for calendar year 1952, was paid directly to commercial shipping interests.

In addition to the ships assigned directly to MSTS, 130 laid-up Victory ships in the NDRF were broken out by the Maritime Administration and assigned under time-charters to private shipping firms for charter to MSTS.

Ships of MSTS not only provided supplies but also served as naval auxiliaries. When the U.S. X Corps went ashore at Inchon in September 1950, thirteen USNS cargo ships, twenty-six chartered American and thirty-four Japanese-manned merchant ships, under the operational control of the MSTS, participated in the invasion.

Sealift responsibilities were accomplished on short notice during the Korean War. Initially American troops lacked the vital equipment to fight the North Koreans, but military and commercial vessels quickly began delivering the fighting tools needed to turn back the enemy. According to MSTS, seven tons of supplies were needed for every Marine or soldier bound for Korea and an additional one for each month thereafter. Cargo ships unloaded supplies around the clock, making Pusan a bustling port. The success of the U.S. Merchant Marine during this crisis hammered home to critics the importance of maritime preparedness and the folly of efforts to scuttle the merchant fleet.

In addition to delivering equipment to American forces, more than ninety percent of all American and other United Nations' troops supplies and equipment were delivered to Korea through MSTS with the assistance of commercial cargo vessels.[42]

The U.N. forces fought back and with the success of General Douglas MacArthur's plan to cut the Communist forces in half by landing at Inchon, the North Koreans were in retreat. The success was short-lived for the People's Republic of China entered the war in November 1950 with over 100,000 troops. U.N forces were then on retreat moving eastward to the coastal ports of Hungnam and Wonsan. Now the process of evacuation of troops, materiel and refugees fleeing from North Korea began.

Generally described as an "amphibious operation in reverse," the evacuation of Hungnam encompassed the safe withdrawal of the bulk of UN forces in eastern North Korea. It was the largest sealift since the 1945 Okinawa operation. In barely two weeks, over a hundred-thousand military personnel, 17,500 vehicles and 350,000 measurement tons of cargo were pulled out. In comparison with the retreat in central and western Korea, little was left behind. Even broken-down vehicles were loaded and lifted out. Also departing North Korea through Hungnam were some 91,000 refugees, a large number, but not nearly as many as had gathered to leave.[43]

The statistics involved in this massive evacuation were incredible and are a credit to the U.S. Merchant Marine.

"In an operation reminiscent of Dunkirk: 193 shiploads rescued 105,000 U.N. troops; 91,000 refugees; 350,000 MT of cargo; and 17,500 vehicles from encirclement and delivered them to the port of Pusan. One ship in particular, the SS *Meredith Victory* under the command of Capt. Leonard P. La Rue, activated from the NDRF, operated by Moore-McCormick Lines, and licensed to carry twelve passengers, transported over 14,000 refugees in one single voyage. First mate D. S. Savastio, with nothing but first aid training, delivered five babies during the three-day passage to Pusan. Ten years later, the Maritime Administration honored the crew by awarding them a Gallant Ship Award."[44]

Summarizing the U.S. merchant marine's contribution in the Korean War, MARAD (Maritime Administration) released a Fact Sheet demonstrating the U.S. merchant marine's "key role" in the effort:

> The merchant marine moved 2,600,000 tons of cargo, petroleum products not included, from Continental United States to the Pacific Theater. 80 percent of this cargo was carried in privately Operated American-flag vessels.
>
> Merchant ships moved 300 times more cargo than air transports.

Approximately 80 privately-owned vessels were placed into service.

130 government-owned vessels were removed from the National Defense Reserve Fleet. These vessels were manned by American seamen and put into operation by private American shipping companies.

Foreign flag vessels provided 6 percent of the dry cargo traffic to the war zone.

The redeployment of thousands of U.S. troops and their equipment from Northeast Korea was an overwhelming success due to the efforts of the American merchant ships. These accomplishments received high praise and commendation from Admiral C.T. Joy, Commander of all U.S. Naval forces in the Far East.

The successful removal of several hundred thousand tons of equipment and supplies by privately-owned American merchant ships resulted in a congratulatory message to A. F. Junker, USN, Commander of the Military Sea Transportation Service for Western Pacific.

Charles S. Thomas, Secretary of the Navy during the Korean conflict said:

In every war, the merchant marine has played a vital, though sometimes unpublicized role. The war in Korea is the most recent example. Every fighting man sent to Korea was accompanied by 5 tons of supplies and it took 64 pounds of supplies and equipment every day to keep him there. Five million passengers, 22,000,000 tons of petroleum products and 52,000,000 tons of dry cargo were transported to, from and within the Korean Theater to support that war.[45]

The Vietnam War

While primarily a guerilla war, the war in Vietnam also included carrier-plane bombardment, destroyer-battleship bombardment, ground attack, mine laying, riverboat warfare, etc. As action became more intensified, units of the Air Force, Army, Coast Guard, Marines and Navy all became involved. And, finally recognized as America's 4th line of defense, the American merchant marine was called upon, once again, to transport personnel and supplies to the Far East. As in the past, America was not prepared for war because the merchant marine had declined.

After Vietnam was partitioned in 1954, refugees from the North had to be evacuated to South Vietnam. In "Operation Passage to Freedom, which lasted from August 1954 to May 1955, thirty-nine MSTS transports carried many of the 293,000 Vietnamese who emigrated by sea from North to South Vietnam."[46]

As the war expanded, problems surfaced with the inadequacy of ships and manpower available. In February 1966, a Congressional inquiry was held to examine why the U.S. merchant marine had declined. The first item dealt with was the "deficiencies in the merchant marine as exposed by the Southeast Asia logistics problem in the Vietnam War."[47]

The primary question was whether the U.S. merchant marine was strong enough to be the fourth arm of America's defense. The Chief of Naval Operations, Admiral David A. McDonald made a study based on a survey sent to his flag officers on the readiness of the merchant marine for auxiliary needs. The findings of this study were that many of the ships were becoming obsolete.[48]

Secretary of Defense, Robert S. McNamara's responded: "the existing fleet, plus the construction program and the Reserve fleet appeared 'adequate to our need.'"[49] His statement was immediately contested by the Shipbuilders Council of America. The Council stated, "that the reserve fleet contained only a small percentage of vessels 'worthy of reactivation, and even then the rehabilitated ships are said to be uneconomic and unreliable.'"[50]

Later that month, Joseph Curran, President of the National Maritime Union and Chairman of the AFL-CIO Maritime Committee said that McNamara was keeping classified the number of ships necessary for military commitment. Two reasons were given: one, "that the Secretary of Defense does not want the people to know just how inadequate our merchant marine is" and, two "that it would expose our weaknesses to our enemies."[51]

Another problem that surfaced was that as more ships were diverted to the Far East, a shortage of engineers, deck officers, and skilled unlicensed personnel developed. The steamship companies and union officials "attributed the shortage to a refusal of local draft boards to defer such men despite appeals based on the allegation that the role of the officers operating ships into war areas was essential at a time of national emergency."[52]

The reason for not having enough new ships was that the U.S. government was not supporting a 1956 program goal of building twenty-five new ships per year. Recent new funding had resulted in sixteen to seventeen ships per year being built and only thirteen ships were budgeted for 1967.[53]

As the war progressed, huge amounts of manpower, supplies and war materiel needed to be shipped.

The Military Sea Transportation Service had the job of bringing war supplies to Vietnam — 10,000 miles from the Pacific coast. MSTS had four customers to serve: the Army, Air Force, Navy and Marine Corps. MSTS ships were staffed by "civilian" crews, but carried ninety-five percent of the supplies used by our Armed Forces in Vietnam including bombs and ammunition into combat zones under fire. Crew members were given Navy grades and rank identification in event of enemy capture.[54]

There were many types of ships utilized by MSTS in the Vietnam War. They included fast unloading roll-on/roll-offs (RO/ROs), aircraft ferries, barges, cargo (standard break-bulk and container) ships, troop transports, tank landing ships, tankers and tugs. "At the height of the war, MSTS operated a fleet of 527 reactivated World War II ships and chartered vessels managed by offices in the United States, Japan, and South Vietnam."[55]

One type of ship was the Victory ship built in World War II. MSTS took about 100 Victory ships out of the National Defense Reserve Fleet (mothball fleet), repaired them, and assigned them to private companies for operation to carry ammunition across the Pacific. MSTS carried guns, tanks, trucks, trains, riverboats, barges, helicopters, bombers, fighters, reconnaissance planes, food, fuel, and medical supplies. By 1965 MSTS had 300 freighters and tankers supplying Vietnam, with an average of seventy-five ships and over 3,000 merchant mariners in Vietnamese ports at any given time.[56]

Between 1965 and 1969, MSTS carried 7.6 million tons of supplies for the Air Force, about half going directly to Vietnam, the rest to staging areas in the Pacific. MSTS delivered the goods "Special Express" and kept some of its nineteen ammunition ships anchored offshore near combat areas as floating warehouses to ease storage problems experienced by the Air Force. SEA Express was the name of the program which delivered other Air Force supplies from Oakland, California to Saigon between 1965 and 1967, in an average of twenty-three days.

In 1965, US Coast Guard Squadron One, composed of seventeen patrol boats was sealifted to the Philippines for Vietnam duty on the SS *Pioneer Myth*, SS *Transcaribbean*, SS *Aloha State*, and the SS *Ocean Cloud*. MSTS delivered bulldozers, cranes, steel and cement for use by Navy Seabees. MSTS and the Merchant Marine transported oil and aviation gas to support Navy fleet operations.

In 1968 MSTS sealifted 19 million tons (39 billion pounds) of cargo to Vietnam for the Army at a cost of $570 million. The MSTS *Corpus Christi Bay*, which housed an Army aviation-maintenance battalion, was positioned as necessary along the coast of Vietnam to provide aircraft maintenance facilities. [57]

In September of 1970 MSTS was renamed Military Sealift Command (MSC). The Military Sealift Command:

> ... is an operating force of the United States Navy. It is a Navy command, staffed predominantly by a civilian work force. The nucleus ships of the Military Sealift Command have status as a Navy fleet. The Commander, Military Sealift Command, reports directly to the Chief of Naval Operations as a fleet commander. Originally known as the Military Sea Transportation Service (MSTS), the Military Sealift Command (MSC) was established in October 1949 to provide, under one authority, the control, operation

and administration of all ocean transportation for the Department of Defense. Vessels of the nucleus fleet are Navy-owned and manned by civil service marine personnel. Ships carry the designation USNS — United States Naval Ship. This is to distinguish them as "in service" ships rather than commissioned ships of the Navy. The ships are easily identified by their blue and gold stack markings.

The Military Sealift Command Mission is five fold: MSC provides immediate sealift capability to support military contingency plans and other national emergencies. It is responsible for planning and being capable of expansion in time of war. It provides peacetime ocean transportation of personnel and cargoes of the Department of Defense worldwide. The command meets all requirements of the Department of Defense for ocean shipping for purposes other than transportation. Finally, MSC operates Navy fleet support ships (oilers, tugs, stores ships) providing underway replenishment and ocean towing.[58]

As a result of a trial conducted in 1972, MSC became involved in the operations of the Naval Fleet Auxiliary Force (NFAF). The oiler USNS *Taluga* became MSC's first NFAF ship, crewed by 105 civilian mariners and a small detachment of Navy communication specialists. This experiment proved the value of civilian-crewing aboard fleet support ships — freeing highly-trained military personnel for service on warships while simultaneously reducing costs and increasing productivity. By the end of the decade, MSC was operating more than twenty NFAF ships.[59]

The war began to wind down as the North Vietnamese began their march southward in the spring of 1975. The Navy now called upon MSC to evacuate refugees and South Vietnamese soldiers fleeing southward.

By April 10, MSC had transported to Phu Quoc 130,000 American and Vietnamese refugees. At the end of the month, the South Vietnamese defenders at Saigon gave way to a powerful North Vietnamese offensive. With Communist occupation of all South Vietnam now virtually certain, President Gerald Ford ordered Operation Frequent Wind, the final evacuation of Saigon. Anticipating just such an order, MSC had filled its ships with food, water, and medicine and stationed Marine security detachments on board. In concert with the U.S. Seventh Fleet, which began lifting refugees by helicopter from Saigon out to the offshore flotilla, MSC took on board a growing flood of refugees. Between April 29 and May 2, when the operation ceased, the MSC ships embarked more than 50,000 evacuees. MSC ships, the Seventh Fleet contingent, and a flotilla of twenty-six Vietnam Navy ships embarking 30,000 Vietnamese sailors and their families then set sail for the Philippines.[60]

From 1964 until the end of the war, some ninety-three ships and mariners were involved in various forms of action including: air attack, ambush, capture, explosions, grenades and rocket grenades, gunfire, mines, rocket attack, shells and sniper fire. A casualty list of fifty-five dead or MIA mariners has been developed by Professor Michael Gillen of Pace University assisted by the editors of the American Merchant Marine at War website.[61]

The act entitling ocean-going merchant mariners of World War II veteran's status occurred only after a long battle and resulted in partial benefits in 1988. Despite the highest death rate of all the services and being sworn-in military auxiliaries subject to the Uniform Military Code of Justice, these valiant patriots were not considered veterans. The same lack of consideration is attached to the Vietnam War in that the mariners who served lack veteran status.

The American Merchant Marine at War website has concisely expressed a final comment concerning the mariners who died or who are missing in action during the Vietnam War:

> U.S. Merchant Marine served on ships that brought supplies to Vietnam during "The War Without a Front." They brought mail, Hueys, ammunition, food, medical supplies, and more. They brought the troops in and brought home many of those named on the Vietnam Memorial, "The Wall." These mariners were killed by mines, rockets, snipers, and explosions. Some are Missing in Action and presumed dead. They paid the Supreme Sacrifice while serving their country. They should be recognized as veterans. Their names belong on The Wall.[62]

Shortly after the Vietnam War ended, there was still one more involvement for the U.S. Merchant Marine; the *Mayaguez* Incident in May of 1975.

ENDNOTES

Prelude

1. "United States Unemployment Rates, 1890 to 1988. *Historical Statistics of the United States*, Series D 85-86: Unemployment: 1890 to 1970: 21 April 2006. http://members. aol.com/amatthaeus/diploma/bl.htm.

Chapter 1 – Cambodia and the Khmer Rouge

1. Raoul Marc Jennar, "Contemporary Cambodian Borders," (1997 Thesis) in Michelle Vachon's, "Defining Cambodia," *Cambodian Daily* 14-15 February 2004.

2. U.S. Department of State, "Background Note: Cambodia," *Working Paper Sites of Political Science: Country Biography Index* 9 May 2006. http://workingpapers.org/country/cambodia. htm.

3. "Khmer Rouge," *Wikipedia the Free Encyclopedia* 6 December 2005. http://en.wilipedia.org/wiki/Khmer_Rouge.

4. U.S. Department of State, Ibid.

5. Ibid.

6. Ibid.

7. "Khmer Rouge," Ibid.

8. Jennar.

9. Department of Defense – Joint Chiefs of Staff, "DIA Intelligence Appraisal," *After Action Report: U.S. Military Operation SS* Mayaguez/*Koh Tang Island 12-15 May 1975, 1.*

10. U.S. House of Representatives, *Seizure Of The* Mayaguez *Part IV* (Washington: USGPO, October 4, 1976), 115.

11. Ibid, 115-116.

12. Ibid, 116.

13. Ibid.

Chapter 2 – The S.S. *Mayaguez*

1. "North Carolina Shipbuilding Company, Wilmington, N.C.: Record of WW II Shipbuilding," *Maritime Business Strategies, LLC* 8 September 2006. http://.coltoncompany.com/shipbldg/ussbldrs/wwii/merchanshipbuilders/northcarolina.htm.

2. Ibid.

3. L.A. Sawyer and W.H. Mitchell, *From America To United States: The History of the Long-range Merchant Shipbuilding Program of the United States Maritime Commission, Part Two* (Kendal: World Ship Society, 1981), 43.

4. Edward R. Murrow, "All-Container Ship Welcomed by Port on Her Debut," *New York Times* 13 January 1960, 94.

5. John P. Callahan, "Container Vessel Off On First Run," *New York Times* 30 January 1960, 42.

6. Ibid.

7. "Venezuelans Drop Container Ship Ban," *New York Times* 21 February 1960, S16.

8. "Grace Line Near Caracas Accord," *New York Times* 11 September 1960, 138.

9. "History of the Pacific Air Forces," 1 July 1974 – 31 Dec. 1975, 1978. Control Number TS- HOA-T6-135, 426.

Chapter 3 – May 12, 1975, Gulf of Thailand

1. U.S. House of Representatives, *Seizure of The* Mayaguez

Part IV, Reports of the Comptroller General of the United States (Washington, DC: USGPO, 4 Oct. 1976), 115-116.

2. Edmund Newton, "Daily Closeup: Four Days in May," *New York Post* 29 August 1975.

3. Ibid.

4. Stephen Zarley, *My Experience aboard the SS* Mayaguez, August 1975.

5. U.S. House of Representatives, Hearings Before The Subcommittee On International Political And Military Affairs …, *Seizure of The* Mayaguez Part II (Washington, DC: USGPO, 19-25 June, 25 July 1975), 184-186.

Chapter 4 – Military Reconnaissance
1. U.S. House of Representatives, *Seizure of the* Mayaguez *Part IV*, Reports of the Comptroller General of the United States (Washington, DC: USGPO, 4 Oct. 1976), 116.

2. Ibid.

3. Ibid, 72-73.

4. Command History Branch Office of the Joint Secretary Headquarters, *Commander In Chief Pacific Command History: Appendix VI – The S.S.* Mayaguez *Incident* (San Francisco, CINPAC, 1976), 13.

5. Ibid, 13-14.

6. Ibid, 14.

7. Ibid, 15.

8. U.S. House of Representatives, *Seizure of the* Mayaguez *Part IV*, 73.

Chapter 5 – May 12, 1975, Washington, D.C.
1. U.S. House of Representatives, *Seizure of the* Mayaguez *Part IV*, Reports of the Comptroller General of the United States (Washington: USGPO, 4 Oct. 1976), 117.

2. National Security Council Meeting Minutes, May 12, 1975, Box 1, National Security Advisor. National Security Council Meetings File, Gerald R. Ford Library. http://www.ford.utexas.edu/library/document/ncsmin/750512n.htm.

3. Gina Chon and Lor Chandara, "Mission Impossible: Twenty-Five Years Ago the US Fought its Last Battle Against the Indochinese Communists …," *The Cambodia Daily WEEKEND* 20-21 May 2000.

4. U.S. House of Representatives, Ibid.

5. Walter J. Wood, "'Mayday' for the *Mayaguez*," *Proceedings of the United States Naval Institute* Vol. 102 No. 11, November 1976, 94-95.

6. U.S. House of Representatives, Ibid, 118.

Chapter 6 – May 13, 1975, Gulf of Thailand

1. *Seizure Of The* Mayaguez *Part II*, Hearings Before The Subcommittee On International Political And Military Affairs …(Washington, DC: USGPO, 19-25 June, 25 July 1975), 237., 186-187.

2. Stephen Zarley, *My Experience aboard the SS* Mayaguez, August 1975, 6.

3. *Seizure of the* Mayaguez Part II, 187.

4. *Seizure of the* Mayaguez Part IV, 118

5. *Part II*, Ibid.

6. *Part IV*, 119.

7. Stephen Zarley, 6-7.

Chapter 7 – Morning, May 13, 1975, Washington, D.C.

1. *National Security Council Meeting Minutes*, May 13, 1975 (Morning) Box 1, National Security Advisor. National Security Council Meetings File, Gerald R. Ford Library. http://www.ford.utexas.edu/library/DOCUMENT/NSCMIN/750513a.htn 1-17.

2. U.S. House of Representatives, *Seizure of the* Mayaguez *Part IV*, Reports of the Comptroller General of the United States (Washington: USGPO, 4 Oct. 1976), 113.

3. Part IV, 118.

4. Ibid, *Seizure Of The* Mayaguez *Part II*, Hearings Before The Subcommittee On International Political And Military Affairs …(Washington, DC: USGPO, 19-25 June, 25 July 1975), 237.

5. Part IV, 113..

6. Ibid.

7. Jan Forsgren, "Cambodia: Final Battle – The *Mayaguez* Rescue Operation," *Aeroflight Information* 20 November 2004 http://www.aeroflight.co.uk/aa-eastasia/cambodia/cam-maya1. htm

Chapter 8 – Evening, May 13. 1975. Gulf of Thailand

1. U.S. House of Representatives, *Seizure of The* Mayaguez *Part II*, Hearings Before The Subcommittee On International Political And Military Affairs …(Washington, DC: USGPO, 19-25 June, 25 July 1975), 188.

2. Stephen Zarley, *My Experience Aboard the SS* Mayaguez, August, 1975, 8-9.

3. U.S. House of Representatives, *Seizure of the* Mayaguez *Part IV,* Reports of the Comptroller General of the United States (Washington, D.C.: USGPO, 4 Oct. 1976), 119.

Chapter 9 – Evening, May 13. 1975, Washington, D.C.

1. *National Security Council Meeting Minutes*, May 13, 1975 (Evening) Box 1, National Security Advisor. National Security Council Meetings File, Gerald R. Ford Library. http://www.ford. utexas.edu/library/DOCUMENT/MSCMIN/750513a.htm 1-23.

2. U.S. House of Representatives, *Seizure of the* Mayaguez *Part IV*, 114.

3. Ibid.

4. Ibid.

5. Ibid.

6. Ibid.

Chapter 10 – Morning, May 14, 1975, Gulf of Thailand.

1. U.S. House of Representatives, *Seizure of The* Mayaguez *Part II*, Hearings Before The Subcommittee On International Political And Military Affairs …(Washington, DC: USGPO, 19-25 June, 25 July 1975), 188-189.

2. Stephen Zarley, *My Experience aboard the SS* Mayaguez August, 1975, 10-12.

3. U.S. House, 189-190.
4. Zarley, 13.
5. U.S. House, 190.
6. Zarley, Ibid.
7. U.S. House, 190-191.
8. Zarley, 15.

Chapter 11 – Afternoon, May 14, 1975, Gulf of Thailand
1. U.S. House of Representatives, *Seizure of the* Mayaguez *Part II…*, Hearings Before The Subcommittee On International Political And Military Affairs …191-193.
2. Stephen Zarley, *My Experience aboard the SS* Mayaguez August 1975, 15-17.
3. U.S. House of Representatives, *Seizure of the* Mayaguez *Part IV*, 121.
4. Ibid, 122.
5. Ibid.
6. *Part II*, 193-195.

Chapter 12 – Plan of Attack
1. U. S. House of Representatives, *Seizure of the* Mayaguez *Part IV*, Reports of the Comptroller General of the United States (Washington, DC: USGPO, 4 Oct. 1976), 123.
2. Ibid.
3. Ibid, 123-124.
4. U.S. House of Representatives, *Seizure of the* Mayaguez *Part II* Hearings Before The Subcommittee On International Political And Military Affairs …(Washington, DC: USGPO 19-25 June, 25 July 1975), 238.
5. *Part IV*, 89.
6. Ibid, 89-90.
7. Ibid, 90.
8. Ibid.
9. Ibid.
10. Ibid.
11. Ibid, 90-91.

12. Ibid.

13. Ibid, 91.

14. *Part II*, 238.

15. *Part IV*, 124.

Chapter 13 – SS *Greenville Victory*

1. Department of the Navy – Naval Historical Center, "Greenville Victory," *Dictionary of American Naval Fighting Ships* 5 June 2007. http://www.history.navy.mil/danfs/g8/greenville_victory.htm.

2. "Welcome Home USNS *Greenville Victory*," (Pamphlet), 11 July 1975.

3. *46th Artillery Group (Redstone): Seventh Army Artillery*, 5 June 2007. http://www.usarmygermany.com/Units/FieldArtillery/USAREUR_46th%20Broup.htm.

4. Department of the Navy, Ibid.

5. "Welcome Home USNS *Greenville Victory*."

6. Raymond Iacobacci, Interview with author, September 2005.

7. Raymond Iacobacci, Master - USNS *Greenville Victory*, "Refugee Evacuation, Report 1-75," to Commander, Military Sealift Command, Far East, 09 April 1975.

8. Raymond Iacobacci, Interview.

9. Iacobacci, "Refugee Report 1-75"…

10. Raymond Iacobacci, Interview.

11. Refugee Report.

12. Raymond Iacobacci, Master - USNS *Greenville Victory*, "Refugee Evacuation Report 5-75," to Commander, Military Sealift Command, Far East, 7 May 1975.

13. Raymond Iacobacci, USNS *Greenville Victory*, "Message to COMSCFE Yokohama …," 2 May 1975.

Chapter 14 – The Merchant Marine Volunteers

1. Raymond Iacobacci, Master - USNS *Greenville Victory*, To: COMSC – Washington DC, "*Mayaguez* Rescue Mission," 20 May 1975.

2. Clinton H. Harriman, "Report of SS *Mayaguez* Incident," May 1975.

3. Karl P. Lonsdale, Email to author, 21 July 2007.

4. Michael, A. Saltwick, "Report of SS *Mayaguez* Incident," May 1975.

5. Robert A. Griffin, Ibid..

6. Epifanio Rodriguez, Ibid.

7. Herminio Rivera, Ibid.

Chapter 15 – U-Tapao Air Base

1. Raymond Iacobacci, Master - USNS *Greenville Victory*, To: COMSC – Washington DC, "*Mayaguez* Rescue Mission," 20 May 1975.

2. Clinton H. Harriman, "Report of SS *Mayaguez* Incident," May 1975.

3. Karl P. Lonsdale, Ibid.

4. Ibid, Email to author, 21 July 2007.

5. Michael A. Saltwick, "Report of SS *Mayaguez* Incident," May 1975.

6. Robert A. Griffin, Ibid.

7. Epifanio Rodriguez, Ibid.

8. Herminio Rivera, Ibid.

9. Thomas K. Noble, Jr., Letter to author, 13 March 2008.

Chapter 16 – Assault on Koh Tang

1. U.S. House of Representatives, *Seizure of the* Mayaguez *Part IV,* Reports of the Comptroller General of the United States (Washington, D.C.: USGPO 4 Oct. 1976), 92.

2. Ibid, 125.

3. Ibid.

4. Dan Hoffman, Interview with Aaron Bowden of Wild Eyes Productions for the History Channel Documentary *Heroes Under Fire: Deadly Reckoning.* 12 May 2005. Updated by letters to author.

5. Allen Bailey, Letter to author, 30 December 2008.

6. Larry Barnett, Interview with Aaron Bowden …, Ibid.

7. Thomas K. Noble, Jr., Letter to author, 13 March 2008.
8. Barnett, Interview …, Ibid.
9. Morris, Ibid.
10. Hoffman.
11. Barnett.
12. Morris.

Chapter 17 – Recapture of the SS *Mayaquez*
1. Karl P. Lonsdale, "Report of SS *Mayaguez* Incident," May 1975.
2. Ibid, Email to author, 21 July 2007.
3. Clinton H. Harriman, "Report of SS *Mayaguez* Incident," May 1975.
4. Michael A. Saltwick, Ibid.
5. Raymond Iacobacci, Master - USNS *Greenville Victory*, To: COMSC – Washington, DC, "*Mayaguez* Rescue Mission," 20 May 1975.
6. Karl P. Lonsdale, Ibid.
7. Clinton H. Harriman, Ibid.
8. Lonsdale, Ibid.
9. Saltwick, Ibid.
10. Robert A. Griffin, Ibid.
11. Epifanio Rodriguez, Ibid.
12. Herminio Rivera, Ibid.
13. Harriman, Ibid.
14. Lonsdale, Ibid.
15. Saltwick, Ibid.

Chapter 18 – The *Mayaguez* Crew Returns
1. U.S. House of Representatives, *Seizure of the* Mayaguez, Part IV, Reports … (Washington, D.C.: USGPO, 4 Oct. 1976) 125.
2. Thomas K. Noble, Jr., Letter to author, 13 March 2008.
3. Part IV, Ibid.
4. U. S. House of Representatives, *Seizure of the Mayaguez Part II*, Hearings Before The Subcommittee On The International

Political And Military Affairs ... *Seizure of the* Mayaguez ...,
198-201.

5. Raymond Iacobacci, Master - USNS Greenville Victory,
To: COMSC – Washington, DC, "*Mayaguez* Rescue Mission,"
20 May 1975.

6. U.S. House, 202.

7. Robert A. Griffin, "Report of SS *Mayaguez* Incident,"
May 1975.

8. Epifanio Rodriquez, Ibid.

9. Herminio Rivera, Ibid.

10. Clinton H. Harriman, Ibid.

11. Karl P. Lonsdale, Ibid.

12. Michael A. Saltwick, Ibid.

13. U.S. House, 202-203.

14. Ibid, 223.

15.Iacobacci.

16.Steven Zarley, *My Experiences Aboard the SS* Mayaguez,
August 1975.

Chapter 19 – Koh Tang Island, May 15, 1975

1. U. S. House of Representatives, *Seizure of the Mayaguez
Part IV*, Reports of the Comptroller General of the United States
(Washington, DC: USGPO, 4 Oct. 1976), 125.

2. Ibid, 125-126.

3. Thomas K. Noble, Jr., Letter to author, 13 March 2008.

4. U.S. House, 126.

5. Richard G. Head, et al, *Crisis Resolution: Presidential
Decision Making in the* Mayaguez *and Korean Confrontations*
(Boulder, Colorado: Westview Press, Inc., 1978), 141.

6. Larry Barnett, Interview with Aaron Bowden of Wild
Eyes Productions for the History Channel Documentary *Heroes
Under Fire: Deadly Reckoning* 12 May 2005. Updated by letters
to author.

7. *History Of The Pacific Air Forces,* 1 Jul. 74 – Dec. 1975,
TS-HOA-76-135, 1978, 453.

8. Noble.

9. U.S. House, Ibid.

10. A.J.C. Lavalle, *The Vietnamese Air Force* ... (USAF Southeast Asia Monograph Series Vol. 3, Monographs 4 and 5) Washington, DC: USGPO, 1977, 148-149.

11. Fred Morris, Interview with Aaron Bowden ..., Ibid.

12. Dan Hoffman, Ibid.

Chapter 20 – Celebration

1. U.S. House of Representatives, *Seizure of the* Mayaguez *Part IV*, Reports of the Comptroller General of the United States (Washington, DC: USGPO, 4 Oct. 1976), 98.

2. Ibid, 59.

3. Sam H. Moore, Communication to the Master USNS *Greenville Victory*, 20 May 1975.

4. J. William Middendorf II, Communication to USNS Ships – *Miller*, *Greenville Victory*, and *Kimbro*, 23 May 1975.

5. Karl P. Lonsdale, Email to author, 20 July 2007.

6. J. William Middendorf II, Letter of Navy Award of Merit for Group Achievement, 9 July 1975.

7. Sam H. Moore, *Welcome Home USNS* Greenville Victory Ceremony (Address) 11 July 1975.

8. Frank B. Guest, Jr., *Welcome Home* ... Ibid.

9. Raymond Iacobacci, Ibid.

Chapter 21 – Aftermath

1. U.S. House, Ibid, 59-61.

2. Glenn T,. Starnes, *The Mayaguez Incident: A Failure in Operational Leadership* (Newport, RI: Naval War College, 1995), 15-16.

3. Peter J. Kelly, "Raids and National Command: Mutually Exclusive!" *Military Review* 60 (Apr. 1980), 26.

4. Starnes, 16.

5. Fred Morris, Interview with Aaron Bowden of Wild Eyes Productions for the History Channel Documentary *Heroes Under Fire: Deadly Reckoning* 12 May 2005. Updated by letters to author.

6. Larry Barnett, Interview with Aaron Bowden of Wild Eyes Productions for the History Channel Documentary *Heroes Under Fire: Deadly Reckoning,* 12 May 2005. Updated by letters to author.

7. Michael Harris, "S.F. Visit: Mayaguez Skipper Says Ford Was Right," 7 October 1976.

Chapter 22 – Missing in Action
1. Peter C. Brown (Maj.), "Investigation to Inquire into the Circumstances Surrounding the Missing in Action Status in the Cases of Private First Class Gary C. Hall USMC, Lance Corporal Joseph N. Hargrove USMC and Private Danny G. Marshall USMC," to Commanding General USMC HQs San Francisco (Ref. MARCORCASPROCMAN, Par 7004) 7 June 1975, 2-3.

2. Ibid, 4-6.
3. Ibid, Statement of LCpl. John S. Standfast, Enclosure 8.
4. Ibid, Statement of PFC Andrew F. Piechna, Enclosure 14.
5. Ibid, Statement of PFC David M. Wagner, Enclosure 18.
6. Ibid, Statement of Private Mario R. Gutierrez, Enclosure 19.
7. Brown, 6-7.
8. Ibid, 7.
9. Koh Tang Radio Disc 2, *After Action Recordings*, Koh Tang Beach Veterans Organization, 2007.
10. Interview with Capt. Mike E. Stahl (Part 6151B), *After Action Recordings,* Koh Tang Beach Veterans Organization, 2007.
11. Koh Tang Radio Traffic, Ibid.
12. Interview with Capt. James Davis, (Part 6119B), *After Action Recordings*, Ibid.
13. Thomas K. Noble, Jr., Letter to author, 13 March 2008.

Chapter 23 – Thirty-five Years Later
1. "Mission Overview: What we do at JPAC," JPAC – Joint Prisoners of War, Missing in Action Accounting Command, 26

February 2008. http://www.jpac.pacom.mil/index.php?page=-mission_overview.

2. Ibid.

3. Ibid.

4. Ibid.

5. Mather, Paul C., "Refugee Report, Sighting of Two Skeletons: Mayaguez Related Death, Joint Casualty Resolution Center, Reference T83-044, 25 April 1983.

6. "Van de Geer, Richard," Compiled by Task Force Omega, Inc, 29 February 2008. http://www.taskforceomegainc.org/v019.html.

7. Lance Radebaugh, "USS *Badger* 1071 – The *Mayaguez* Incident," 18 February 2008. http://ussbadger-1071.org/menus/mayaguez.html.

8. "Vander de Geer."

9. Joint Field Activity Report (Unclassified) Case # 1998 DRI, 5 June 1996.

10. "Vander de Geer."

11. Monte Marchant, "Joint POW/MIA Accounting Command (JPAC) Success on their latest dig in Koh Tang," Koh Tang Beach Veterans, 23 February 2008. http://www.kohtang.com.

12. Brian DeSantis, "Joint POW/MIA Accounting Press Release," #08-02, 10 March 2008.

13. "Dig Update, Koh Tang Beach Club Veterans," 18 March 2009 <http://www.kohtank.com/new_page_1.htm>

Appendix A

1. "Targeting Ho Chi Minh Trail," *The Nautilus Institute* 20 February 2006. http://nautilus.org/VietnamFOIA/background/HoChiMinhTrail.html.

2. "Ho Chi Minh Trail," *Spartacus* 20 February 2006. http://www.spartacus.schoolnet.co.uk/VNhotrail.htm.

3. Huong, Le. "Women's stories of liberation," *Vietnam News Vietnam News Agency* 20 February 2006. http://vietnamnews.vnagency.com.vn/showarticle.php?num=01WAR240405.

4. Department of the Navy –Naval Historical Center, "USS *Maddox* (D-D-731), 1944-1972 — Actions in the Gulf of Tonkin, August 1964." 28 February 2006. http://www.history.navy.mil/photos/sh-usn/usnsh-m/dd731-k.htm.

5. Ibid, "Tonkin Gulf Crisis, August 1964." 13 July 2005, 14 March 2006. http://www.history.navy.mil/faqs/faq120-1.htm.

6. "Gulf of Tonkin Incident (Documents-Audio Recordings, Photos," Vietnam War Gulf of Tonkin Documents <http//www.paperlessarchives.com/vw_gulf_of_tonkin.html>

7. Department of the Navy …

8. John Prados, "Essay: 40th Anniversary of the Gulf of Tonkin Incident," *The National Security Archive* 14 March 2006. http://www.gwu.edu/~nsarchiv/MSAEBB/NSAEBB132/essay.htm.

9. Ibid.

Appendix B – History of the Wartime U.S. Merchant Marine

1. Donald Chidsey, *The American Privateers* (New York: Dodd, Mead & Company, 1962), 32.

2. Edgar Stanton Maclay, *A History of American Privateers* (Freeport, NY: Books For Libraries Press, 1970), iii.

3. Eloise Engle and Arnold S. Lott, *America's Maritime Heritage* (Annapolis, MD: Naval Institute Press, 1975), 55.

4. Horodysky, "Privateers or Merchant Mariners in the Revolutionary War," Ibid, 10 June 2006. http://www.usmm.org/revolution.html.

5. Horodysky.

6. Michael A. Palmer, "The Navy: The Continental Period, 1775-1890," *A History Of The U.S. Navy – Naval Historical Center* 13 June 2006. http://www.history.navy.mil/history/history2.htm.

7. Engle, 93.

8. Maclay, 225.

9. Ibid.

10. Engle, 100.

11.Robert D. Paulus, "Pack Mules and Surf Boats: Logistics in the Mexican War," in *Army Logistician* Nov/Dec. 1997, 11 July 2006. http://www.almc.army.mil/alog/issues/NOVDec9//MS210.htm.

12.Alvin P. Stauffer, "The Quartermaster's Department and the Mexican War: Supply of the First American Overseas Expeditionary Force," *Quarter Master Review* May-June 1950, 11 July 2006. http://www.qmfound.com/quartermaster_department_mexican_war.htm.

13. Paulus.

14. Maclay, 503.

15. Horodysky, "Merchant Marine in the Civil War," Ibid 20 June 2006. http://www.usmm.org/civilwar.html.

16. Ibid.

17. Ibid.

18. Winthrop L. Marvin, *The American Merchant Marine: Its History And Romance From 1620 To 1902* (Charles Scribner's Sons: New York, 1919), 338-339.

19. Horodysky.

20. Engle, 212.

21. Ibid, 213.

22. Horodysky, "American Merchant Marine in Spanish-American War," Ibid. http://www.usmm.org/spanishamerican.html.

23. Charles Oscar Paullin, *Paullin's History of Naval Administration*, (Annapolis, MD: U.S. Naval Institute, 1968).

24. Paulus, "From Santiago to Manila: Spanish-American War Logistics," in *Army Logistician* July/August 1998, 12 July 2006. http://www.almc.army.mil/ALOG/issues/JulAug98/MS305.htm.

25. "Sell Wartime Ships," *Business Week* 17 July 1937, 42.

26. Engle, 221.

27. U.S. Department of Commerce Maritime Administration, *The United States Merchant Marine: A Brief History* 1972, 3.

28. Horodysky, "Merchant Marine in World War I," Ibid. http://usmm.org/WW1.html.

29. U.S. Department of Commerce Maritime Administration, Ibid.

30. U.S. Department of Commerce, Ibid.

31. Horodysky, "U.S. Merchant Ships Sunk or Damaged in World War II," Ibid. 10 August 2006. http://www.usmm.org/shipsunkdamaged.html.

32. U.S. Department of Commerce Maritime Administration, Ibid.

33. Horodysky, *U.S. Merchant Marine in World War II: First to Go Last to Return, Higher Casualty Rate* (Berkeley, CA: American Merchant Marine at War Organization, 2000)

34. Emory S. Land, *The United States Merchant Marine at War* (Washington, DC: War Shipping Administration, 1946), 64.

35. Horodysky, "U.S. Merchant Ships Sunk or Damaged ..." Ibid.

36. Ibid, "U.S. Merchant Marine Casualties during World War II," Ibid, 9 August 2006. http://www.usmm.org/casualty.html.

37. Ibid "U.S. Merchant Maine in WW II," Ibid. http://www.usmm.org/ww2.html.

38. U.S. Department of Commerce Maritime Administration, Ibid, 4.

39. "Ready Reserve Force (RRF)," *FAS Military Analysis Network: U.S. Navy Ships* 15 August 2006. http://www.fas.org/man/dod-101/sup/ship/rrf.htm.

40. Salvatore R. Mercogliano, "One Hundred Years in the Making: The Birth of Military Sea Transportation Service (MSTS)," *American Merchant Marine at War* 10 July 2006. http://www.usmm.org/msts.html.

41. Department of Defense, "The Merchant Marines in the Korean War: Fact Sheet," *The United States Of America Korean War Commemoration* 30 May 2006. http://korea50.army.mil/history/factsheets/merchant_marines.shtml.

42. Ibid.

43. Department Of The Navy – Naval Historical Center, "The Korean War, 1950-1953: The Hungnam Evacuation, 10-24 December 1950," 10 August 2000, 18 August 2006. http://www. history.navy.mil/photos/events/kowar/50-chin/hungnam.html.

44. Mercogliano, "Korea: The First Shot (Military Sea Transportation Service in the Korean War)," *American Merchant Marine at War* 30 May 2006. http://www.usmm.org/msts/korea. html.

45. Department of Transportation MARAD, "JUST THE FACTS: The American Merchant Marine in the Koran Conflict," 30 May 2006. http://www.marad.gov/education/history/korea/ JUST%20THE%20FACTS.html.

46. Edward J. Marolda, "Military Sealift Command," Department Of The Navy – Naval Historical Center, 26 August 2003, 7 June 2006. http://www.history.navy.mil/wars/vietnam/ msc.htm.

47. George Horne, "Maritime Inquiry To Begin Tuesday: House Panel Will Investigate Merchant Marine Decline – U.S. Aid to Be Studied," *New York Times* 6 February 1966, S21.

48. Ibid.

49. Ibid.

50. Ibid.

51. Warner Bamberger, "Curran Questions Fleet's Adequacy: Charges McNamara Keeps Vietnam Needs Secret," *New York Times* 20 February 1966, S13.

52. John P. Callahan, "Officer Shortage At Sea Is Feared: Unions Say Draft Is Taking Men Essential on Ships," *New York Times* 11 December 1965, 66.

53. "Cargo Loss Laid To Vietnam War: Diversion to Saigon Said to Cost Merchant Tonnage," *New York Times* 9 March 1966, 81.

54. Horodysky, "U.S. Merchant Marine, Military Sea Transportation Service, and Military Sealift Command in Vietnam," *American Merchant Marine at War* 6 July 2005. http://www.usmm.org/vietnam.html.

55. Marolda.

56. Horodysky.

57. Ibid.

58. "The United States Navy Military Sealift Command," Change of Command Ceremony, (Pamphlet), 15 June 1979.

59. "MSC Timeline 1970-1979," *Military Sealift Command* 21 August 2006. http://www.msc.navy.mil/N00p/7079.htm.

60. Marolda.

61. Horodysky.

62. Ibid.

ABOUT THE AUTHOR

Gerald Reminick is a Professor of Library Services at the Grant Campus Library, Suffolk County Community College, Brentwood, New York. He received his Bachelor of Science degree from Adelphi University in 1967, a Master of Arts from State University of New York (SUNY) at Stonybrook in 1975 and a Master of Science in Library and Information Science at Long Island University in 1979.

He is an associate member of the Edwin J. O'Hara and Kings Point chapters of the American Merchant Marine Veterans.

BIBLIOGRAPHY

Bailey, Allen. Letter to author. December 30, 2008.

Bamberger Warner. "Curran Questions Fleet's Adequacy: Charges McNamara Keeps Vietnam Needs Secret." *New York Times* 20 February 1966, S13.

Barnett, Larry. Interview with Aaron Bowden of Wild Eyes Productions for the History Channel Documentary *Heroes Under Fire: Deadly Reckoning,*12 May 2005. Updated by letters to author.

Brown, Peter C. "Investigation to Inquire into the Circumstances Surrounding the Missing in Action Status in the Cases of Private First Class Gary C. Hall USMC, Lance Corporal Joseph N. Hargrove USMC and Private Danny G. Marshall USMC," to Commanding General USMC HQs San Francisco (Ref. MARCORCASPROCMAN, Par 7004) 7 June 1975, 2-3.

— Ibid. Statement of Private Mario R. Gutierrez, Enclosure 19.

— Ibid. Statement of PFC Andrew F. Piechna, Enclosure 14.

— Ibid. Statement of LCpl John S. Standfast, Enclosure 8.

— Ibid. Statement of PFC David M. Wagner, Enclosure 18.

Butwell, Richard. "Vietnam War," *Encyclopedia Americana* 2005 ed., Vol. 28, 112b. "Vietnam War." *Wikipedia* 1 March 2006. http://en.wikipedia.org/wiki/Vietnam_war.

Callahan, John P. "Container Vessel Off On First Run," *New York Times* 30 January 1960, 42.

— "Officer Shortage At Sea Is Feared: Unions Say Draft Is Taking Men Essential on Ships." *New York Times* 11 December 1965, 66.

"Cargo Loss Laid To Vietnam War: Diversion to Saigon Said to Cost Merchant Tonnage." *New York Times* 9 March 1966, 81.

Chidsey, Donald. *The American Privateers.* New York: Dodd, Mead & Company, 1962.

Chon, Gina and Lor Chandara, "Mission Impossible: Twenty-Five Years Ago the US Fought its Last Battle Against the Indochinese Communists …." *The Cambodia Daily WEEKEND* 20-21 May 2000.

Command History Branch Office of the Joint Secretary Headquarters, *Commander In Chief Pacific Command History: Appendix VI – The S.S.* Mayaguez *Incident.* San Francisco: CINPAC, 1976.

Davis, James (Interview - Part 6119B). *After Action Recordings.* Koh Tang Beach Veterans Organization, 2007. Courtesy Gerald R. Ford Library and the Koh Tang Beach Veterans.

Department of Defense – Joint Chiefs of Staff, "DIA Intelligence Appraisal." *After Action Report: U.S. Military Operation SS* Mayaguez */ Koh Tang Island* 12-15 May 1975.

Department of Defense, "The Merchant Marines in the Korean War: Fact Sheet." *The United States Of America Korean War Commemoration* 30 May 2006 http://korea50.army.mil/history/factsheets/merchant_marines.shtml.

Department of Transportation MARAD, "JUST THE FACTS: The American Merchant Marine in the Koran Conflict." 30 May 2006. http://www.marad.gov/education/history/korea/JUST%20THE%FACTS.html.

Department of the Navy – Historical Center, "Greenville Victory." *Dictionary of American Naval Fighting Ships* 5 June 2007. http://www.history.navy.mil/danfs/g8/greenville_victory.htm.

— "The Korean War, 1950-1953: The Hungnam Evacuation, 10-24 December 1950." 10 August 2000, 18 August 2006. http://www.history.navy.mil/photos/events/kowar/50-chin/hungnam.html

— "Tonkin Gulf Crisis, August 1964." 13 July 2005, 14 March 2006. http://www.history.navy.mil/faqs/faq120-1.htm

— "USS *Maddox* (D-D-731), 1944-1972—Actions in the Gulf of Tonkin, August 1964." 28 February 2006. http://www.history.navy.mil/photos/sh-usn/usnsh-m/dd731-khtm.

DeSantis, Brian. Joint POW/MIA Accounting Press Release #08-02. 10 March 2008. "JPAC Arrival Ceremony Set For March 14, 2008."

"Dig Update, Koh Tang Beach Club Veterans," 18 March 2009 <http://www.kohtang.com/new_page_1.htm>

Engle, Eloise and Arnold S. Lott. *America's Maritime Heritage.* Annapolis, MD: Naval Institute Press, 1975.

Ford, Gerald R. *A Time To Heal: The Autobiography of Gerald R. Ford.* New York: Harper & Row, 1979.

Forsgren, Jan, "Cambodia: Final Battle – The *Mayaguez* Rescue Operation." *Aeroflight Information* 20 November 2004. http://www.aeroflight.co.uk/aa-eastasia/cambodia/cam-maya1,htm.

46th Artillery Group (Redstone): Seventh Army Artillery, 5 June 2007. http://www.usarmygermany.com/Units/FieldArtillery/USAREUR_46th%20Arty%20Grouphtm.

"Grace Line Near Caracas Accord." *New York Times* 11 September 1960, 138.

Griffin, Robert A. "Report of the SS *Mayaguez* Incident, May 1975.

Guest Jr., Frank B. *Welcome Home USNS* Greenville Victory Ceremony (Address) 11 July 1975.

Guilmartin Jr., John F. *A Very Short War.* College Station: Texas A&M University Pr., 1995.

"Gulf of Tonkin Incident (Documents - Audio Recordings - Photos)," Vietnam War Gulf of Tonkin Documents <http://www.paperlessarchives.com/vw_gulf_of_tonkin.html>

Harriman, Clinton H. "Report of the SS *Mayaguez* Incident." May 1975.

Harris, Michael "S.F. Visit: Mayaguez Skipper Says Ford Was Right," 7 October 1976.

Head, Richard G. et al. *Crisis Resolution: Presidential Decision Making in the* Mayaguez *and Korean Confrontations.* Boulder, Colorado: Westview Press, Inc., 1978.

Hendricks, John B. Email to James Miller, 16 March 2005. Courtesy of James Miller.

"History of the Pacific Air Forces." 1 July 1974 – 31 Dec. 1975, 1978. Control Number TS- HOA-T6-135, 426.

"Ho Chi Minh Trail." *Spartacus* 20 February 2006. http://www.spartacus.schoolnet.co.uk/VNhotrail.htm.

Hoffman, Dan. Interview with Aaron Bowden of Wild Eyes Productions for the History Channel Documentary *Heroes Under Fire: Deadly Reckoning.* 12 May 2005. Updated by letters to author.

Horne, George. "Maritime Inquiry To Begin Tuesday: House Panel Will Investigate Merchant Marine Decline – U.S. Aid to Be Studied." *New York Times* 6 February 1966, S21.

Horodysky, Dan and Toni. "American Merchant Marine in Spanish-American War." *American Merchant Marine at War.* http://www.usmm.org/spanishamerican.html.

—   "Merchant Marine in the Civil War." Ibid 20 June 2006. http://www.usmm.org/civilwar.html.

—   "Merchant Marine in World War I." Ibid. http://www.usmm.org/ww1.html.

—   "Privateers or Merchant Mariners in the Revolutionary War." Ibid, 10 June 2006. http://www.usmm.org/revolution.html.

— "U.S. Merchant Marine Casualties during World War II." Ibid, 9 August 2006. http://www.usmm.org/casualty.html.

— "U.S. Merchant Marine in World War II." 12 June 2006 Ibid. http://www.usmm.org/www2.html.

— *U.S. Merchant Marine in World War II: First to Go Last to Return, Higher Casualty Rate.* Berkeley, CA: American Merchant Marine at War Organization, 2000.

— "U.S. Merchant Marine, Military Sea Transportation Service, and Military Sealift Command in Vietnam." *American Merchant Marine at War* 6 July 2005. http://www.usmm.org/vietnam.html.

— "U.S. Merchant Ships Sunk or Damaged in World War II." Ibid. 10 August 2006. http://www.usmm.org/shipsunkdamaged.html.

Huong, Le. "Women's stories of liberation." *Vietnam News Vietnam News Agency* 20 February 2006. http://vietnamnews.vnagency.com.vn/showarticle.php?num=01WAR240405.

Iacobacci, Raymond. Master - USNS *Greenville Victory*, To COMSC – Washington DC, "Mayaguez Rescue Mission." 20 May 1975.

— Interview with author. September 2005.

— "Message to COMSCFE Yokohama ...." 2 May 1975.

— "Refugee Evacuation, Report 1-75." to Commander, Military Sealift Command, Far East, 9 April 1975.

— "Refugee Evacuation Report 5-75." to Commander, Military Sealift Command, Far East, 7 May 1975.

Jennar, Raoul Marc. "Contemporary Cambodian Borders." (1997 Thesis) in Michelle Vachon's, "Defining Cambodia," *Cambodian Daily* 14-15 February 2004.

Joint Field Activity Report – Investigation of the Reported Burial Sites (Unclassified) Case # 1998 DRI, 5 June 1996.

Kelly, Brian J. *Situation Critical: Seized at Sea.* (Videotape) Henniger Productions, 2000.

Kelly, Peter J. "Raids and National Command: Mutually

Exclusive!" *Military Review* 60 (Apr. 1980), 26.

"Khmer Rouge." *Wikipedia the Free Encyclopedia* 6 December 2005. http://en.wikipedia.org/wiki/khmer_Rouge.

Koh Tang Radio Disc 2, *After Action Recordings*, Koh Tang Beach Veterans Organization, 2007. Courtesy Gerald R. Ford Library and the Koh Tang Veterans.

Land, Emory S. *The United States Merchant Marine at War.* Washington, DC: War Shipping Administration, 1946.

Lavalle, A.J.C. *The Vietnamese Air Force 1951-1975: An Analysis Of Its Role In Combat and Fourteen Hours at Koh Tang.* (USAF Southeast Asia Monograph Series Vol. 3, Monographs 4 and 5) Washington, DC: USGPO, 1977.

Lonsdale, Karl P. Email to author. 21 July 2007.

—— "Report of the SS *Mayaguez* Incident." May 1975.

"MSC Timeline 1970-1979." *Military Sealift Command* 21 August 2006. http://www.msc.navy.mil/N00p/7079.htm.

Maclay, Edgar Stanton. *A History of American Privateers.* Freeport, NY: Books For Libraries Press, 1970.

Marchant, Monte. "Joint POW/MIA Accounting Command (JPAC) Success on their latest dig in Koh Tang." Koh Tang Beach Veterans, 23 February 2008. http://www.kohtang.com.

Marolda, Edward J. "Military Sealift Command." Department Of The Navy – Naval Historical Center, 26 August 2003, 7 June 2006. http://www.history.navy.mil/wars/vietnam/msc.htm.

Marvin, Winthrop L. *The American Merchant Marine: Its History And Romance From 1620 To 1902.* Charles Scribner's Sons: New York, 1919.

Mather, Paul C. "Refugee Report, Sighting of Two Skeletons: Mayaguez Related Death."Joint Casualty Resolution Center, Reference T83-044. 25 April 1983.

Mercogliano, Salvatore R. "Korea: The First Shot (Military Sea Transportation Service in the Korean War)." *American*

Merchant Marine at War 30 May 2006. http://www.
usmm.org/msts/korea.html.

— "One Hundred Years in the Making: The Birth of
Military Sea Transportation Service (MSTS)." *American
Merchant Marine at War* 10 July 2006. http://www.
usmm.org/msts.html.

Middendorf II, J. William. Communication to USNS Ships –
Miller, *Greenville Victory*, and *Kimbro*, 23 May 1975.

— Letter of Navy Award of Merit for Group Achievement,
9 July 1975.

"Mission Overview: What we do at JPAC." JPAC – Joint
Prisoners of War, Missing in Action Accounting
Command, 26 February 2008. http://www.jpac.pacom.
mil/index.php?page=mission_overview.

Moore, Sam H. Communication to the Master USNS *Greenville
Victory*, 20 May 1975.

— *Welcome Home USNS* Greenville Victory Ceremony
(Address) 11 July 1975.

Morris, Fred. Interview with Aaron Bowden of Wild Eyes
Productions for the History Channel Documentary
Heroes Under Fire: Deadly Reckoning 12 May 2005.
Updated by letters to author.

Mueller, Theodore H. *Chaos Theory and the Mayaguez Crisis.*
Defense Technical Information Center, FT. Belvoir, VA:
U.S. Department of Defense, 1990.

Murrow, Edward R. "All-Container Ship Welcomed by Port on
Her Debut." *New York Times* 13 January 1960, 94.

National Security Council Meeting Minutes. May 12, 1975, Box
1, National Security Advisor. National Security Council
Meetings File, Gerald R. Ford Library. http://www.ford.
utexas.edu/library/document/nscmin/75051n.htm.

— May 13, 1975 (Morning) Box 1, National Security
Advisor. National Security Council Meetings File,
Gerald R. Ford Library. http://www.ford.utexas.edu/
library/DOCUMENT/NSCMIN/750513a.htm 1-17.

— May 13, 1975 (Evening) Box 1, National Security

Advisor. National Security Council Meetings File, Gerald R. Ford Library. http://www.ford.utexas.edu/library/DOCUMENT/NSCMIN/750513a.htm 1-23.

—   May 14, 1975 Ibid. http://www.ford.utexas.edu/library/document/nscmin/75051n.htm.

Nessen, Ron. *It Sure Looks Different from the Inside.* Chicago: Simon & Schuster, 1978.

Newton, Edmund. "Daily Closeup: Four Days in May." *New York Post* 29 August 1975.

Noble, Thomas K. Letter to author. 13 March 2008.

"North Carolina Shipbuilding Company, Wilmington, N.C.: Record of WW II Shipbuilding." *Maritime Business Strategies, LLC* 8 September 2006. http://www.coltoncompany.com/shipbldg/ussbldrs/wwii/merchantshipbuilders/northcarolina.htm.

Palmer, Michael A. "The Navy: The Continental Period, 1775-1890." *A History Of The U.S. Navy – Naval Historical Center* 13 June 2006. http://www.history.navy/mil/history/history2.htm.

Paulus, Robert D. "From Santiago to Manila: Spanish-American War Logistics." in *Army Logistician* July/August 1998, 12 July 2006. http://www.almc.army.mil/ALOG/issues/JulAug98/MS305.htm.

—   "Pack Mules and Surf Boats: Logistics in the Mexican War." in *Army Logistician* Nov/Dec. 1997, 11 July 2006. http://www.almc.army.mil/ALOG/issues/NovDec97/MS305.htm.

Prados, John. "Essay: 40th Anniversary of the Gulf of Tonkin Incident." *The National Security Archive* 14 March 2006. http://www.gwu.edu/~nsarchiv/NSAEBB/NSABB132/essay.htm.

Radebaugh, Lance. "USS Badger 1071 – The Mayaguez Incident." 18 February 2008. http://www.ussbadger-1071.org/menus/mayaguez.html.

"Ready Reserve Force (RRF)." *FAS Military Analysis Network: U.S. Navy Ships* 15 August 2006. http://www.fas.org/man/dod-101/sup/ship/rrf.htm.

Rivera, Herminio. "Report of the SS Mayaguez Incident." May 1975.

Rodriguez, Epifanio. "Report of the SS *Mayaguez* Incident." May 1975.

Rowan, Roy. *The Four Days of* Mayaguez. New York: W.W. Norton, 1975.

Saltwick, Michael, A. "Report of SS *Mayaguez* Incident." May 1975.

Sawyer L.A. and W.H. Mitchell. *From America To United States: The History of the Long-Range Merchant Shipbuilding Program of the United States Maritime Commission Part Two.* Kendal: World Ship Society, 1981.

"Sell Wartime Ships." *Business Week* 17 July 1937, 42.

Stahl, (Capt.) Mike E. (Interview - Part 6151B). *After Action Recordings.* Koh Tang Beach Veterans Organization, 2007. Courtesy Gerald R. Ford Library and the Koh Tang Beach Veterans.

Starnes, Glenn T.. *The Mayaguez Incident: A Failure in Operational Leadership.* Newport, R.I.: Naval War College, 1995.

Stauffer, Alvin P. "The Quartermaster's Department and the Mexican War: Supply of the First American Overseas Expeditionary Force." *Quarter Master Review* May-June 1950, 11 July 2006. http://www.qmfound.com/quartermaster_department_mexican_war.htm.

Stockdale, Jim and Sybil. *In Love and War.* New York: Bantam Books, 1985.

"Targeting Ho Chi Minh Trail." *The Nautilus Institute* 20 February 2006. http://www.nautilus.org/VietnamFOIA/background/HoChiMinhTrail.html.

"The United States Navy Military Sealift Command." Change of Command Ceremony, (Pamphlet), 15 June 1979.

"United States Unemployment Rates, 1890 to 1988. *Historical Statistics of the United States,* Series D 85-86:

Unemployment: 1890 to 1970: 21 April 2006. http://members.aol.com/amatthaeus/diplom/b1.htm.

U.S. Department of Commerce Maritime Administration, *The United States Merchant Marine: A Brief History,* 1972.

U.S. Department of State. "Background Note: Cambodia." *Working Paper Sites of Political Science: Country Biography Index* 9 May 2006. http://workingpapers.org/country/cambodia.htm.

U.S. House of Representatives. *Seizure of the* Mayaguez *Part I.* Hearings before the Committee On International Relations and its Subcommittee On International Political And Military Affairs, 94th Congress, First Session, May 14 and 15, 1975. Washington, DC: USGPO, 1975.

— *Seizure of the* Mayaguez *Part II.* Hearings before the Subcommittee On International Political And Military Affairs of the Committee On International Relations, 94th Congress, First Session, June 19, 25, and July 25, 1975. Washington, DC: USGPO, 1975.

— *Seizure of the* Mayaguez *Part III.* Hearings before the Subcommittee On International Political and Military Affairs of the Committee on International Relations, 94th Congress, First Session, July 31 and September 12, 1975. Washington, DC: USGPO, 1975.

— *Seizure of the* Mayaguez *Part IV.* Reports of the Comptroller General of the United States Submitted to the Subcommittee on International Political and Military Affairs, Committee on International Relations, 94th Congress, Second Session, October 4, 1976. Washington DC: USGPO, 1976.

"USS *Coral Sea* (CV-43)." *Wikipedia* 30 January 2007. http://en.wikipedia.org/wiki/USS_Coral_Sea_(CV-43).

"Van de Geer, Richard." Compiled by Task Force Omega, Inc., 29 February 2008. http://www.taskforceomegainc.org/v019.html.

"Venezuelans Drop Container Ship Ban." *New York Times* 21 February 1960, S16.

"Welcome Home USNS *Greenville Victory.*" (Pamphlet), 11 July 1975.

Wetterhahn, Ralph. *The Last Battle: The* Mayaguez *Incident and the End of the Vietnam War.* New York: Carroll & Graf Publishers, Inc, 2001.

— "Lost and Found." *Popular Science* March 2000: 8.

— "Missing in Action." *Popular Science* August 1998: 46-54.

Wilson, Robert J. *Too Joint or Not Too Joint: An Analysis of U.S. Joint Military Operatives.* Washington DC: National War College, March 1984.

Wood, Walter J., "'Mayday' for the *Mayaguez.*" *Proceedings of the United States Naval Institute* Vol. 102 No. 11, November 1976, 94-95.

Zarley, Stephen. *My Experiences Aboard the SS* Mayaguez, August 1975.

Index